# The
# CCNA™ Routing and Switching Cram Sheet

This Cram Sheet contains the distilled, key facts about CCNA Routing and Switching. Review this information right before you enter the test room, paying special attention to those areas where you need the most support. You can transfer any of these facts onto a blank sheet of paper before beginning the exam.

## INTERNETWORKING BASICS

1. The primary advantage of bridging is increased bandwidth available on a segment because of the decreased number of devices in the collision domain.

2. Switches have the same basic functionality as bridges but usually have more ports. Each switch port is a separate collision domain, and each port provides dedicated bandwidth.

3. Virtual local area networks (VLANs) can be used to make a group of switch ports into a separate, isolated LAN. Routing is required for communication between VLANs.

4. VLANs can function across multiple switches when they are connected by a trunk connection. Inter-switch linking (ISL) is used to create a trunk connection between Fast Ethernet ports on Cisco switches.

5. Switches make it possible to run Ethernet devices in full-duplex mode. In full-duplex mode, two devices share the Ethernet wire exclusively, enabling faster throughput because no collisions are possible.

6. Store-and-forward switching reads the entire frame before making a forwarding decision; cut-through switching reads only the first six bytes—the destination media access control (MAC) address—to make a forwarding decision. Store-and-forward switching performs error checking; cut-through switching does not.

7. The primary advantages of routers are:
   - Allow you to connect dissimilar LANs
   - Provide multiple paths to a destination network
   - Allow the interconnection of large and complex networks

8. Connection-oriented communication uses a nonpermanent path for data transfer. It involves three steps: establish the connection, transfer the data, and terminate the connection. Connectionless communication uses a permanently established link.

## OPEN SYSTEMS INTERCONNECT (OSI) MODEL

9. The layers of the OSI model are 7-application, 6-presentation, 5-session, 4-transport, 3-network, 2-data link, and 1-physical.

10. Encapsulation, or tunneling, takes frames from one network system and places them inside frames from another network system.

11. The presentation layer concerns itself with data representation, data encryption, and data compression. It supports different protocols for text, data, sound, video, graphics, and images such as ASCII, MIDI, MPEG, GIF, and JPEG.

12. The session layer establishes, manages, and terminates sessions between applications. Network file system (NFS), structured query language (SQL), and remote procedure calls (RPCs) are examples of session layer protocols.

13. The transport layer sits between the upper and lower layers of the OSI model. The transport layer

performs flow control by buffering, multiplexing, and parallelization. It provides end-to-end data transport services by:

- Segmenting upper-layer applications
- Establishing an end-to-end-connection
- Sending segments from one end host to another
- Ensuring reliable data transport

14. The primary functions of the network layer of the OSI model are path determination and packet switching. In addition, remember that the network layer is the domain of routing.

15. The primary functions of the data link layer of the OSI model are:

- Allows the upper layers of the OSI model to work independently of the physical media
- Performs physical hardware addressing
- Provides optional flow control
- Generates error notification

## ROUTER BASICS

16. EXEC includes the following:

- Context-sensitive help for syntax checking, command prompting, and keyword completion. Use the question mark (?) to activate context-sensitive help.
- Command history that provides a record of recent commands. Use the Up and Down Arrow keys to scroll through the history list. Tab completes a partially entered command.
- Enhanced editing that enables commands retrieved from command history to be changed quickly then re-executed. The **terminal editing** and **terminal no editing** commands enable and disable enhanced editing.

17. Examine the status of a router with the following commands: **show version**, **show memory**, **show protocols**, **show running-config** (or **write terminal**), **show startup-config** (or **show configuration**), **show interfaces**, and **show flash**.

18. The Cisco Discovery Protocol (CDP) displays summary information about directly connected devices and operates at the data link layer. The **show cdp neighbors** command displays ID, local and remote port, holdtime, platform, and capability information. The **show cdp entry <device id>** command displays information about a specific device including all layer 3 addresses and Internetwork Operating System (IOS) versions.

## ROUTER CONFIGURATION

19. The command to back up a router configuration file (copy a configuration file from a router to a Trivial File Transfer Protocol [TFTP] server) is **copy running-config tftp**. The command to restore a configuration file (copy a configuration file from a TFTP server to a router) is **copy tftp running-config**.

20. The commands to set the enable, enable secret, console, and auxiliary passwords on a router are as follows:

- **Router(config)#enable *password***
- **Router(config)#enable secret *password***
- **Router(config)#line aux *0*** and **Router (config-line)#login** and **Router(config-line)#password *password***
- **Router(config)#line con *0*** and **Router (config-line)#login** and **Router(config-line)#password *password***
- **Router(config)#line vty *0 4*** and **Router (config-line)#login** and **Router(config-line)#password *password***

21. To create a banner for a router and a description for an interface, use the **banner motd** (message of the day) and **description** commands.

## ROUTING PROTOCOLS

22. Convergence occurs when all routers in an internetwork agree on optimal routes. A routing loop occurs when a packet bounces back and forth between two or more routers. A routing loop is sometimes called counting to infinity.

23. Distance vector routing protocols send all of their route tables to their neighbors. Link state protocols send the state of their own interfaces to every router in the internetwork.

24. Counting to infinity is a problem for distance vector routing protocols. It can be eliminated or mitigated by using the following techniques: maximum hop count, split horizon, route poisoning, and hold-down timers.

25. Router resource usage, bandwidth consumption, and update synchronization are problems for link state routing protocols. They can be eliminated or reduced by using the following techniques:

- Lengthening update frequency
- Exchanging route summaries
- Using time stamps or sequence numbers

# CCNA™
# Routing and Switching

## Second Edition

Jason Waters
Matthew J. Rees
Jeffrey T. Coe

**CCNA™ Routing and Switching Exam Cram, Second Edition**

**Limits of Liability and Disclaimer of Warranty**

The author and publisher of this book have used their best efforts in preparing the book and the programs contained in it. These efforts include the development, research, and testing of the theories and programs to determine their effectiveness. The author and publisher make no warranty of any kind, expressed or implied, with regard to these programs or the documentation contained in this book.

The author and publisher shall not be liable in the event of incidental or consequential damages in connection with, or arising out of, the furnishing, performance, or use of the programs, associated instructions, and/or claims of productivity gains.

**Trademarks**

Trademarked names appear throughout this book. Rather than list the names and entities that own the trademarks or insert a trademark symbol with each mention of the trademarked name, the publisher states that it is using the names for editorial purposes only and to the benefit of the trademark owner, with no intention of infringing upon that trademark.

The Coriolis Group, LLC
14455 N. Hayden Road
Suite 220
Scottsdale, Arizona 85260

(480)483-0192
FAX (480)483-0193
www.coriolis.com

Library of Congress Cataloging-in-Publication Data
Coe, Jeffrey T.
    CCNA routing and switching exam cram / by Jeffrey T. Coe, Matthew J. Rees, and Jason Waters.— 2nd ed.
    p. cm.
    Includes index.
    ISBN 1-57610-628-4
    1.  Electronic data processing personnel--Certification. 2.  Telecommunication--Switching systems--Examinations--Study guides.  I.  Rees, Matthew J.  II.  Waters, Jason.  III.  Title.
    QA76.3 .C636 2000
    004.6'6—dc21
                                            00-031607
                                            CIP

Printed in the United States of America
10 9 8 7 6 5 4

**President and CEO**
Keith Weiskamp

**Publisher**
Steve Sayre

**Acquisitions Editors**
Jeff Kellum
Shari Jo Hehr

**Marketing Specialist**
Cynthia Caldwell

**Project Editor**
Lynette Cox

**Technical Reviewer**
Ariel Silverstone

**Production Coordinator**
Wendy Littley

**Cover Designer**
Jesse Dunn

**Layout Designer**
April Nielsen

The Coriolis Group, LLC • 14455 North Hayden Road, Suite 220 • Scottsdale, Arizona 85260

# *ExamCram.com* Connects You to the Ultimate Study Center!

Our goal has always been to provide you with the best study tools on the planet to help you achieve your certification in record time. Time is so valuable these days that none of us can afford to waste a second of it, especially when it comes to exam preparation.

Over the past few years, we've created an extensive line of *Exam Cram* and *Exam Prep* study guides, practice exams, audio training, and interactive training. To help you study even better, we have now created an e-learning and certification destination called **ExamCram.com**. (You can access the site at **www.examcram.com**.) Now, with every study product you purchase from us, you'll be connected to a large community of people like yourself who are actively studying for their certifications, developing their careers, seeking advice, and sharing their insights and stories.

I believe that the future is all about collaborative learning. Our **ExamCram.com** destination is our approach to creating a highly interactive, easily accessible collaborative environment, where you can take practice exams and discuss your experiences with others, sign up for features like "Questions of the Day," plan your certifications using our interactive planners, create your own personal study pages, and keep up with all of the latest study tips and techniques.

I hope that whatever study products you purchase from us—*Exam Cram* or *Exam Prep* study guides, *Practice Tests, Flash Cards, Personal Trainers*, or one of our interactive Web courses—will make your studying fun and productive. Our commitment is to build the kind of learning tools that will allow you to study the way you want to, whenever you want to.

Help us continue to provide the very best certification study materials possible. Write us or email us at **learn@examcram. com** and let us know how our study products have helped you study. Tell us

**Visit ExamCram.com now to enhance your study program.**

about new features that you'd like us to add. Send us a story about how we've helped you. We're listening!

Good luck with your certification exam and your career. Thank you for allowing us to help you achieve your goals.

Keith Weiskamp
President and CEO

# Look for these other products from The Coriolis Group:

**CCNA Routing and Switching Exam Prep**
Mark Poplar, Jason Waters, Shawn McNutt, David Stabenaw

**CCNA Routing and Switching Practice Tests Exam Cram**
Robert Gradante

**CCNA Routing and Switching Exam Cram Flash Cards**
Robert Gradante

**CCNA Routing and Switching Audio Review**
Jason Waters

**CCNA Routing and Switching Value Pack**
CIP Author Team

**CCNA Routing and Switching Exam Cram Personal Trainer**
CIP Author Team

*This book is dedicated to my friends and family.*
*—Jason Waters*

*This book is dedicated to my family, Christine, and Luke.*
*You are the most special people in the world.*
*—Matthew J. Rees*

*This book is dedicated to Brenda, Daniel, Jackee, Jessica, my family and friends.*
*I will always remember your love and support for me.*
*—Jeffrey T. Coe*

≈

# About the Authors

Jason Waters is a network consultant based in the Chicago area. He has designed and administered networks for a wide range of companies, including ISPs, insurance companies, and banks. Certifications include CCNA, MCSE, MCP+I, and A+.

Jason is entirely self-taught and has been growing with the industry ever since learning to program on his Commodore 64 and running a BBS in the pre-Internet days. When he is not strapped to his PC, Jason enjoys adventure travel such as backpacking across Europe or trekking in Peru. He also frequents renaissance festivals and is a collector of replica medieval arms and armor. Jason lives in Palatine, IL and can be reached at **jwaters@iname.com.**

Matthew J. Rees is a consultant with Calence, Inc. in Tempe, Arizona. He has worked in a diverse set of technical environments ranging from software development and testing to Wide Area Network design and implementation. Matthew has expertise in network planning, international network design, internetworking technologies, year 2000 network requirements, voice and data network integration, network modeling, campus design, and local and wide area network installation and testing. He has worked with a diverse set of Fortune 100 clients; however, Matthew's primary clientele has been telecommunications companies. Matthew currently holds a Cisco Certified Network Professional (CCNP) certification. He is also pursuing other Cisco internetworking certifications.

Jeffrey T. Coe is a network security consultant with Calence, Inc. in Tempe, Arizona. He has over ten years of experience in various information technologies, including applications development and support, database and distributed systems architecture design, and enterprise-wide application and network security. His technical experience includes designing and implementing computer networks for Fortune 500 companies using network protocols such as Frame Relay, SMDS, IP, IPX, STUN and SNA. In addition, Jeffrey has designed and implemented fault tolerant LAN architectures for call centers, Web complexes and third-party connectivity. Jeffrey currently holds Cisco Certified Network Professional (CCNP), Cisco Security Specialist and Certified Information Systems Security Professional (CISSP) certifications.

# Acknowledgments

I would like to express my thanks to everyone at the Coriolis team for giving me the opportunity to work on this project. Thanks to Jeff Kellum, Lynette Cox, and Wendy Littley for pulling this whole thing together. Thanks also to April Eddy, copyeditor, and Ariel Silverstone, technical editor, for their help.

There are numerous other people who have given me support—professional and personal—throughout this project. You have my sincere gratitude. Thanks Mom and Dad, your love and continual encouragement have enabled me to accomplish things I never thought possible. Thanks also to the rest of my family—Jimmy, Heidi, my grandparents, and everyone else. Dawn—thank you for all your help and patience throughout this process—I certainly could not have done this without you in my life. I love you all! I also want to thank several people—co-workers, friends, employers—who have been vital to my career development. Thanks to Tony Young, Joe Danrich, HH Communications, Gary Cortez, Ricardo Bravo, Bill Lang, and SRI. And finally, I want to thank God for making all this possible!
—*Jason Waters*

To begin, I would like to thank Jeff Kellum for presenting me with the opportunity to write this book. This book could not have been possible without the fantastic forum for obtaining knowledge created by Calence, Inc. For everyone at Calence, thanks for your consistent perseverance to achieve excellence. I have grown and gained tremendous personal and technical benefits from having you as colleagues and friends.

This book would have never of reached fruition without the commitment to closing the contract demonstrated by Shari Jo Hehr of The Coriolis Group. We will all benefit from your efforts. To the editor of this book, Lynette Cox, thanks for your time and effort. Also, thank you to Keith Weiskamp for publishing this book, and many thanks to the rest of the team for their excellent work, including Production Coordinator, Wendy Littley; Marketing Specialist, Cynthia Caldwell; Cover Designer, Jesse Dunn; and the Layout Designer, April Nielsen. All of your work should be commended. Special accolades go to Ariel Silverstone and April Eddy for providing relentless technical and editorial advice.

# Acknowledgments

Most importantly, I want to thank my Mom and Dad for always believing in me no matter what walk of life I chose. Words cannot express the confidence you have instilled in me by always being there. To my brother, Dave, I would have always thought that you would have been the first to publish a book. I never owned a Commodore 64 nor a chemistry set, however, it was your love of computers that drew me to this profession. Most of all, though, thanks for never judging me on anything but being a good brother. You're the best, Dave.

Special thanks to my co-author, Jeff Coe, for his tremendous dedication and his technical contributions in helping to write this book.

I could not finish these acknowledgments without identifying those people that sacrificed the most while I was helping to write this book. To my girlfriend, Christine, thank you for being so understanding during this trying experience. Your support and love are the cornerstone of my strength to complete this book. Finally, to my best friend, Luke, thanks for spending time with Geti during my late-nights writing.
—*Matthew J. Rees*

Thanks to the entire team at The Coriolis Group! You've been incredibly professional and patient with me. Thanks Shari Jo Hehr for getting us through the toughest part of the book so that we could start writing. To Lynette Cox, you've been great! Your supervision and people skills kept all of us on track—you were truly the cornerstone of this book. April Eddy, I'm appreciative of your sharp eye in editing the book. Ariel Silverstone, thanks for the terrific technical editing. I'm grateful to have worked with such a terrific team including Keith Weiskamp for publishing our book, Wendy Littley for production coordination, Cynthia Caldwell for marketing (I've already been watching **amazon.com.**), Jesse Dunn for the cover design, and April Nielsen for the layout design. You may have only been doing your job, but I really appreciate the effort you put into this book! I also need to acknowledge Jeff Kellum for his contribution in shuttling different parts of the book back and forth. We would have been in sad shape without you on our team.

Thanks to everyone at Calence! The environment we have is something special. I continue to learn so much from each of you about networking, teamwork and fun, and about doing the job well. I owe a deep heartfelt thanks to my friends at SSCC and those on the block who patiently waited and prayed for me while I worked on this book. I won't forget how you forced me to take a break when you saw I needed one. It encouraged me tremendously since I knew people were vicariously writing through me.

Thanks Mom, Dad, Pam and Cindy! I'm thankful for your input early in the process and for calling me to make sure everything was okay. To Matt Rees, my co-author, thanks for asking me to be involved in this adventure. I owe you big time for challenging me! Without your initiative, this book would still be just a cool idea!

Finally, I want to acknowledge my wife Brenda, and my kids, Daniel, Jackee, and Jessica. You've really been an inspiration during this entire process. You knew precisely when to let me concentrate and when to distract me. I'll always be grateful for your patience, support, and love—it means the world to me.
—*Jeffrey T. Coe*

# Contents at a Glance

# Table of Contents

# Introduction

Welcome to *CCNA Routing and Switching Exam Cram, 2nd Edition*. This book aims to help you get ready to take and pass Cisco Certification Exam 640-507, "Cisco Certified Network Associate 2.0." This introduction explains Cisco's certification programs in general and talks about how the *Exam Cram* series can help you to prepare for Cisco's certification exams.

*Exam Cram* books help you to understand and appreciate the subjects and materials you need to pass Cisco certification exams. *Exam Cram* books are aimed strictly at test preparation and review. They do not teach you everything you need to know about a topic, such as the ins and outs of configuring Integrated Services Digital Network (ISDN) services or all of the nitty-gritty details involved in using routing protocols. Instead, we (the authors) present and dissect the questions and problems we've found that you're likely to encounter on a test. We've worked from Cisco's own training materials, preparation guides, tests, and from a battery of third-party test preparation tools. Our aim is to present as much information as possible about Cisco's certification exams.

Nevertheless, to prepare yourself completely for any Cisco test, we recommend that you begin by taking the self-assessment that immediately follows this introduction. This tool will help you to evaluate your knowledge base against the requirements for a CCNA exam under both ideal and real circumstances.

Based on what you learn from that exercise, you might decide to begin your studies with classroom training or background reading. On the other hand, you might decide to pick up and read one of the many study guides available from Cisco or third-party vendors on certain topics.

We also strongly recommend that you install, configure, and fool around with the software and hardware on which you'll be tested, because nothing beats hands-on experience and familiarity when it comes to understanding the questions you're likely to encounter on a certification test. Book-learning is essential, but hands-on experience is the best teacher of all.

# The Cisco Certification Program

It is important that when you start the Cisco Career Certification process, first determine the technological career path you wish to master. Cisco offers wide variety of certifications; however, they are designed to follow two distinct career paths with multiple tracks along each path. In an effort to summarize the material, this book presents each career path and the tests required for proceeding along each path. Cisco Systems Inc. offers a wide variety of training courses that are designed to facilitate the certification process. Of course you have to pay for these training courses. You can find the recommended training courses and a more in-depth analysis of each test on Cisco's Web page at **www.cisco.com/warp/public/10/wwtraining/certprog/index.html**.

# Career Path 1: Routing and Switching

The routing and switching career path is shown in Table 1.

## Track 1: Network Support

The routing and switching network support certification career path is for professionals who support networks with Cisco local area network (LAN) and wide area network (WAN) routers and switches. This path has three core certifications.

**Table 1    Cisco Routing and Switching CCNA, CCNP, and CCIE Requirements**

**CCNA**

| Only 1 exam required | |
| --- | --- |
| ▶ Exam 640-507 | Cisco Certified Network Associate 2.0 (CCNA) |

**CCNP***

| 4 exams required | |
| --- | --- |
| Exam 640-503 | Routing 2.0 (RTING) |
| Exam 640-504 | Switching 2.0 (SWTCH) |
| Exam 640-505 | Remote Access 2.0 (RMTAC) |
| Exam 640-506 | Support 2.0 (SUPRT) |

* You need to have your CCNA before you become a CCNP.

**CCIE**

| 1 written exam and 1 lab exam required | |
| --- | --- |
| Exam 350-001 | CCIE Routing and Switching Qualification |
| Lab Exam | CCIE Routing and Switching Laboratory |

## Cisco Certified Network Associate (CCNA) 2.0 (CCNA Exam 640-507)

The skills expected of a CCNA are the ability to install, configure, and operate simple-routed LAN, routed WAN, and switched LAN networks.

## Cisco Certified Network Professional (CCNP) 2.0

The skills expected of a CCNP are the ability to install, configure, operate, and troubleshoot complex routed LAN, routed WAN, switched LAN networks, and dial access services. Two different test options are available for achieving the CCNP.

Test option 1:

➤ CCNA Certification (CCNA Exam 640-507)

➤ Foundation 2.0 (Exam 640-509)

➤ Support 2.0 (SUPRT Exam 640-506)

Test option 2:

➤ CCNA Certification (CCNA Exam 640-507)

➤ Routing 2.0 (RTING Exam 640-503)

➤ Switching 2.0 (SWTCH Exam 640-504)

➤ Remote Access 2.0 (RMTAC Exam 640-505)

➤ Support 2.0 (SUPRT Exam 640-506)

The only difference between test option 1 and 2 is the second set of tests required for test option 2. These tests are designed to cover the same material as the Foundation 2.0 Exam in test option 1, but they are broken up to reduce the test time and make the certification process more manageable.

In addition, Cisco offers specialization exams for people who have achieved the CCNP certification. These tests are designed for professionals to demonstrate superior knowledge in specific technical disciplines. These tests include the following specialization:

Security specialization:

➤ Managing Cisco Network Security (MCNS Exam 640-442)

➤ Cisco Enterprise Management Solutions (CEMS Exam 640-601)

➤ Managing Cisco Routed Internetworks (MCRI Exam 640-443)

➤ Managing Cisco Switched Internetworks (MCSI Exam 640-444)

LAN ATM:

➤ Cisco Campus ATM Solutions (CATM 640-446)

Voice access:

➤ Cisco Voiceover Fram Relay (CVOICE Exam 640-447)

SNA solutions:

➤ SNA Foundation (SNAIPF Exam 640-456)

➤ SNA Configuration for Multiprotocol Administrators (SNAM Exam 640-445)

### CCIE—Routing and Switching

The CCIE is the pinnacle of career certifications in the Cisco certification process. The skills expected of a CCIE are the ability to install, configure, operate, and troubleshoot complex routed LAN, routed WAN, switched LAN, and ATM LANE network, and dial access services. Also, a CCIE is expected to diagnose and resolve network faults, use packet/frame analysis and Cisco debugging tools, and document and report the problem-solving processes used. The CCIE exam is split into a written test and a grueling laboratory test:

➤ Routing and Switching CCIE Written Exam

➤ Routing and Switching CCIE Lab Test

For more information about the CCIE Routing and Switching certification, please visit Cisco's CCIE Routing and Switching Web page at **www.cisco.com/warp/public/625/ccie/certifications/routing.html.**

# Career Path 2: Network Design

The routing and switching network design certification career path is for professionals who want to design Cisco-based networks that predominantly include routed LAN, routed WAN, and switched LAN networks. This career path has two core certifications.

## Cisco Certified Design Associate (CCDA)

The skills expected of a CCDA are the ability to design simple routed LAN, routed WAN, and switched LAN networks. The test required to achieve the CCDA certification is as follows:

➤ Design Cisco Networks (DCN Exam 640-441)

## Cisco Certified Design Professional (CCDP) 2.0

The skills expected of a CCDP are to design complex routed LAN, routed WAN, and switched LAN networks. The test assumes prerequisite knowledge and skills to install, configure, and operate these networks. Two different test options are available for achieving the CCDP.

Test option 1:

➤ CCNA Certification (CCNA Exam 640-507)

➤ CCDA Certification (CCDA Exam 640-441)

➤ Foundation 2.0 (Exam 640-509)

➤ Cisco Internetworking Design 3.0 (CID 3.0 Exam 640-025)

Test option 2:

➤ CCNA Certification (CCNA Exam 640-507)

➤ CCDA Certification (CCDA Exam 640-441)

➤ Routing 2.0 (RTING Exam 640-503)

➤ Switching 2.0 (SWTCH Exam 640-504)

➤ Remote Access 2.0 (RMTAC Exam 640-505)

➤ Cisco Internetworking Design 3.0 (CID 3.0 Exam 640-025)

The only difference between test option 1 and 2 is the third set of tests required for test option 2. These tests are designed to cover the same material as the Foundation 2.0 Exam in test option 1, but they are broken up to reduce the test time and make the certification process more manageable.

# Career Path 3: WAN Switching Network Design and Support

The WAN switching network design and support career path is designed for professionals who focus on WAN switching, such as Internet Service Providers (ISPs) and carriers. Two tracks are available in the WAN switching network design and support career path.

## Track 1: Network Support

The routing and switching network support certification career path is for professionals who configure, operate, troubleshoot, and manage WAN switched networks. The exams are designed to test required skills in the following areas:

➤ Media and telephony transmission techniques, error detection, and time division multiplexing (TDM)

➤ Knowledge of Frame Relay and ATM

➤ Knowledge of Cisco-specific technologies, including WAN switch platforms, applications, architectures, and interfaces

➤ Knowledge of service provider technology, including packet encapsulation and network-to-network interconnections

## CCNA (WAN Switching)

The skills expected of a CCNA (WAN switching) are the ability to install WAN switches IPX, IGX, BPX, AXIS, Shelf, and modems. The test required to achieve the CCNA WAN switching certification is:

➤ CCNA WAN Exam 640-410

## CCNP (WAN Switching)

The skills expected of a CCNP (WAN switching) are the ability to configure, operate, troubleshoot, and manage WAN switched networks. Three different test options are available for achieving the CCNP (WAN switching).

Test option 1:

➤ CCNA-WAN Switching Certification (CCNA Exam 640-410)

➤ BPX Switch and Service Configuration (BSSC Exam 640-425)

➤ MGX ATM Concentrator Configuration (MACC Exam 640-411)

➤ Multiband Switch and Service Configuration (MSSC Exam 640-419)

➤ Cisco StrataView Plus (CSVP Exam 640-422)

Test option 2:

➤ CCNA-WAN Switching Certification (CCNA Exam 640-410)

➤ Cisco WAN Switch Service Networking (CWSSN Exam 640-424)

➤ Cisco WAN Switch Configuration (CWSC Exam640-423)

➤ Cisco StrataView Plus (CSVP Exam 640-422)

Test option 3:

➤ CCNA-WAN Switching Certification (CCNA Exam 640-410)

➤ Network Operations for BPX/AXIS Products (BNOC Exam 640-414)

➤ Network Operations for IGX Products (NNOC Exam 640-415)

➤ Cisco StrataView Plus (CSVP Exam 640-422)

# Track 2: Network Design

The skills expected of the network design track are the ability to design and implement ATM and frame networks, troubleshoot existing WAN switched networks, and manage traffic and voice technologies.

## CCDP (WAN Switching)

The skills expected of a CCDP (WAN switching) are the ability to design and implement an ATM network with CBR, ABR, and VBR traffic and a frame relay network using Committed Information Rate (CIR) and MIR traffic parameters; troubleshoot an existing WAN switched network; and manage traffic and voice technologies. The test required to achieve the CCDP certification is as follows:

➤ Designing Switched WAN Voice Solutions (DSWVS Exam 640-413)

## CCIE (WAN Switching)

The CCIE is the pinnacle of career certifications in the Cisco certification process. The skills expected of a CCIE are the ability to implement an ATM network (with CBR, ABR, and VBR traffic) and a frame relay network (using CIR and MIR traffic parameters), troubleshoot an existing WAN switched network, and manage traffic and voice technologies. The CCIE is split into a written test and a grueling laboratory test:

➤ WAN Switching CCIE Written Exam

➤ WAN Switching CCIE Lab Test

For more information about the CCIE WAN switching certification, visit Cisco's CCIE WAN switching Web page at **www.cisco.com/warp/public/625/ccie/certifications/wan.html**.

The many different career tracks in the certification process are designed to meet the requirements of a variety of career fields. Most of you will want to proceed down the routing and switching network support or network design career tracks; these are the most mainstream certifications. Those of you who need to proceed down the WAN switching career path will be working in that type of environment. The ultimate goal of any one of these tracks is to achieve the CCIE certification. This is a noble achievement, and the marketplace recognizes the value of CCIEs.

# Taking a Certification Exam

You can register for the CCNA 2.0 exam online through Sylvan Prometric's Web site at **www.2test.com**.

You can also call 1-800-829-NETS to register for the exam. We strongly recommend that you take the time to review Cisco's Exam Web sites mentioned previously. The cost of the exam is $100 that can be paid by credit card, personal check, or money order.

You will be taking the test at a Sylvan Prometric Testing Center at the location you choose. When you arrive at the testing location, sign in with the test coordinator and have two forms of identification ready, one of which must be a photo ID. The test coordinator will give you a set of rules for you to read and abide by during the test. You will also receive some scratch paper and a pencil, or a dry-erase board and marker. The amount of scratch paper required to take the test will vary for each individual, but we recommend that you get as much as possible to be safe. If you are given a dry-erase board, ask for two of them so you don't have to erase previously written material to make extra room for notes or calculations during the test. The test coordinator will take you to a room with a number of computer stations divided by walls. You will have the option of taking a tutorial on the exam before the time starts for the test. If this is your first Cisco test, we recommend that you review this material.

A Cram Sheet has been provided at the beginning of the text with material that most often appears on the test. If it helps you, write down as much as you can remember on your scratch paper before taking the test. You can use the time provided to take the tutorial to make these notes. The test will consist of 65 questions, and you will be given 75 minutes to complete the exam. Strategies for time management are provided in the next section. Remember to take a deep breath and have confidence in yourself. If you have spent the time studying the material in this book, you will be well-equipped to tackle the test head on.

After you have completed the test, the results of your test will be available online immediately. After you have received your passing score, you will be prompted to print your results. *Do print your results*. Don't go any further until you have seen a printed copy of your results, because this is your only true verification that you have passed the exam. After you have seen this printout, conclude the exam, and see the test coordinator.

## CCNA Exam Test Format

The CCNA exam uses the typical certification test format of asking multiple-choice questions with one or more answers per question. What makes some questions more difficult is that more than five answer choices are listed, reducing the power of eliminating answers and choosing from the remaining answers. The nice part is that the number of required answers is given for each question.

The test consists of 65 questions and requires a score of 822 on a scale of 300 to 1,000 to pass. The test questions can be grouped into eight topics, all of which are covered in this book. We have attempted to estimate the number of questions that are taken from each subject area to give you an idea of where to focus the majority of your time; however, the percentage of questions that will appear for any topic will most certainly vary. We have developed this list from taking the test and talking with other people who have passed the exam.

As you can see, the Open Systems Interconnect (OSI) model, router configuration basics, Transmission Control Protocol/Internet Protocol (TCP/IP), and WAN protocols make up 65 percent of the test. Make sure that you spend extra time learning these concepts. Concentrate especially on the OSI model; without a thorough understanding of it, you will have difficulty passing the test. Also, to develop a foundation for obtaining additional internetworking skills, you need to master these topics.

# Tracking Cisco Certification Status

As soon as you pass any Cisco certification, you'll attain Cisco certification status. Cisco also generates transcripts that indicate which exams you have passed and your corresponding test scores. Cisco will send these transcripts to you. In addition, you will receive a login ID and password that will allow you to track your status on Cisco's Web page.

# How to Prepare for an Exam

The CCNA exam requires test-taking skills that many of us learned in high school or college. This section will be a refresher for many and important for all.

The first thing to focus on during the test is time management. The CCNA exam allows 75 minutes to complete the test. This gives you just over 1 minute per question. Don't worry about how long it takes you to finish an individual question, but divide the test into checkpoints to monitor your progress during the test.

You must answer each question. In fact, the test engine will not let you proceed if you have not selected an answer or if you have not chosen the correct number of answers. You will not be allowed to go back to a question after you've answered it. If you get stuck on a question, check to see how much time you have left and if you are on schedule to finish in adequate time. If you don't have time to spare, make an educated guess and move on.

Another very important item to remember is to read every question and answer it carefully. The CCNA exam has many questions that are not designed to be trick questions; however, they require careful examination of the test question's syntax. Many of the questions refer to exact commands required to implement a function on a router. It is important to know the different syntax and to recognize small differences in commands. This book will highlight areas of the exam that might be tricky.

Make sure to read every answer before choosing one. Often, one answer might sound great; however, another answer will be more correct than the first. Remember to read all of the answers before choosing the best one. In addition, saying questions out loud often makes them easier to understand and, thus, easier to answer.

# About this Book

Each *Exam Cram* chapter follows a regular structure, along with graphic cues about important or useful information. Here's the structure of a typical chapter:

➤ *Opening hotlists* —Each chapter begins with a list of the terms and techniques that you must learn and understand before you can be fully conversant with that chapter's subject matter. We follow the hotlists with one or two introductory paragraphs to set the stage for the rest of the chapter.

➤ *Topical coverage* —After the opening hotlists, each chapter covers a series of topics related to the chapter's subject title. Throughout this section, we highlight topics or concepts that are likely to appear on a test using a special Exam Alert layout, like this:

 This is what an Exam Alert looks like. Normally, an Exam Alert stresses concepts, terms, software, or activities that are likely to relate to one or more certification test questions. For that reason, we think any information found offset in Exam Alert format is worthy of unusual attention on your part. Indeed, most of the information that appears on the Cram Sheet appears as Exam Alerts within the text.

Pay close attention to material flagged as an Exam Alert; although all of the information in this book pertains to what you need to know to pass the exam, we have flagged certain items that are really important. You'll find what appears in the meat of each chapter to be worth knowing, too, when preparing for the test. Because this book's material is very condensed, we recommend that you use this book along with other resources to achieve the maximum benefit.

In addition to the Exam Alerts, we have provided tips that will help you to build a better foundation for CCNA knowledge. Although the information may not be on the exam, it is certainly related and will help you to become a better test taker.

This is how tips are formatted. Keep your eyes open for these, and you'll become a networking guru in no time.

➤ *Practice questions* —Although we talk about test questions and topics through-out each chapter, this section presents a series of mock test questions and explanations of both correct and incorrect answers. We also try to point out especially tricky questions by using this special icon:

➤ *Trick questions* —Ordinarily, this icon flags the presence of a particularly de-vious inquiry, if not an outright trick question. Trick questions are calculated to be answered incorrectly if not read more than once and very carefully. Although they're not ubiquitous, such questions make regular appearances on the Cisco exams. That's why we say that exam questions are as much about reading comprehension as they are about knowing your material inside out and backwards.

➤ *Details and resources* —Every chapter ends with a section titled "Need to Know More?" This section provides direct pointers to Cisco and third-party re-sources who offer more details on the chapter's subject. In addition, this sec-tion tries to rank or at least rate the quality and thoroughness of the topic's coverage by each resource. If you find a resource you like in this collection, use it, but don't feel compelled to use all the resources. On the other hand, we recommend only resources we use on a regular basis, so none of our recom-mendations will be a waste of your time or money (but purchasing them all at once probably represents an expense that many network administrators and would-be CCNAs, CCNPs, and CCIEs might find hard to justify).

The bulk of the book follows this chapter structure slavishly, but we'd like to point out a few other elements. Chapter 17 includes a sample test that provides a good review of the material presented throughout the book to ensure that you're ready for the exam. Chapter 18 provides an answer key to the sample test that appears in Chapter 17. Additionally, you'll find the glossary, which explains terms, and an index that you can use to locate terms as they appear in the text.

Finally, the tear-out Cram Sheet attached next to the inside front cover of this *Exam Cram* book represents a condensed and compiled collection of facts and tips that we think you should memorize before taking the test. Because you can dump this information out of your head onto a piece of paper before taking the exam, you can master this information by brute force—you need to remember it only long enough to write it down when you walk into the test room. You might even want to look at it in the car or in the lobby of the testing center just before you walk in to take the test.

# How to Use this Book

If you're preparing for a first-time test, we've structured the topics in this book to build on one another. Therefore, some topics in later chapters make more sense after you've read earlier chapters. That's why we suggest that you read this book from front to back for your initial test preparation. If you need to brush up on a topic or get ready for a second try, use the index or table of contents to go straight to the topics and questions that you need to study. Beyond helping you prepare for the test, we think you'll find this book useful as a tightly focused reference to some of the most important aspects of routing and switching.

Given all of the book's elements and its specialized focus, we've tried to create a tool that will help you to prepare for—and pass—Cisco Exam 640-507, "Cisco Certified Network Associate 2.0." Please share your feedback about the book with us, especially if you have ideas about how we can improve it for future test takers. We'll consider everything you say carefully, and we'll respond to all suggestions.

Send your questions or comments to us at **learn@examcram.com**. Please remember to include the title of the book in your message; otherwise, we'll be forced to guess which book you're writing about. And we don't like to guess—we want to *know*! Also, be sure to check out the Web pages at **www.examcram.com**, where you'll find practice tests, information updates, commentary, clarifications, and more on documents for each book that you can either read online or download for later use.

Thanks, and enjoy the book!

# Self-Assessment

The Self-Assessment in this *Exam Cram* book will help you to evaluate your readiness to tackle the Cisco Certified Network Associate (CCNA) certification. It should also help you to understand what you need to know to master the topic of this book, namely, CCNA Exam 640-507. But before you tackle this assessment, let's talk about the information technology (IT) networking profession and understand the opportunity Cisco certifications can create for you.

## IT Networking Opportunities

The demand for experienced and skilled IT networking professionals is forecast to grow tremendously over the next decade. In addition, the supply of skilled IT networking professionals does not meet the current demand, thus requiring IT organizations to pay a premium for these skills. The demand for IT networking professionals at all levels is increasing, and it's creating an opportunity for both the novice and the expert to increase their personal net worth to corporate America.

The beauty of IT networking is that the industry builds from a core set of technical skills into a wide variety of diverse and highly challenging technical focuses. Mastery of the IT networking foundation skills enables an individual to learn more complex subjects at a more rapid pace. Many professionals attempt or are forced to learn the more complex subjects of IT networking before they truly understand the basic networking skills. These people often become frustrated, and their ability to learn new skills is drastically reduced, because they never took the time to master the foundation skills.

The CCNA exam is an excellent starting point or checkpoint for determining if you have mastered the basic skills of IT networking. We cannot emphasize enough the advantages you will realize by mastering these skills before attempting to understand the more complex subjects of IT networking.

Mastering the basic skills before attempting to understand the more difficult technologies is critical to your success. Now for the good news: The CCNA exam is designed for IT networking professionals of all levels. It tests the basic foundations skills required to be successful in the profession.

If you are a novice IT networking professional, this book is focused on assisting you to obtain possibly your first IT certification. If you are an experienced IT professional, this book gives you the opportunity to go back and master the basic skills and substantially increase your ability to learn more complex technologies quickly.

Choosing Cisco Systems Career Certifications as a starting point for your career certification process is the right step. Cisco Systems currently owns 80 percent of the internetworking arena. Cisco is the dominant player in corporate network infrastructures and the Internet. Individuals who have Cisco Certifications find jobs, period.

# CCNAs in the Real World

In the next section, we describe an ideal CCNA candidate, knowing full well that only a few real candidates will meet this ideal. In fact, our description of that ideal candidate might seem downright scary. But take heart: Although the requirements to obtain CCNA certification may seem pretty formidable, they are by no means impossible to meet. You should be keenly aware, however, that it does take time, require some expense, and consume substantial effort to get through the process.

You can get all the real-world motivation you need from knowing that many others have gone before, so you will be able to follow in their footsteps. If you're willing to tackle the process seriously and do what it takes to obtain the necessary experience and knowledge, you can take—and pass—all the certification tests involved in obtaining a CCNA. In fact, we've designed this *Exam Cram* to make it as easy on you as possible to prepare for these exams. But prepare you must!

# The Ideal CCNA Candidate

Just to give you some idea of what an ideal CCNA candidate is, here are some relevant statistics about the background and experience such an individual might have. Don't worry if you don't meet these qualifications or even come very close—this is a far from an ideal world, and where you fall short is simply where you'll have more work to do.

➤ Academic or professional training in network theory, concepts, and operations.

➤ Two years or more of professional networking experience in a LAN environment, including experience with Ethernet, token ring, modems, switches, and other networking media. This must include installation, configuration, upgrade, and troubleshooting experience.

➤ Two years or more in a WAN environment that includes hands-on experience with Frame Relay, High-level Data Link Control (HDLC), or Integrated Services Digital Network (ISDN) architecture, installation, configuration, maintenance, and troubleshooting.

➤ A thorough understanding of key networking protocols, routing protocols, and addressing, including Transmission Control Protocol/Internet Protocol (TCP/IP), Internet Packet Exchange/Sequence Packet Exchange (IPX/SPX), Routing Information Protocol (RIP), and Interior Gateway Routing Protocol (IGRP).

Fundamentally, this boils down to a bachelor's degree in computer science, plus three years of work experience in a technical position involving network design, installation, configuration, and maintenance. We believe that well under half of all certification candidates meet these requirements and that, in fact, most meet less than half of these requirements—at least, when they begin the certification process. Many have survived this ordeal and have been certified, and you can survive it too—especially if you heed what our Self-Assessment can tell you about what you already know and what you need to learn.

# Put Yourself to the Test

The following series of questions and observations is designed to help you figure out how much work you must do to pursue CCNA certification and what resources to consult on your quest. Be absolutely honest in your answers, or you'll end up wasting money on exams that you're not yet ready to take. You'll not find right or wrong answers, only steps along the path to certification. Only you can decide where you really belong in the broad spectrum of aspiring candidates.

Two things should be clear from the outset:

➤ Even a modest background in computer science will be helpful.

➤ Hands-on experience with Cisco products and technologies is an essential ingredient to certification success.

## Educational Background

1. Have you ever taken any computer-related classes? [Yes or No]

    ➤ If Yes, proceed to Question 2.

    ➤ If No, proceed to Question 3.

2. Have you taken any networking concepts or technologies classes? [Yes or No]

➤ If Yes, you will probably be able to handle networking terminology, concepts, and technologies. If you're rusty, brush up on basic networking concepts and terminology, especially the Open Systems Interconnect (OSI) model, TCP/IP, IPX/SPX, and networking technologies such as Ethernet, token ring, fiber distributed data interface (FDDI), and WAN links.

➤ If No, you might want to read one or two books in this topic area. The two best books that we know of are *Computer Networks, 3rd Edition*, by Andrew S. Tanenbaum (Prentice Hall, 1996, ISBN 0133499456) and *Computer Networks and Internets*, by Douglas E. Comer (Prentice Hall, 1997, ISBN 0132390701).

➤ Skip to the next section, "Hands-on Experience."

3. Have you done any reading about networks? [Yes or No]

➤ If Yes, review the requirements stated in the first paragraphs after Question 2. If you meet those requirements, move on to the next section, "Hands-on Experience."

➤ If No, consult the recommended reading list. A strong background will help you to prepare for the CCNA exam better than just about anything else.

# Hands-on Experience

The most important key to success on all of the Cisco tests is hands-on experience, especially with Cisco routers. If we leave you with only one realization after taking this Self-Assessment, it should be that you can't find any substitute for time spent installing, configuring, and using the various Cisco equipment on which you'll be tested repeatedly and in depth.

4. Have you installed, configured, and worked with Cisco routers? [Yes or No]

➤ If Yes, make sure that you understand addressing, TCP/IP, IPX/SPX, and routing protocols. Be sure to study WAN services like Frame Relay and ISDN.

➤ If you haven't worked with Cisco routers, we recommend that you obtain access to at least two routers, so that you can exercise the concepts that you will be learning.

5. Have you installed, configured, and worked with Cisco switches? [Yes or No]

➤ If Yes, make sure that you understand the concepts and benefits of network segmentation and the types of LAN switching.

➤ If No, you will need to obtain access to a switch.

Before you even think about taking any Cisco exam, make sure that you've spent enough time with the related equipment and software to understand how to install, configure, monitor, and troubleshoot it. This will help you during the exam and in real life.

## Testing Your Exam-Readiness

Whether you attend a formal class on a specific topic to get ready for an exam or use written materials to study on your own, some preparation for the CCNA certification exam is essential. At $100 a try, pass or fail, you want to do everything you can to pass on your first try. That's where studying comes in.

For any given subject, consider taking a class if you've tackled self-study materials, taken the test, and failed anyway. The opportunity to interact with an instructor and fellow students can make all the difference in the world, if you can afford that privilege. For information about Cisco classes, visit the Training and Certification Web page at **www.cisco.com/training** or **www.geotrain.com** (use the "Locate a Course" link).

If you can't afford to take a class, visit the Training and Certification Web page anyway, because it also includes pointers to free practice exams and other self-study tools. Even if you can't afford to spend much at all, you should still invest in some low-cost practice exams from commercial vendors, because they can help you to assess your readiness to pass a test better than any other tool. All of the following Web sites offer practice exams online:

➤ The Coriolis Group's Study Resource Center at **www.examcram.com/studyresource/practiceexam**.

➤ CCPrep.com at **www.ccprep.com** (requires membership)

➤ Network Study Guides at **www.networkstudyguides.com** (pay as you go)

6. Have you taken a practice exam on your chosen test subject? [Yes or No]

➤ If Yes and you scored 70 percent or better, you're probably ready to tackle the real thing. If your score isn't above that crucial threshold, keep at it until you break that barrier.

➤ If No, obtain all of the free and low-budget practice tests you can find (see the previous list) and get to work. Keep at it until you can break the passing threshold comfortably.

When it comes to assessing your test readiness, no better way exists than to take a good-quality practice exam and pass with a score of 70 percent or better. When we're preparing ourselves, we shoot for 80-plus percent, just to leave room for the "weirdness factor" that sometimes shows up on Cisco exams.

# Assessing Readiness for Exam 640-507

In addition to the general exam-readiness information in the previous section, you can do several things to prepare for the CCNA exam. As you're getting ready for Exam 640-507, visit the Cisco Web site at **www.cisco.com**. Its open forum or technical tips sections are great places to ask questions and get good answers or to watch the questions that others ask (along with the answers, of course).

For OSI model, TCP/IP, and basic router configuration preparation in particular, we'd also like to recommend that you check out one or more of the following resources as you prepare to take Exam 640-507:

➤ Shawn McNutt, Mark Poplar, Jason Waters, David Stabenaw. *CCNA Routing and Switching Exam Prep*. The Coriolis Group, Scottsdale, AZ, 2000. ISBN 1-57610-440-0.

➤ Chappell, Laura. *Introduction to Cisco Router Configuration*. Cisco Systems Inc., MacMillan Publishing Company, Indianapolis, IN, 1998. ISBN 0-7645-3186-7.

➤ Comer, Douglas. *Internetworking with TCP/IP: Principles, Protocols, and Architecture, Vol. 1*. Prentice Hall, Englewood Cliffs, NJ, 1995. ISBN 0-1321-6987-8.

➤ Stallings, William. *Handbook of Computer Communications Standards: The Open Systems Interconnection (OSI Model and OSI-Related Standards), Vol. 1*. Prentice-Hall, Englewood Cliffs, NJ, 1990. ISBN 0-02415-521-7.

Stop by your favorite bookstore or online bookseller to check out one or more of these resources.

One last note: It makes sense to stress the importance of hands-on experience in the context of the CCNA exam. As you review the material for that exam, you'll realize that hands-on experience with the various router configuration and monitoring commands is invaluable.

# Onward, through the Fog

When you've assessed your readiness, undertaken the right background studies, obtained the hands-on experience that will help you to understand the products and technologies at work, and reviewed the many sources of information to help you to prepare for a test, you'll be ready to take a round of practice tests. When your scores come back positive enough to get you through the exam, you're ready to go after the real thing. If you follow our assessment regime, you'll not only know what you need to study, but when you're ready to make a test date. Good luck!

# Cisco Career Certification Exams

**Terms you'll need to understand:**

✓ Radio button

✓ Checkbox

✓ Exhibit

✓ Multiple-choice question formats

✓ Careful reading

✓ Process of elimination

**Techniques you'll need to master:**

✓ Preparing to take a certification exam

✓ Practicing (to make perfect)

✓ Making the best use of the testing software

✓ Budgeting your time

✓ Saving the hardest questions until last

✓ Guessing (as a last resort)

✓ Breathing deeply to calm frustration

Exam taking is not something that most people anticipate eagerly, no matter how well prepared they are. In most cases, familiarity helps ameliorate test anxiety. In plain English, this means that you will probably not be as nervous when you take your fourth or fifth Cisco certification exam as when you take your first.

Whether it is your first exam or your tenth, understanding the details of exam taking (how much time to spend on questions, the environment you will be in, and so on) and the exam software will help you to concentrate on the material, rather than on the setting. Likewise, mastering a few basic exam-taking skills should help you to recognize—and perhaps even outfox—some of the tricks and gotchas you are bound to find in some of the exam questions.

This chapter, besides explaining the exam environment and software, describes some proven exam-taking strategies that you can use to your advantage.

# The Exam Situation

When you arrive at the exam testing center, you must sign in with an exam coordinator and show two forms of identification, one of which must be a photo ID. After you have signed in and your time slot arrives, you will be asked to deposit any books, bags, or other items you brought with you. Then, you will be escorted into a closed room. Typically, the room will be furnished with one to half a dozen computers, and each workstation will be separated from the others by dividers designed to keep you from seeing what is happening on someone else's computer.

You will be furnished with a pen or pencil and a blank sheet of paper, or, in some cases, an erasable plastic sheet and an erasable felt-tip pen. You are allowed to write any information you want on both sides of this sheet. Before the exam, memorize as much of the material that appears on the Cram Sheet (inside the front cover of this book) as you can and write that information on the blank sheet as soon as you are seated in front of the computer. You can refer to your rendition of the Cram Sheet anytime you like during the test, but you will have to surrender the sheet when you leave the room.

Most test rooms feature a wall with a large picture window. This permits the exam coordinator standing behind it to monitor the room, to prevent exam takers from talking to one another, and to observe anything out of the ordinary that might happen. The exam coordinator will have preloaded the appropriate Cisco certification exam—for this book, that's Exam 640-507—and you will be permitted to start as soon as you are seated in front of the computer.

All Cisco certification exams allow a certain maximum amount of time in which to complete the work (this time is indicated on the exam by an on-screen counter/clock, so you can check the time remaining whenever you like). Exam 640-507 consists of 65 randomly selected questions. You may take up to 75 minutes to complete the exam. To pass, you are required to achieve a score of 822 or better on a scale of 300 to 1,000.

All Cisco certification exams are computer-generated and use a multiple-choice format. From time to time, you may be prompted to enter actual configuration commands as if you were at the command-line interface. It is important not to abbreviate the commands in any way when this type of question is posed. Although this may sound quite simple, the questions are constructed not only to check your mastery of basic facts and figures about Cisco router configuration, but also to require you to evaluate one or more sets of circumstances or requirements. Often, you will be asked to give more than one answer to a question. Likewise, you might be asked to select the best or most effective solution to a problem from a range of choices, all of which are technically correct. Taking the exam is quite an adventure, and it involves real thinking. This book shows you what to expect and how to deal with the potential problems, puzzles, and predicaments.

# Exam Layout and Design

Some exam questions require you to select a single answer, whereas others ask you to select multiple correct answers. The following multiple-choice question requires you to select a single correct answer. Following the question is a brief summary of each potential answer and why it is either right or wrong.

## Question 1

What is the key piece of information on which routing decisions are based?

- ○ a. Source network layer address
- ○ b. Destination network layer address
- ○ c. Source MAC address
- ○ d. Destination MAC address

Answer b is correct. The destination network layer, or layer 3, address is the protocol-specific address to which this piece of data is to be delivered. The source network layer address is the originating host and plays no role in getting the information to the destination; therefore, answer a is incorrect. The source and destination MAC addresses are necessary for getting the data to the router or to the next hop address, but they are not used in pathing decisions; therefore, answers c and d are incorrect.

This sample question format corresponds closely to the Cisco certification exam format—the only difference on the exam is that answer keys do not follow questions. To select an answer, position the cursor over the radio button next to the answer, and then click the mouse button to select the answer.

Let's examine a question that requires choosing multiple answers. This type of question provides checkboxes rather than radio buttons for marking all appropriate selections.

## Question 2

---

Which of the following services exist at the application layer of the TCP/IP model? [Choose the three best answers]

❑ a. SMTP

❑ b. FTP

❑ c. ICMP

❑ d. ARP

❑ e. TFTP

---

Answers a, b, and e are correct. SMTP, FTP, and TFTP all exist at the application layer of the TCP/IP model. Answer c is incorrect because ICMP exists at the Internet layer of the TCP/IP model. Answer d is incorrect because ARP exists at the network interface layer of the TCP/IP model.

For this type of question, more than one answer is required. As far as the authors can tell, such questions are scored as wrong unless all of the required selections are chosen. In other words, a partially correct answer does not result in partial credit when the test is scored. For Question 2, you have to check the boxes next to items a, b, and e to obtain credit for a correct answer. Notice that picking the right answers also means knowing why the other answers are wrong!

These two basic types of questions can appear in many forms; they constitute the foundation on which all of the Cisco certification exam questions rest. More complex questions include so-called *exhibits*, which are usually network scenarios, screen shots of output from the router, or pictures from the course materials. For some of these questions, you will be asked to make a selection by clicking on a checkbox or radio button on the screenshot itself. For others, you will be expected to use the information displayed therein to guide your answer to the question. Familiarity with the underlying utility is your key to choosing the correct answers.

Other questions involving exhibits use charts or network diagrams to help document a workplace scenario that you will be asked to troubleshoot or configure. Careful attention to such exhibits is the key to success. Be prepared to toggle frequently between the exhibit and the question as you work.

# Using Cisco's Exam Software Effectively

Unlike some exams by Cisco and other companies, the CCNA 2.0 exam software does not allow you to mark questions or review them later. You may not skip questions or go back to them later. In fact, the test engine will not let you proceed if you have not selected an answer or if you have not chosen the correct number of answers.

With this in mind, time management is very important during the test. You cannot save difficult or lengthy questions to do at the end of the exam. For this reason, it will be helpful to monitor your progress by checking the clock periodically during the test. Make sure that you are one-third of the way through the test when one-third of your time is up. The test has 65 questions and allows 75 minutes, so that gives you just over 1 minute per question.

# Exam-Taking Basics

The most important advice about taking any exam is this: Read each question carefully. Some questions are deliberately ambiguous, some use double negatives, and others use terminology in incredibly precise ways. The authors have taken numerous exams—both practice and live—and have missed at least one question in nearly every one because they did not read the question closely or carefully enough.

Here are some suggestions for how to deal with the tendency to jump to an answer too quickly:

➤ Make sure you read every word in the question. If you find yourself jumping ahead impatiently, go back and start over.

➤ As you read, try to restate the question in your own terms. If you can do this, you should be able to pick the correct answers much more easily.

➤ When returning to a question after your initial read-through, read every word again; otherwise, your mind can fall quickly into a rut. Sometimes, revisiting a question after turning your attention elsewhere lets you see something you missed, but the strong tendency is to see what you have seen before. Try to avoid that tendency at all costs.

➤ If you return to a question more than twice, try to articulate to yourself what you do not understand about the question, why the answers do not appear to make sense, or what appears to be missing. If you reflect on the subject for a while, your subconscious might provide the details that are lacking or you might notice a trick that will point to the right answer.

➤ Breathe. Deep rhythmic breathing is a stress reliever. Breathe in for a count of four, hold it for two, and then exhale for a count of four. You will be surprised how this can clear your mind of the frustration that clouds it and allow you to regain focus.

Above all, try to deal with each question by thinking through what you know about Cisco routers and their configuration—the characteristics, behaviors, facts, and figures involved. By reviewing what you know (and what you have written down on your information sheet), you will often recall or understand things sufficiently to determine the answer to the question.

# Question-Handling Strategies

Based on exams the authors have taken, some interesting trends have become apparent. For questions that require a single answer, two or three of the answers will usually be obviously incorrect, and two of the answers will be plausible—of course, only one can be correct. Unless the answer leaps out at you (if it does, reread the question to look for a trick; sometimes those are the ones you are most likely to get wrong), begin the process of answering by eliminating those answers that are most obviously wrong.

Things to look for in obviously wrong answers include spurious menu choices or utility names, nonexistent software options, and terminology you have never seen. If you have done your homework for an exam, no valid information should be completely new to you. In that case, unfamiliar or bizarre terminology probably indicates a bogus answer.

Numerous questions assume that the default behavior of a particular utility is in effect. If you know the defaults and understand what they mean, this knowledge will help you cut through many Gordian knots.

As you work your way through the exam, another counter that Cisco thankfully provides will come in handy—the number of questions completed and questions outstanding. Budget your time by making sure that you have completed one-quarter of the questions one-quarter of the way through the exam period and three-quarters of them three-quarters of the way through.

If you are not finished when 70 minutes have elapsed, use the last 5 minutes to guess your way through the remaining questions. Remember, guessing is potentially more valuable than not answering; blank answers are always wrong, but a guess may turn out to be right. If you do not have a clue about any of the remaining questions, pick answers at random. The important thing is to submit an exam for scoring that has an answer for every question.

# Mastering the Inner Game

In the final analysis, knowledge breeds confidence, and confidence breeds success. If you study the materials in this book carefully and review all of the exam prep questions at the end of each chapter, you should become aware of those areas where additional learning and study are required.

Next, follow up by reading some or all of the materials recommended in the "Need to Know More?" section at the end of each chapter. The idea is to become familiar enough with the concepts and situations you find in the sample questions that you can reason your way through similar situations on a real exam. If you know the material, you have every right to be confident that you can pass the exam.

After you have worked your way through the book, take the practice exam in Chapter 17. This will provide a reality check and help you to identify areas that you need to study further. Make sure that you follow up and review materials related to the questions you miss on the practice exam before scheduling a real exam. Take the real exam only when you have covered all of the ground and feel comfortable with the whole scope of the practice exam.

 If you take the practice exam and do not score at least 75 percent correct, you need additional practice.

Armed with the information in this book and with the determination to augment your knowledge, you should be able to pass the certification exam. You need to work at it, however, or you will spend the exam fee more than once before you finally pass. If you prepare seriously, you should do well. Good luck!

# Additional Resources

A good source of information about Cisco certification exams comes from Cisco itself. Because its products and technologies (and the exams that go with them) change frequently, the best place to go for exam-related information is online.

If you haven't already visited the Cisco Certified Professional site, do so right now. The Cisco Connection Online home page resides at **www.cisco.com/warp/public/10/wwtraining/certprog/index.html**, as shown in Figure 1.1.

*Note: Because things change regularly on the Cisco site, the home page might not be available at this address or it might have been replaced by something new and different. If this is the case, read the sidebar titled "Coping with Change on the Web."*

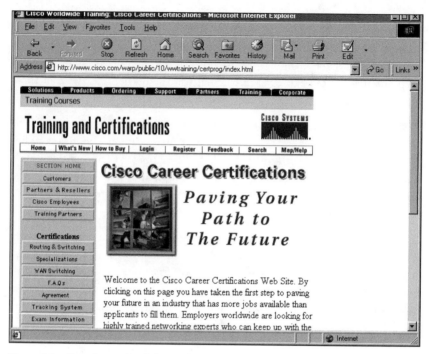

**Figure 1.1** Cisco Connection Online home page.

The menu options in the left column of the home page point to the most important sources of information in the Career Certification pages. Here's what to check out:

➤ *Routing and Switching*—Use this entry to explore the CCIE certification track for routing and switching.

➤ *Specializations*—Use this entry to explore different CCNP specialization options.

➤ *WAN Switching*—Use this entry to explore the CCIE certification track for wide area network (WAN) switching.

➤ *FAQs*—Use this entry to access the most commonly asked questions regarding any Cisco Career Certification.

➤ *Agreement*—Prior to certification, all candidates must complete the certification agreement or Cisco will not recognize them as certified professionals.

➤ *Tracking System*—After you have registered with Sylvan Prometric and taken any Cisco exam, you will be added to a living certification tracking system automatically so that you can keep up with your progress.

➤ *Exam Information*—This entry actually points to a class locator. It should be noted that no book is an adequate replacement for instructor-led, Cisco-authorized training. This entry will assist your efforts to find a class that meets your scheduling needs.

These are just the high points of what's available on the Cisco Certified Professional pages. As you browse through them—and we strongly recommend that you do—you will probably find other informational tidbits that are interesting and compelling.

## Coping with Change on the Web

Sooner or later, all the information we have shared with you about the Cisco Certified Professional pages and the other Web-based resources mentioned throughout the rest of this book will go stale or be replaced by newer information. In some cases, the Uniform Resource Locators (URLs) you find here might lead you to their replacements; in other cases, the URLs will go nowhere, leaving you with the dreaded "404 File not found" error message. When that happens, do not give up.

There's always a way to find what you want on the Web if you are willing to invest some time and energy. Most large or complex Web sites—and Cisco's qualifies on both counts—offer a search engine. Looking back at Figure 1.1, you can see that a Search field appears along the top edge of the page. As long as you can get to Cisco's site (it should stay at **www.cisco.com** for a long while yet), you can use this tool to help you find what you need.

The more focused you can make a search request, the more likely the results will include information you can use. For example, you can search for the string "training and certification" to produce a lot of data about the subject in general, but if you are looking for the preparation guide for Exam 640-507, "CCNA Routing and Switching," you will be more likely to get there quickly if you use a search string similar to the following:

```
"Exam 640-507" AND "preparation guide"
```

Finally, feel free to use general search tools—such as **www.search.com**, **www.altavista.com**, and **www.excite.com**—to search for related information. The bottom line is this: If you can't find something where the book says it lives, intensify your search.

# Internetworking
# Concepts Overview

. . . . . . . . . . . . . . . . . . . . . . . . . . . . . . . . . . . . . . . .

### Terms you'll need to understand:

✓ Local area network (LAN)

✓ Wide area network (WAN)

✓ Bridge

✓ Switch

✓ Router

### Techniques you'll need to master:

✓ Learning the advantages of LAN segmentation

✓ Identifying the network congestion problem in Ethernet networks

✓ Understanding LAN segmentation using bridges

✓ Learning the benefits of network segmentation with bridges

✓ Understanding LAN segmentation using switches

✓ Learning the benefits of network segmentation with switches

✓ Understanding the features and benefits of Fast Ethernet

✓ Learning the guidelines and distance limitations of Fast Ethernet

The first step in preparing for CCNA certification is making sure you have a solid understanding of basic networking concepts. You will rely on these fundamentals as you learn to design and configure Cisco routed and switched internetworks. You will need to understand different network topologies, transmission media, and protocols. In addition, you must know the components that make up a network—hubs, bridges, routers, switches, etc. This chapter will provide an overview of these basic internetworking concepts.

# Networking Fundamentals

This section will briefly review several basic networking concepts that are the building blocks to CCNA study. Ideally, you should recognize and understand most of the material in this section, using it only as a review. If these concepts are not familiar, make sure you study this section and master this material before progressing.

The network consists of several components—the physical connections between devices; the intermediate devices that facilitate transmission such as hubs, routers, and switches; and the protocols used to make everything work. You will examine the following components that make network communication possible:

➤ *Transmission media*—The physical connection between devices

➤ *Media access method*—The rules that define how a device can access the transmission media

➤ *Data transmission methods*—What types of data messages can be sent

➤ *Network transport methods*—The standards, such as Ethernet, that define the media, access, and transmission methods and form a complete system for moving data

## Transmission Media

At the bottom of the Open Systems Interconnect (OSI) model are the layers that define how a network is physically connected—the wires that carry data from one device to another. This network component is called the *transmission media*. It is important to note that wire is not the only type of transmission media. Several newer technologies, such as microwave, radio, and infrared, use air as the transmission medium.

The most common types of wire-based transmission media are:

➤ *Twisted pair copper cable*—This is a popular wiring type for local area networks (LANs). Individual copper wires are twisted together to prevent electromagnetic interference (EMI). These twisted pairs of wires are wound together and have an outer casing. Twisted pair is very inexpensive and flexible. Most buildings are pre-wired with unshielded twisted pair (UTP) copper cable because it's the same wire used for telephone service. Twisted pair network cables can reliably transmit data to a length of 100 meters. There's another type of twisted pair cable that adds an additional foil shield wrapping between the copper pairs and the outer casing—shielded twisted pair (STP). This provides additional protection against EMI.

The American National Standards Institute classifies twisted pair cable into different "categories" based on the data rate it can sustain. The most common types of cables you will see are Category 3 and Category 5 (also called CAT 3 or CAT 5). CAT 3 is the minimum cable type required for voice systems and 10Mb Ethernet. CAT 5 is required to support Fast Ethernet. Most newer buildings are being pre-wired with CAT 5 cable. However, many existing cable plants are wired with CAT 3 cable.

➤ *Coaxial cable*—Coaxial cable comes in two forms: thick and thin. Thick cable (also called *ThickNet*) was one of the first types of wire used to connect computers. This type of wire is rigid and thus difficult to work with. The other type of coaxial cable, Thin or *ThinNet* is easier to work with because of its flexibility. Coaxial cable can support longer distances than twisted pair.

➤ *Fiber-optic cable*—Fiber-optic is the newest type of cable available for wiring networks. It consists of a glass core that is encased by a plastic outer covering. Instead of electrical current, fiber-optic cable carries laser light. It can transport data much further than other wiring types—miles instead of feet. It is also immune to EMI. The disadvantages are its cost and difficulty to install and work with.

# Media Access Methods

Most networks today are built using some type of shared media. That is, all the devices on the network are connected to the same physical wire, whether it's twisted pair, coaxial, or fiber-optic. Only one device can access the media at a given time, so there must be some way for devices to share the available media (also called a channel).

A *media access method* is a rule or set of rules that define how devices can share a single media channel. The most common media access methods currently in use are:

➤ *Contention*—Contention is an access method in which devices access the media on a first-come, first-served basis. All devices are contending for the single media channel. The most common type of contention method is *carrier sense multiple access with collision detection* (CSMA/CD). This type of access method is used by Ethernet. Whenever the device needs to send data, it listens to the channel to find out if it is available. If so, the data is sent. If not, it will wait until the channel is free. The problem with this method is that two devices may check the channel at the same time, both detecting that it is free, and both may send data at the same time. When this happens, a collision occurs, and both devices must retransmit the data.

➤ *Token passing*—Token passing is an access method that is used in ring-connected networks. A signal called the *token* is passed from device to device around the ring, so that data can only be transmitted over the media when a device has the token. The token passing method eliminates collisions and retransmissions. However, the disadvantage is that more processing power is required, and problems can occur if the ring is broken by a malfunctioning device.

➤ *Polling*—Polling is an access method that relies on a central device to control access to the network. Before a device can transmit data onto the network, it must check with this central device, known as a *media access administrator* or *channel access administrator*.

## Data Transmission Methods

Once a network device has access to the shared media, how does it format the data in order to get the data to its intended recipient? The answer to this depends on whether the data needs to be sent to a single device or multiple devices on the network. Remember, because all devices are connected to the same physical media, all the devices may "see" all the packets, regardless of their intended recipient. Each device will examine the packet to determine its recipient. If the packet is addressed to a different device, it will get dropped. There are three methods by which data packets are addressed and transmitted onto the network: unicast, multicast, and broadcast.

➤ *Unicast*—A unicast packet is one that is sent directly from one device to another. Each network device is identified by a unique hardware address (MAC address), and only the machine whose address matches will process the packet.

➤ *Multicast*—A multicast packet needs to be sent to more than one recipient. This is accomplished by addressing each packet to a multicast group address. Hosts wishing to receive the packet must join this multicast group. Multicasts are typically used with multimedia applications, such as delivering video and audio to end users on a network. IP multicasting applications use Class D addresses to address packets. Class D IP addresses range from 224.0.0.0 to 239.255.255.255. (IP Addressing will be discussed in detail in Chapter 10.)

➤ *Broadcast*—A broadcast packet is sent to all receiving devices on the network. A special address is used in place of the recipient's hardware address, indicating that the packet is intended for all network devices.

# Network Standards

Several network standards have been developed that define specific topologies, media, access methods, and transmission methods. These standards incorporate all of these aspects into a single solution for moving data across a network. Three of the most common standards are: Ethernet, token ring, and ATM.

➤ *Ethernet*—Ethernet has become, by far, the most common standard for local area networks (LANs). Ethernet uses coaxial, twisted pair, or fiber-optic cable to transmit data using CSMA/CD contention. It operates at the speed of 10Mbps (10 million bits per second). There are faster versions of Ethernet as well—Fast Ethernet operates at 100Mbps, and Gigabit Ethernet operates at 1,000Mbps. Devices are connected either on a bus or star topology.

 Ethernet uses a three-part naming convention. Common Ethernet specifications include 10baseT, 100baseT, and 10baseFL. First is a number indicating the speed (in Mbps), such as 10 or 100. Second is the signaling type, which in almost all cases is baseband, or base. Finally, there is a value indicating the physical media type. For example, T indicates twisted-pair, and F indicates fiber media.

➤ *Token ring*—Token ring was developed by IBM in the 1970s and is still a common network type in use today. Devices on a token ring network are connected in a ring topology. Typically, they are connected to a multistation access unit (MSAU) that simulates the ring topology. Token ring uses either coaxial cable or twisted pair to transmit data using the token passing method of media access. It operates at speeds up to 16Mbps.

➤ *ATM*—Asynchronous Transfer Mode (ATM) is a newer network standard that can be used for extremely high-speed data transport over long distances. It uses a star topology, and relies on polling as the media access method. An ATM switch is the central hub of the star and acts as the channel access administrator. ATM can use coaxial or fiber-optic cable at speeds from 200Mbps to over 1Gbps (1 billion bits per second).

# The OSI Model

As computers and networks have evolved since the 1960s, a wide variety of software and hardware components have been developed to enable computers to share data. Luckily for everyone, the International Organization for Standardization (ISO) created the Open Systems Interconnect (OSI) reference model to promote interconnectivity between different developers and vendors of computer equipment. This model divides the functions of networking—moving data from one device to another—into seven distinct and separate tasks or layers.

Each of the seven layers within the OSI model represents a specific and separate network function. Standards and protocols have been defined for each layer. These protocols sit one atop the other and, as a whole, can be considered a protocol stack. When two systems are communicating over the network, data is being sent down the protocol stack at the sending device and back up the protocol stack at the receiving device. This division of separate network functions in a stack provides the following benefits:

➤ The interrelated aspects of network operations are divided into simpler components.

➤ Complex internetworking components can be divided into discrete subsets.

➤ Hardware and software engineers can focus their designs and development efforts in a modular fashion.

➤ Enhancements to one area are isolated from another area.

➤ Standard interfaces for plug-and-play compatibility between vendors can be defined.

For example, the OSI model details how data should be communicated from a word processing application residing on one computer through a network medium (like a copper wire) to a word processing application residing on another computer. The specific network layers and functions within the OSI model are described in Table 2.1.

*Note: Layers 1 and 2 of the OSI model are implemented through hardware and software; layers 3 through 7 are implemented in software.*

The OSI model will be described in detail in Chapters 3 and 4.

# Problems Associated with the Expanding Network

Most of the technologies you're studying in preparation for the CCNA exam were developed as a means to solve some of the problems that existed in traditional LANs. We will use Ethernet as the basis for discussion in the following section due to its dominance in the marketplace.

Ethernet is an efficient and reliable means of sharing data between computers when used in the environment for which it was designed. At the time this standard was developed, typical networks rarely exceeded a few hundred devices, and 4Mbps or 10Mbps was adequate bandwidth to support the network applications being used.

Now, compare that with the needs of today's typical mid- to large-sized corporate network. The number of network devices requiring support is often in the thousands. In addition, newer applications are demanding ever-increasing amounts of bandwidth to support applications such as realtime voice or video conferencing.

| Table 2.1 | The OSI model. | |
|---|---|---|
| **Layer Number** | **Layer Name** | **Layer Function** |
| 7 | Application layer | Provides network services to a user application program. It is the highest layer in the model and is the closest to the user. |
| 6 | Presentation layer | Provides data representation, data encryption, and data compression. It ensures that data sent from and arriving to the application layer is readable. |
| 5 | Session layer | Establishes, maintains, and terminates sessions between applications. |
| 4 | Transport layer | Segments and reassembles data into a data stream. |
| 3 | Network layer | Determines the optimal way to move data from one place to another within the network. |
| 2 | Data link layer | Provides physical transmission across the network medium. Also called the link layer. |
| 1 | Physical layer | Provides the electrical, mechanical, procedural, and functional means for establishing and maintaining the physical link among systems. |

# Latency

One of the first issues that must be addressed when dealing with an expanding local area network is the fact that all devices are sharing the same physical media. As more devices are placed on the wire, chances become greater and greater that the wire will be busy as each device requires access. The time during which the device must wait for access to the wire is called *latency*.

As you can imagine, there's a certain threshold where adding new devices begins to noticeably impact performance. The actual number of devices that can be supported varies greatly, depending on the types of network applications being used.

# Collisions

Collisions are another problem for an overcrowded Ethernet network. By design, a network device must check to make sure the wire is free before transmitting data. However, there is a small chance that every time a device transmits data, another device will transmit data at exactly the same time and a collision will occur. In this event, both devices stop, wait a random amount of time and try to retransmit the data. Collisions are not necessarily a bad thing. By design, they will happen in an Ethernet network. However, a high collision rate can seriously impact network performance, and the likelihood of a collision happening increases with each new device added into the network.

In order to combat the problem created by collisions in an Ethernet network, you must segment the network into smaller collision domains. This can be accomplished by using bridges, switches, or routers.

## Broadcasts

Another issue related to overcrowding an Ethernet segment is the *broadcast storm*. A broadcast is a frame sent to every device on the segment. As such, it requires every network interface card (NIC) to process the frame, regardless of whether the frame is actually intended for that device.

Broadcasts are a very important component in today's network-enabled operating systems, because they are typically used to help users find resources. However, more hosts on a segment mean more broadcasts that must be processed by every machine on the segment. Excessive broadcasts can have a very negative impact on network performance.

Segmenting the network into separate broadcast domains can alleviate broadcast problems. A router is often used to accomplish this.

*Note: Switches can also be used to segment a network into separate broadcast domains by using VLANs. However, for devices to communicate between VLANs, a router is required.*

# Network Hardware Roles

The problems of network congestion can be addressed by segmenting the network into smaller sections. There are three tools commonly used in today's networks to perform this segmentation: bridges, routers, and switches. In the following section, you will take a look at the role each device plays within a network infrastructure.

## Hubs

Hubs are non-intelligent devices operating at layer 1 (physical layer) of the OSI model. Hubs are used at the lowest level of desktop connectivity. Actually, many companies are phasing out hubs for desktop connectivity in favor of a switch port for every device.

A hub can be thought of as a physical extension to the Ethernet wire. A hub does not view or process any data that crosses it. It simply receives data on any wire plugged into it, and electronically repeats this data to all other wires.

The characteristics of hubs can be summarized as follows:

➤ All devices share bandwidth.

➤ All devices are in the same collision domain.

➤ All devices are in the same broadcast domain.

# Bridges

A *bridge* is used to physically separate a LAN into multiple segments. A bridge operates at layer 2 (data link layer) of the OSI model, making installation simple because a bridge is transparent to higher-layer protocols like Transmission Control Protocol/Internet Protocol (TCP/IP) and Internet Packet Exchange (IPX). All that is required to make a bridge work is plugging a segment into each of its ports and turning it on.

Each port on a bridge constitutes a separate segment. A single device can be plugged into a port, thus getting its own segment. Or, a hub can be plugged into a bridge port, connecting any devices on the hub to its own segment. Each segment becomes a separate *collision domain*. For this reason, a bridge can be a simple and effective way to improve the performance of a network experiencing excessive line utilization or collisions. Broadcasts, however, are still forwarded to all segments. These characteristics are summarized as follows:

➤ Each segment is a separate collision domain.

➤ All segments are in the same broadcast domain.

Because it is a layer 2 device, all bridging decisions are based on layer 2 hardware media access control (MAC) addresses. By listening to all frames on each segment, the bridge learns which devices are present on each segment, and builds a *forwarding table* based on this information. Figure 2.1 shows an example of a network that is separated into two segments with a bridge.

When a device on segment 1 sends out a frame for a host on segment 2, the bridge will forward the frame. However, if the same host sends a frame to a computer on its own segment, the bridge will simply drop the frame because it will be picked up by the destination computer without the aid of the bridge. The bridge only sends a frame to a segment if it is destined for a host on that segment.

By using this method of segmentation, the network functions as if everything were on one big segment—but with line-utilization and collision rates reduced in each segment.

So far, we've been describing the behavior of bridging when dealing with unicast frames. How does a bridge handle multicast or broadcast frames?

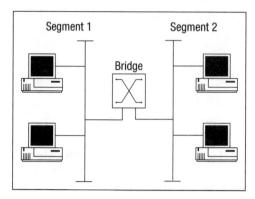

**Figure 2.1** Bridge.

The answer to this question lies in the fact that, by nature, a bridge is a transparent device. That is, the bridge must make many smaller segments function exactly like one large segment would. For this reason, any broadcast or multicast frames are still sent to all segments connected to the bridge.

The most important message to understand about bridges is the way they deal with different types of traffic. Bridges simply forward non-local and broadcast traffic. They drop local traffic because an Ethernet bridge assumes the frame has already reached its destination.

## Switches

*Switching* is a major enhancement to bridging. A switch provides much of the same functionality as a bridge, because both are layer 2 devices. In addition, both solve collision problems, and both forward all broadcasts and multicasts. Like the bridge, switching can be implemented into most existing network infrastructures with little or no upgrading or reconfiguration. Like a bridge, a switch offers the following characteristics:

➤ Each segment is a separate collision domain.

➤ All segments are in the same broadcast domain.

Compared to bridges, switching offers increased throughput performance, port density, and greater flexibility. Switches provide higher port densities than bridges, so network administrators typically place fewer users on each switch port. The term port density refers to the number of ports on one physical device—in this case, a switch. Minimizing the number of users per port increases the total bandwidth available per user. In most cases, each computer or server is given its own port, thereby granting it dedicated access to the physical media. In the case of Ethernet technology, servers or users realize 10Mb, 100Mb, or even 1,000Mb of bandwidth. Furthermore, most switches are capable of providing full-duplex media access. It is the architecture of the switch that allows the tremendous rates and high port densities.

Switching technology will be examined in detail in Chapters 5 and 6.

Each port on a switch provides dedicated bandwidth. For example, if five devices are plugged in to a Fast Ethernet switch, all five devices can utilize the full 100Mbps of bandwidth.

# Routers

Routers are another tool that can be used to segment a network. Routers operate at layer 3 (network layer) of the OSI model. Unlike bridges, which are virtually transparent and easy to implement, routers are much more intrusive in a network. They forward and filter packets based on layer 3 addresses, such as IP addresses. This means that a network addressing scheme must be carefully planned and laid out before you can successfully implement routers into a network.

One important feature that distinguishes a router from a bridge or switch is the fact that it does not forward broadcasts by default. Like a bridge, a router creates separate collision domains, but also creates separate broadcast domains. In comparison to a hub, bridge, or switch, a router has the following characteristics:

➤ Each segment is a separate collision domain.

➤ Each segment is a separate broadcast domain.

Whereas bridging and switching physically segment LANs, routing provides a method to isolate traffic into logically and physically distinct LANs. Why do we want to do this? Logically separating LANs allows for different types of LAN technologies (token ring, FDDI, Ethernet, etc.) to communicate with one another without concern for the LAN technology being used. You have seen that bridges can provide some options for connecting dissimilar LANs; however, the functionality bridges provide is dwarfed in comparison to that provided by routers. Routers provide the intelligence necessary for the interconnection of complex networks.

Routers provide the logic for implementing security, fragmenting packets, converting between technologies, and a variety of other functions. Routers don't concern themselves with individual hosts on a network, but focus on taking the best path to the network of a host. Routers only have to determine the best way to forward a packet to a destination network. Furthermore, routers effectively terminate LAN broadcast domains.

The additional functionality included in routers does not come without costs. The amount of latency for sending packets across routers is estimated at 30 to 40 percent more than that of a LAN media. These numbers have been drastically reduced with the introduction of new technologies into routers. However, the amount of time required to make layer 3 decisions continues to be higher than layer 2 decisions.

In summary, the advantages of routing are that they:

➤ Connect dissimilar LANs

➤ Provide multiple paths to a destination network

➤ Allow for a richer set of functionality than that of bridges and switches

➤ Allow for the interconnection of large and complex networks

The disadvantages of routers in comparison to bridges and switches are that they:

➤ Increase latency to forward packets

➤ Increase maintenance complexity

# Increasing Throughput in an Ethernet Network

Ethernet continues to be the most popular LAN transport method for network computer users. The simplicity and flexibility of Ethernet has allowed it to evolve faster than competing technologies, like token ring. Many people did not believe that Ethernet was capable of scaling to meet the increasing bandwidth demand of network users. However, organizations and standard bodies have proven these doubters wrong with the introduction of faster and faster Ethernet technology. Ethernet has scaled from 10Mbps to *Fast Ethernet* (100Mbps) to speeds of *Gigabit Ethernet* (1,000Mbps) and may soon support speeds of up to 10,000Mbps.

## Fast Ethernet

When Fast Ethernet was in the nascent stages, two competing theories developed regarding the proper architecture to implement to achieve the higher speeds. The first theory maintained that the current CSMA/CD network access method would scale to the desired higher speeds. The second theory developed a new access method, which could be implemented with token ring as well as Ethernet technologies. These two methods are as follows:

➤ *100BaseT*—Ethernet using *unshielded twisted pair* (*UTP*) or *shielded twisted pair* (*STP*) cabling. This method is compatible with the Institute of Electrical and Electronics Engineers (IEEE) Ethernet specification 802.3.

➤ *100VG-AnyLAN*—Provides for 100Mb token ring and Ethernet over 4-pair UTP. This technology has not been adopted very quickly due to its noncompliance with existing IEEE standards, such as IEEE 802.3.

The 100BaseT technology has been adopted and termed as Fast Ethernet. However, Fast Ethernet has many different flavors. Although the media access standard specified by IEEE 802.3 does not change, a few variations of physical hardware implementation exist. The different hardware offerings are as follows:

➤ *100BaseTX*—Fast Ethernet with category 5 cabling

➤ *100BaseFX*—Fast Ethernet with fiber-optic cabling

➤ *100BaseX*—Fast Ethernet with either fiber or category 5 cabling

The distance limitations of Fast Ethernet are dependent on the physical media chosen as the transport. As was mentioned earlier, fiber optics and category 5 cabling are the predominant transport media in use today. Table 2.2 details the distance limitations with fiber-optic and category 5 cabling.

The distance limitations can be extended with the use of repeaters to amplify the signal. In addition, many breakthroughs in fiber-optic cable are being developed, allowing distance limitations to be increased to 5 to 10Km.

# Full-Duplex and Half-Duplex Ethernet

Ethernet traditionally operated in *half-duplex mode* because of the technological limitation of shared access to the physical media. Half-duplex allows a device to either send or receive transmissions at any time but not both at the same time. Half-duplex designates that one wire in the twisted pair transmits while the other wire listens for collisions. Because Ethernet is built upon the CSMA/CD media access technology, any time a device in half-duplex mode sends a frame, it must listen to determine if the frame collided with another frame. If a collision occurs, the device must resend the frame to ensure that it reaches its destination. In the traditional hub environment, all devices shared the physical media, so the possibility for a collision was present. Thus, it was necessary to implement half-duplex Ethernet.

With the introduction of switches, it became possible to give a device a dedicated physical piece of the logical LAN. The device no longer has to worry about listening to determine if a frame collides. Collisions are not possible, because each device has access to its own physical network. So manufacturers included the

| Table 2.2 | Distance limitations of Fast Ethernet with fiber-optic and category 5 cabling. | |
|---|---|---|
| Media Type | Media Description | Distance Limitation |
| Category 5 cable | 2 pairs of STP or UTP | 100m |
| Fiber-optic cable | 62.5 micron multimode fiber | 400m |
| Fiber-optic cable | Single mode fiber | 10Km |

capability of running Ethernet in full-duplex mode with their Ethernet inter-faces. Devices could now simultaneously send and receive messages on both wires, because the second wire no longer is used to listen for collisions. This is why Fast Ethernet (100Mb) sometimes is listed as having the capability of transmitting at 200Mb. In this scenario, a device is receiving and transmitting at 100Mb speeds, with a combined throughput of 200Mb.

 No collisions will be generated when two devices are communicating in full duplex Ethernet mode.

# Practice Questions

## Question 1

Which of the following are advantages of using a bridge to segment a LAN? [Choose the two best answers]

□ a. A bridge isolates local traffic to only one physical segment of the LAN.

□ b. A bridge logically segments a LAN, therefore isolating non-local and broadcast traffic from local traffic.

□ c. A bridge can extend the physical distance of a LAN by amplifying the electrical signal of the physical media.

□ d. A bridge provides security and a high level of protocol conversion capabilities.

Answers a and c are correct. A bridge isolates local traffic to its originating physical segment. It also can extend the physical media by amplifying the electrical signal between two physically segmented LANs. Answer b is incorrect because a bridge does not logically separate LANs. Therefore, broadcast traffic is forwarded to all nodes on the logical LAN. In addition, non-local LAN traffic must be forwarded at a minimum between the physical LAN of the originating and destination nodes. Answer d is incorrect because bridges do not provide security or a high level of protocol conversion capabilities. Bridges do provide limited protocol conversion capabilities between token ring and Ethernet LANs.

## Question 2

How many of the following are advantages of routing compared to bridging and switching? [Choose the two best answers]

□ a. Routing provides the functionality to allow complex networks with dissimilar technologies to be connected.

□ b. Reduced latency.

□ c. Routing provides a higher level of security.

□ d. Routing allows faster throughput than bridges and switches because it does not have to consider layer 3 addressing.

Answers a and c are correct. Routing provides a rich set of functionality when compared to bridges and switches. The ability of routers to identify the best path between two networks (using different technologies and layer 3 addressing schemes) allows routers to interconnect complex and dissimilar networks. Routers also increase the level of security on networks. Answer b is incorrect because routers typically have higher latency when compared to bridges and switches. Answer d is incorrect because switches and bridges usually have a higher throughput than routers.

## Question 3

> Which technology has the slowest forwarding rates?
>
> ○ a. Routing
>
> ○ b. Bridging
>
> ○ c. Switching

Answer a is correct. Routing has slower forwarding rates when compared to bridging and switching due to the fact that routers must process more data per frame (they must examine up to layer 3) than bridges or switches (they process up to layer 2).

## Question 4

> Which of the following statements regarding Ethernet technology is true?
>
> ○ a. Fast Ethernet provides 1,000Mb of throughput performance.
>
> ○ b. Ethernet technology must be employed using category 5 cabling.
>
> ○ c. Half-duplex Ethernet provides greater throughput than full-duplex Ethernet.
>
> ○ d. Full-duplex Ethernet technology doubles the amount of throughput compared to half-duplex technology.

Answer d is correct. Full-duplex Ethernet technology allows users to double the amount of throughput. This is accomplished by allowing devices to use both wires for transmitting or receiving frames. Answer a is incorrect because Fast

Ethernet provides 100Mb of throughput, not 1,000Mb. Answer b is incorrect because Ethernet technology can be implemented on a variety of physical media, not just category 5 cable. However, category 5 cable is the predominant physical media in use today with Ethernet. Answer c is incorrect because half-duplex provides a lower throughput than does full-duplex.

## Question 5

> Which of the following are characteristics of hubs? [Choose the two best answers]
>
> ❑ a. All segments are in the same collision domain.
>
> ❑ b. Each segment is a separate collision domain.
>
> ❑ c. All segments are in the same broadcast domain.
>
> ❑ d. Each segment is a separate broadcast domain.

Answers a and c are correct. With hubs (as opposed to bridges, switches, and routers), all devices share bandwidth and are part of a single collision domain and broadcast domain. For this reason, answers b and d are incorrect.

## Question 6

> Which of the following are characteristics of bridges? [Choose the two best answers]
>
> ❑ a. All segments are in the same collision domain.
>
> ❑ b. Each segment is a separate collision domain.
>
> ❑ c. All segments are in the same broadcast domain.
>
> ❑ d. Each segment is a separate broadcast domain.

Answers b and c are correct. In a bridge, each port (segment) is a separate collision domain. However, broadcasts are forwarded across all bridged ports, so all segments are in the same broadcast domain. Therefore, answers a and d are incorrect.

## Question 7

Which of the following are characteristics of switches? [Choose the two best answers]

❏ a. All segments are in the same collision domain.

❏ b. Each segment is a separate collision domain.

❏ c. All segments are in the same broadcast domain.

❏ d. Each segment is a separate broadcast domain.

Answers b and c are correct. Like bridges, each port on a switch is a single collision domain, but all ports are in the same broadcast domain. For this reason, answers a and d are incorrect.

## Question 8

Which of the following are characteristics of routers? [Choose the two best answers]

❏ a. All segments are in the same collision domain.

❏ b. Each segment is a separate collision domain.

❏ c. All segments are in the same broadcast domain.

❏ d. Each segment is a separate broadcast domain.

Answers b and d are correct. Each port on a router is both a separate collision and broadcast domain. This is one advantage of using routers as opposed to bridges or switches. Answers a and c are incorrect.

## Question 9

You have connected 10 PCs to a Fast Ethernet switch. Each PC is plugged into a single switch port. All PCs are equipped with 10/100 NICs. How much bandwidth is available to each PC?

○ a. 100Mbps

○ b. 10Mbps

○ c. 1Mbps

○ d. 1Mbps

Answer a is correct. A Fast Ethernet switch provides dedicated bandwidth to each port. This is unlike hubs, which share bandwidth among all ports. By definition, Fast Ethernet runs at 100Mbps. Note that if these PCs were connected through a single switch port, they would share the 100Mbps available to that port.

# Need to Know More?

 McNutt, Shawn, Mark Poplar, Jason Waters, and David Stabenaw. *CNNA Routing and Switching Exam Prep.* The Coriolis Group, Scottsdale, AZ, 2000. ISBN 1-57610-440-0. This book is a great complement to the CNNA Cram book. It has expanded coverage and detailed information about CNNA exam topics.

 Chappell, Laura. *Introduction to Cisco Router Configuration.* Cisco Systems Inc., Macmillan Publishing Company, 1998. ISBN 0-7645-3186-7. This book provides a great overview of the concepts tested on the CCNA exam.

 Ford, Merilee, H. Kim Lew, Steve Spanier, and Kevin Downes. *Internetworking Technologies Handbook 2ⁿᵈ Edition.* Macmillan Publishing Company, 1998. ISBN 1-56205-102-3. This book is full of resourceful information on Internetworking Technologies.

 Lammle, Todd, Donald Porter, and James Chellis. *CCNA Cisco Certified Network Associate.* Sybex Network Press, Alameda, CA, 1999. ISBN 0-7821-2381-3. This book is a great supplement for learning the technologies tested on the CCNA exam.

 Syngress Media, with Richard D. Hornbaker, CCIE. *Cisco Certified Network Associate Study Guide.* Osborne/McGraw-Hill, Berkeley, CA, 1998. ISBN 0-07882-487-7. Another great book for review before taking the CCNA exam.

 Visit **www.cisco.com/univercd/cc/td/doc/product/software/ios113ed/113ed_cr/switch_c/xcisl.htm** for a great article entitled *Configuring Routing between VLANs with ISL Encapsulation.*

# The OSI Model: Upper Layers

## Terms you'll need to understand:

- ✓ Open Systems Interconnect (OSI) model
- ✓ Protocol
- ✓ Protocol data unit (PDU)
- ✓ Peer-to-peer communication
- ✓ Encapsulation
- ✓ De-encapsulation
- ✓ Session
- ✓ Handshake
- ✓ Congestion
- ✓ Flow control
- ✓ Buffering
- ✓ Multiplexing
- ✓ Parallelization

## Techniques you'll need to master:

- ✓ Identifying and describing the functions of each of the seven layers of the OSI model
- ✓ Identifying at least three reasons why the industry uses a layered model
- ✓ Describing peer-to-peer communication
- ✓ Contrasting data encapsulation and data de-encapsulation
- ✓ Explaining the five conversion steps of data encapsulation
- ✓ Describing the different types of flow control

This chapter provides an overview of the OSI model. It also highlights the layers within the OSI model and provides detailed information regarding the upper layers of the OSI model, application, presentation, session, and transport.

# The OSI Model

Computers and programs that share and move data must use common protocols to communicate effectively. A *protocol* is simply a formal description of a set of rules and conventions that defines how devices on a network must exchange information. If a wide variety of protocols for data communication exists, linking computers into networks becomes extremely difficult. As a result, computer vendors began developing their own protocols. Because protocols were being developed rapidly and for different computer platforms, some vendors developed more than one.

This situation led to the creation of standards for the various computer platforms and systems. In 1984, the International Organization for Standardization (ISO) released the OSI reference model to help computer vendors create interoperable network equipment. (See the following note.) Since then, the OSI reference model has become the primary architectural model for intercomputer communication. Most network vendors now relate their products to the OSI reference model in order to educate customers about the product's features and capabilities. Each technology addressed in this book can be mapped to one of the layers in the OSI model. As a result, the OSI model is a valuable tool available for people who need to learn about network technologies.

*Note: ISO does not stand for International Standards Organization. ISO is not an acronym for anything. The International Organization for Standardization borrowed its name from the Greek word isos, which means equal. Creating an acronym for the organization's three official languages (English, French, and Russian) would be incredibly difficult.*

## A Layered Network Model

In Chapter 2, you were briefly introduced to the idea of and purpose for a layered approach in developing networking standards. The problem of moving data among different computer systems over a network is significant. Using a divide-and-conquer approach, the OSI reference model addresses this problem by dividing one large problem into seven smaller, more self-contained problems. The solution to each of the seven problems comes in the form of a layer within the OSI model. This layered approach does not constrain or define how a vendor's implementation should be; it simply provides a framework in which vendors can build their specific products. In other words, a network implementation or product does not conform to the OSI model, but it conforms to the standards and protocols developed from the OSI model.

## Peer-to-Peer Communication

Each layer in a single system uses its own layer protocols to communicate with its peer layer in another system. The peer layers between systems communicate by exchanging *protocol data units (PDUs)*, that is, *peer-to-peer communication*. Figure 3.1 illustrates peer-to-peer communication between two systems.

Layers within the OSI model exchange different types of PDUs. Transport layers in different systems exchange segments, network layers exchange packets, data link layers exchange frames, and physical layers exchange bits. All PDUs exchanged between the other layers are generally referred to as data.

In Figure 3.1, the dashed horizontal lines with arrows illustrate the peer-to-peer communication between systems. Layers within different systems must interact and communicate with their peer layers. For example, the network layer within system A must communicate with the network layer within system B. However, the OSI model's layering precludes direct communication between peers. Even the physical layers cannot communicate directly and must communicate over the network.

As a result, each layer in the OSI model must provide services to the layer directly above it and receive services from the layer directly beneath it. In other words, the

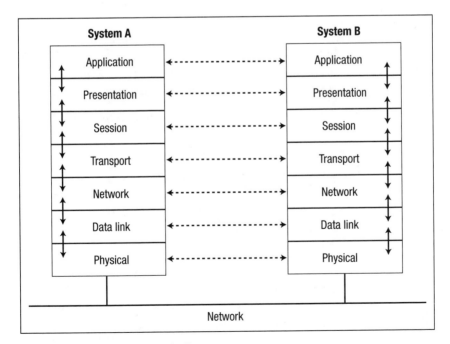

**Figure 3.1**    Peer-to-peer communication.

layers within a system interact and communicate hierarchically. In Figure 3.1, the vertical lines with arrows illustrate this type of communication. For example, the network layer within system A must rely on the data link layer within system A to accomplish this task.

## Encapsulation and De-Encapsulation

For peer-to-peer communication to occur, data must move through the layers within a single system before traversing the network to another system. For example, the application layer must send its PDUs to the presentation layer. The presentation layer then sends its PDUs to the session layer, and so on down the protocol stack until the physical layer sends bits across the network.

Each layer (source layer), however, includes control information with its PDUs that informs its peer layer (destination layer) what should be done with the PDU. This control information is included in a PDU by the source layer through a process known as *encapsulation*. The control information is read and processed by the destination layer through a process know as *de-encapsulation*. During the encapsulation process, a layer adds header information to the data it received from the layer directly above it. In some cases, a layer will add information to the end of the data block; this is known as a trailer. In either case, the layer then passes the newly created package of data to the layer directly beneath it, as shown in Figure 3.2.

During the encapsulation process, the information changes from layer to layer as each layer adds header information to the PDU it receives from the layer directly above it. Although header information is added as the information moves down the protocol stack, the contents or original data does not change. In other words, the original data continues to be wrapped and header information added as it is sent from layer to layer. Figure 3.2 illustrates an internetwork example (beginning at the session layer) that includes a five-step conversion process:

1. A user creates an email message. The upper layers convert and format the message for use on the internetwork. The message is sent from the session layer to the transport layer as data.

2. The transport layer receives the data, converts the data into segments, and includes header information with each segment to ensure that the email systems at both ends of the internetwork can communicate reliably. The transport layer sends the segments (segment header and data) to the network layer.

3. The network layer receives the segments from the transport layer, converts the segments into packets, and adds its header information, that is, logical source and destination addresses, to each packet. The network layer then sends the packets (packet header and segments) to the data link layer.

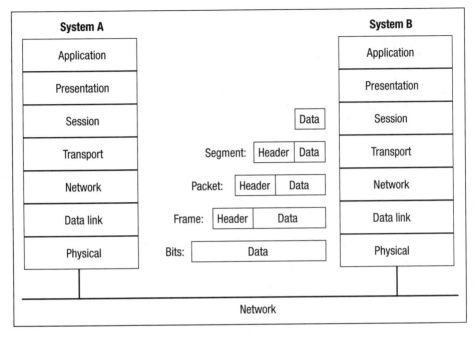

**Figure 3.2**    The encapsulation process.

4. The data link layer receives the packets from the network layer, converts the packets into frames, and adds its header information, that is, physical source and destination addresses, to each frame. The data link layer then sends the frames (frame header and packets) to the physical layer.

5. The physical layer receives the frames from the data link layer and converts the frames into a pattern of electrical voltages that represent 0s and 1s. The 0s and 1s (or *bits*) can then be transmitted on the network medium.

 When the entire process of encapsulation and de-encapsulation involves taking data from one network system and placing it inside frames from another network system, it is called tunneling.

The de-encapsulation process takes place whenever a system receives bits on the network. De-encapsulation is simply the reverse of encapsulation: A layer reads its corresponding header information, processes the header, removes the header information, and, if necessary, sends the PDU to the layer directly above it for further processing. The encapsulation and de-encapsulation processes can occur several times on a single data stream during its transmission across an internetwork to its final destination.

It is important to understand all functions of a given layer.

# Application Layer

The application layer (layer 7) is the layer closest to the user. Because it is the highest layer in the OSI model, it does not provide services to other layers, but it does communicate with user applications and select the appropriate network applications for those user applications. In addition, layer 7 identifies and establishes the availability of application resources in order to synchronize applications, negotiate error recovery, and provide data integrity.

Table 3.1 lists common user and network applications.

Any of the user applications can require services from one or more of the network applications. For example, a database application on one server may require remote access to a database on another server and, also, the ability to transfer database information between the two.

Alternatively, some user applications can include network application functions. For example, a word processor application that includes the network components necessary to email files (a network application) would be considered an application at layer 7 of the OSI model.

# Presentation Layer

The presentation layer (layer 6) ensures that information received from the application layer is readable by the application layer of the destination peer. Simply put, the presentation layer concerns itself primarily with how the data is represented to the application. The presentation layer accomplishes this task by performing several functions:

➤ It performs code formatting and conversion to ensure that applications have readable information.

| Table 3.1 Common user and network applications. | |
|---|---|
| **User Application** | **Network Application** |
| Word processing | Email |
| Spreadsheet | File Transfer Protocol (FTP) |
| Presentation graphics | Client/server process |
| Database | Remote access |
| Computer-aided design | Telnet/rlogin |

➤ It negotiates data transfer syntax between applications that use different data formats.

➤ It performs data encryption and decryption to ensure that the data cannot be viewed or altered by unauthorized parties.

➤ It performs data compression to make optimal use of its channel (a single communication path on a system).

The primary services provided by the presentation layer are data representation, data encryption, and data compression.

The presentation layer must support a wide variety of data types. Table 3.2 lists some of the common data types and standards supported in layer 6 of the OSI model.

It is important to know the different standards at the presentation layer.

# Session Layer

The session layer (layer 5) establishes, manages, and terminates sessions between applications. A *session* consists of a dialogue between presentation layers on two or more systems. The session layer also synchronizes and coordinates service requests and responses between the systems. Common layer 5 protocols include:

➤ *Network file system (NFS)*—Developed by Sun Microsystems, NFS provides transparent remote access to network resources via TCP/IP on Unix workstations.

➤ *Structured query language (SQL)*—Developed by IBM, SQL provides a simple method of accessing information on local or remote systems.

| Table 3.2 Presentation layer data types and standards. | |
| --- | --- |
| **Data Type** | **Standards** |
| Text and data | ASCII, EBCDIC, Encrypted |
| Sound and video | MIDI, MPEG, QuickTime |
| Graphics and images | PICT, TIFF, GIF, JPEG |

➤ *Remote procedure call (RPC)*—RPCs are procedures that are built on a client and executed on a local or remote server.

*Note: The application, presentation, and session layers provide standardization so that applications can share data and communicate with one another more easily. Layers 7, 6, and 5 do not concern themselves with how the data will arrive at its destination.*

# Transport Layer

The transport layer (layer 4) is situated between the upper and lower layers. Layer 4 is not concerned with applications, data presentation, or session management. As its name implies, the transport layer provides end-to-end data transport services to the upper layers. To further clarify, layer 4 provides the following services to the upper layers:

➤ It segments upper-layer applications.

➤ It establishes an end-to-end connection.

➤ It sends segments from one end host to another.

➤ It ensures reliable data transport.

## Segment Upper-Layer Applications

One service provided by the transport layer is the capability to segment upper-layer applications. Layer 4 accomplishes this task by transporting the data segment by segment. Each segment created is autonomous. Different applications send successive segments on a first-come, first-served basis to the transport layer. The applications can destine the segments for a single system or several different systems. To illustrate, a file transfer can occur between two different systems. Conversely, a single email message may be sent to one or more recipients. The transport layer tracks and manages the various segments sent to and from both applications using port numbers. These port numbers are standard for each application and must be set by the application before the transport layer receives the segment. Because the source and destination applications use predefined port numbers, the transport layers at the source and destination systems can pass the segments easily to and from the appropriate upper-layer applications.

## Establish End-to-End Connections

The second service that the transport layer provides is establishing an end-to-end connection between the source and destination systems. Layer 4 establishes this connection through a series of *handshakes*, which involve one system making a request to another system prior to a connection being established. Handshakes occur during the establishment of a connection between two systems and address matters such as synchronization and connection parameters.

## Send Segments from One Host to Another

Another service that is provided by the transport layer occurs after the connection has been established and data transfer between the two systems has begun. The transport layer is responsible for sending the segments from one system to another and verifying that all of the segments arrive at the destination. As data is transferred between the two systems, data can be discarded for many reasons, but the most common reason is *congestion*. This may occur during data transfer if one computer generates traffic faster than the network can transfer it. Also, if several computers send traffic simultaneously to a single destination or through a single gateway, that destination or gateway may not be able to process the data quickly enough. The transport layer handles congestion by *flow control*, a mechanism that ensures that a sending system does not overwhelm the receiving system with data.

 As the transport layer sends segments from one system to another, it can use any of these three methods of flow control:

➤ Buffering

➤ Multiplexing

➤ Parallelization

### Buffering

The first method of flow control involves *buffering*. Each system has a certain amount of memory available for buffering information. The transport layer of the receiving system ensures that sufficient buffers are available and that data is not transmitted at a rate that exceeds the rate at which the receiving system can process it. When the buffers on the receiving system are full, a "not ready" message is sent to the sending system to suspend data transmission until the data in the buffers has been processed. A "ready" message is sent from the receiving system to the sending system when the data in the buffers has been processed.

### Multiplexing

The second method of flow control involves *multiplexing*. Occasionally, the upper layers require slower service than a channel can provide. As a result, the channel's bandwidth becomes underutilized. In this case, the transport layer multiplexes conversations by interweaving packets from different segments and transmitting them. The transport layer at the receiving end sorts the packets (using the header information that was encapsulated) and re-creates the original segments.

## Parallelization

The third method of flow control involves *parallelization*. If the upper layers require faster service than a channel can provide, the transport layer may be able to combine multiple channels (paralleling the flow of the data) and to increase the effective bandwidth for the upper layers.

*Note: Operating systems (OSs) such as Unix and MVS support parallelization, whereas some personal computer (PC) OSs do not.*

# Ensure Reliable Data Transport

The final service that is provided by the transport layer involves the reliable transport of the segments. Reliable transport depends on a connection-oriented relationship between the sending and receiving systems to ensure that the following tasks are completed successfully:

➤ Send an acknowledgment to the sending system for each segment that was received successfully.

➤ Retransmit any segments that were not acknowledged by the receiving system.

➤ Discard any duplicate segments.

➤ Return segments to their original sequence at the receiving system.

➤ Provide congestion avoidance and control.

Thus, reliable transport ensures that segments are not lost, damaged, duplicated, or received out of sequence. Upon successful receipt of segments, the receiving system sends acknowledgments to the sending system.

# Practice Questions

## Question 1

What is the correct order for the OSI model?

○ a.  Application, session, presentation, transport, network, physical, data link

○ b.  Application, network, presentation, transport, session, physical, data link

○ c.  Application, presentation, session, transport, network, data link, physical

○ d.  Application, network, transport, presentation, session, physical, data link

Answer c is the correct order. Answers a, b, and d are incorrect because they are out of order.

## Question 2

Which of the following tasks is an example of encapsulation?

○ a.  Converting data into ones and zeros for transmission across a physical medium.

○ b.  Performing a CRC check to determine if data needs to be retransmitted.

○ c.  Putting a header and/or trailer on an outgoing frame.

○ d.  Stripping a header and/or trailer from an incoming frame.

Answer c is correct. Encapsulation involves placing control information on an outgoing PDU. The PDU can be a frame, segment, or packet. Answers a and b are incorrect because neither is a function of encapsulation. Answer d is incorrect because it involves stripping control information from a PDU.

## Question 3

> Which of the following layers is most concerned with selecting the appropriate network applications for user applications?
>
> ○ a. Application
>
> ○ b. Presentation
>
> ○ c. Session
>
> ○ d. Transport

Answer a is correct. The application layer provides services for user applications. The presentation layer's chief concern is data representation. The session layer mainly performs session management. The transport layer primarily focuses on aspects of data transport. Therefore, answers b, c, and d are incorrect.

## Question 4

> Which of the following tasks is an example of de-encapsulation?
>
> ○ a. Stripping a header and trailer from an incoming frame.
>
> ○ b. Putting a header and trailer on an incoming segment.
>
> ○ c. Converting data into ones and zeros for transmission across a physical medium.
>
> ○ d. Putting a header and trailer on an outgoing frame.

Answer a is correct. De-encapsulation involves removing control information from incoming PDUs. Answers b and d are incorrect because they involve putting control information on the PDU. Answer c is incorrect because this is not a function of de-encapsulation.

# Question 5

A data, segment, packet, frame, and bits conversion process includes which layers (in order)?

○ a.  Presentation, session, transport, network, physical

○ b.  Session, transport, network, data link, physical

○ c.  Presentation, session, transport, network, data link

○ d.  Session, network, transport, data link, physical

Answer b is correct. The session layer sends data to the transport layer. The transport layer converts the data to segments. The network layer converts segments into packets. The data link layer converts packets into frames. The physical layer converts frames into bits. Therefore, answers a, c, and d are incorrect.

# Question 6

Which of the following layers is most concerned with getting an entire segment through a network from the source to the final destination?

○ a.  Application

○ b.  Presentation

○ c.  Session

○ d.  Transport

Answer d is correct. The transport layer handles different aspects of data transport, including end-to-end communication, sending segments from one host to another, and reliable transport. The application layer provides services for user applications; therefore, answer a is incorrect. The presentation layer's chief concern is data representation; therefore, answer b is incorrect. The session layer mainly performs session management; therefore, answer c is incorrect.

## Question 7

Which of the following is NOT a service provided by the session layer?

- ○ a. Establishing a session
- ○ b. Ensuring that the segment sent is error-free
- ○ c. Ending a session
- ○ d. Keeping the sending and receiving station from sending segments at the same time

Answer b is correct. The session layer provides services to establish sessions, to end sessions, and to manage the dialogue between the sending and receiving stations. Ensuring that the segment sent is error-free is handled within the transport layer. Therefore, answers a, c, and d are incorrect.

## Question 8

Which of the following are NOT services provided by the presentation layer? [Choose the two best answers]

- ❏ a. Data representation
- ❏ b. Data compression
- ❏ c. Dialog management
- ❏ d. Data transmission
- ❏ e. Data encryption

Answers c and d are correct. The session layer handles dialog management; therefore, answer c is correct. The transport layer handles data transmission; therefore, answer d is correct. The presentation layer concerns itself with data representation, data compression, and data encryption. Therefore, answers a, b, and e are incorrect.

# Question 9

> With what is the transport layer of the OSI model concerned? [Choose the three best answers]
>
> ❑  a. Ensuring data reliability
>
> ❑  b. Compressing data
>
> ❑  c. Establishing an end-to-end connection
>
> ❑  d. Segmenting upper-layer applications
>
> ❑  e. Synchronizing service requests

Answers a, c, and d are correct. The transport layer ensures data reliability, establishes end-to-end connectivity, and segments upper-layer applications. The presentation layer performs data compression; therefore, answer b is incorrect. The session layer synchronizes service requests; therefore, answer e is incorrect.

# Question 10

> What does peer-to-peer communication involve?
>
> ○  a.  Each layer communicating with its adjacent layers in a single system.
>
> ○  b.  Each layer communicating with its corresponding layer in a single system.
>
> ○  c.  Each layer communicating with its adjacent layers in another system.
>
> ○  d.  Each layer communicating with its corresponding layer in another system.

Answer d is correct. Peer-to-peer communication occurs when a layer in one system communicates with the same layer in another system. In other words, the network layer in system A communicates with the network layer (its peer layer) in system B. Answers a and b are incorrect because peer-to-peer communication cannot occur with a single system. Answer c is incorrect because peer-to-peer communication does not occur between adjacent layers.

## Question 11

> Reasons why the industry uses a layered model include: [Choose all that apply]
>
> ❑ a. Enhancements for one layer can be isolated from the other layers.
>
> ❑ b. Design and development efforts can be made in a modular fashion.
>
> ❑ c. Network operations and troubleshooting can be simplified.
>
> ❑ d. Standard interfaces can be defined for vendor compatibility.

Answers a, b, c, and d are correct.

# Need to Know More?

 McNutt, Shawn, Mark Poplar, Jason Waters, and David Stabenaw. *CCNA Routing and Switching Exam Prep.* The Coriolis Group, Scottsdale, AZ, 2000. ISBN 1-57610-440-0. This book is a great complement to the CCNA Cram book. It has expanded coverage and detailed information about CCNA exam topics.

 Stallings, William. *Handbook of Computer Communications Standards: The Open Systems Interconnection (OSI Model and OSI-Related Standards).* Vol. 1. Prentice-Hall, Englewood Cliffs, NJ, 1990. ISBN 0-02415-521-7.

 The official Cisco documentation Web site provides more information regarding the OSI model. See the first chapter of the "Networking Fundamentals" Web page at **www.cisco.com/public/documentation.html**.

 Review the Web pages on the OSI model at **http://whatis.com/osi.htm**. These Web pages offer additional information and illustrations on the OSI model.

# The OSI Model: Lower Layers

## Terms you'll need to understand:

✓ Logical link control (LLC) sublayer

✓ Media access control (MAC) sublayer

✓ Synchronous data link control (SDLC)

✓ High-level data link control (HDLC)

✓ Integrated services digital network (ISDN)

✓ Public switched telephone network (PSTN)

✓ Frame Relay

✓ Point-to-point protocol (PPP)

✓ Connection-oriented network services

✓ Service access point (SAP)

✓ Connectionless network services

✓ RS-232

✓ V.35

✓ High-speed serial interface (HSSI)

## Techniques you'll need to master:

✓ Differentiating between connection-oriented and connectionless network services

✓ Describing the differences between data link layer addresses and network layer addresses

✓ Identifying the functions of a network layer address

✓ Identifying the functions of a data link layer address

✓ Identifying the key internetworking functions of the Open Systems Interconnect (OSI) network layer

✓ Describing how the OSI network layer performs its functions in a router

✓ Describing the difference between a routing and a routed protocol

This chapter describes the functions of the physical, data link, and network layers of the OSI model. The information in this chapter focuses on providing the right details to help you study and pass the CCNA exam. In many cases, the information presented will not provide a comprehensive explanation of specific technologies and concepts; however, you'll find a reference to other sources of information on each topic at the end of the chapter.

# Network Layer

The primary purpose of the network layer is to determine the best path from one network to another and to route messages in that direction; therefore, the network layer is considered the domain of routing. The process of routing includes path determination and packet switching. Path determination requires the use of routing protocols to optimize the routing process. In addition, the network layer employs routed protocols that provide a logical two-part addressing scheme to identify paths and assign costs to different destinations. The steps in path determination and packet switching are discussed in the next sections.

 Remember that the primary purposes of the network layer are:

➤ Packet switching

➤ Path determination

## Path Determination

The network layer performs path determination via routers, routing protocols, and routed protocols. A router utilizes a routing protocol to determine the best path between itself and a destination. Typically, routing protocols utilize layer 3 or logical addressing—an inherent part of most routed protocols—to identify and differentiate between two destinations. Before we continue to discuss the process of path determination, let's look at the difference between a routed and a routing protocol.

### Routed Protocols Vs. Routing Protocols

*Routed protocols* are ones you are already familiar with such as TCP/IP and IPX/SPX. More specifically, a routed protocol is one in which the network layer address differentiates between a network and node. This is what allows the protocol to be routed. This is the function performed by IP in the TCP/IP suite, and IPX in the IPX/SPX suite. Routed protocols carry data from end system to end system on the internetwork.

*Routing protocols* are used between routers in an internetwork. They provide a means for routers to share information about the networks they are connected to. The only function of routing protocols is to maintain routing tables. They don't go from end to end on the internetwork, only from router to router. Some examples of routing protocols include Routing Information Protocol (RIP), open shortest path first (OSPF), and enhanced interior gateway routing protocol (EIGRP).

## Logical Addressing

Network layer addressing is most commonly referred to as *logical addressing* (versus the physical addressing of the data link layer). Whereas the physical address of a device cannot be changed without removing or changing the hardware, a logical address can be reconfigured as required. A logical address consists of two parts: the network and the node. Routers use the network part of the logical address to determine the best path to the network of a remote device. Some routing protocols count the number of networks that must be crossed to reach a destination and make that value the cost of the path. For example, Figure 4.1 shows three routers (labeled A through C) supporting four networks. Each connection between a router is labeled with a network number starting at 1 and ending with 4. Table 4.1 shows the routing table of router A.

In this scenario, router A is trying to determine the best path to send a packet to network 4. The routing protocol uses the path with the fewest number of hops

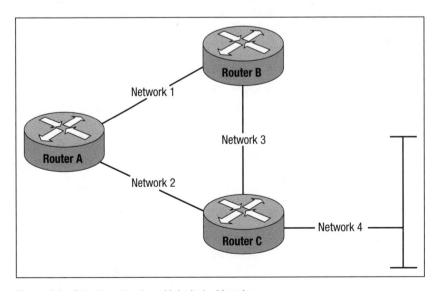

**Figure 4.1**  Path determination with logical addressing.

(networks) between itself and the destination as the metric for determining the optimal route. The routing table provided in Table 4.1 indicates the cost of reaching network 4, which is two hops, by sending the packet to router B, whereas the cost of sending it through router C is only one hop. Because the path with the lowest number of hops is the most desirable for this routing protocol, the packet is forwarded to router C.

The node part of the logical address is used to identify a specific device on a network. To continue the previous example, when router C has received the message destined for network 4, it must determine how to differentiate between all of the nodes on network 4. The router uses the node part of the logical address to determine the physical address of the destination node and sends the message directly to that node.

The utilization of this type of two-part network layer addressing scheme has allowed networks to scale to enormous sizes. Table 4.2 highlights the difference between IP and IPX logical addressing.

 It is very important to be able to distinguish between the network portion and the node portion of IP and IPX addresses.

 Novell IPX addresses do not necessarily have to have eight hexadecimal characters. A Novell IPX address will often use less than eight characters to represent the network address.

*Note: Each address is broken into a network and a node portion. IP uses a 32-bit classfull-addressing scheme; IPX uses up to an 80-bit classless-addressing scheme. The details of IPX and IP are presented in Chapters 7, 8, and 9. Note, however, that IP uses a dotted decimal notation to represent the network and node values, whereas IPX uses a hexadecimal notation. The node portion of the IPX address is the MAC address of the destination node.*

# Routing Protocol Algorithms and Metrics

Routing protocols use algorithms to generate a list of paths to a particular destination and the cost associated with that path. The cost of a path is determined by the values of the metrics used as input to the algorithm. The metrics used differ depending on the routing protocol implemented. Some of the most common

**Table 4.1   Router A's routing table.**

| Destination | Next Hop | Number of Hops |
|---|---|---|
| Network 1 | None | Directly connected |
| Network 2 | None | Directly connected |
| Network 3 | Router B | 1 |
| Network 3 | Router C | 1 |
| Network 4 | Router C | 1 |
| Network 4 | Router B | 2 |

**Table 4.2   IP vs. IPX logical addressing.**

| Protocol | Network | Interface/Node | Example |
|---|---|---|---|
| TCP/IP | Uses up to 30 bits to indicate the network number. | The number of bits used for the node is dependent on the number of bits used for the network. | 172.29.15.4. 172.29 = Network 15.4 = Node |
| Novell IPX | Uses up to 32 bits to indicate the network address. Can be up to 8 hexadecimal characters. | Uses the 48-bit 8 hexadecimal MAC address. | 8BCDF45E.0011.0434.44FF 8BCDF45E = Network 0011.0434.44FF = Interface |

metrics include hop count, link speed, reliability, and MTBF. Metrics are set either administratively or dynamically. The reliability of a circuit is an example of an administratively set metric, because a system administrator is required to set the metric. Hop count is an example of a dynamically set metric, because the routing protocol determines this value by communicating with other routers. When the number of hops changes, this metric will be updated. Metrics and logical addresses are inputs to routing algorithms and a routing table that displays destination network addresses. From these, the best path to take to reach that destination is produced. An illustration of this process is shown in Figure 4.2.

# Packet Switching

The final purpose of the network layer is to perform *packet switching* from one network to another. The process of packet switching refers to a router receiving a packet on one network interface and switching it to another interface in route to its destination. This process relies on the determination of an optimal path by the routing protocol so that the best interface can be identified for reaching the packet's destination. When the best path has been identified, the router takes the packet from one interface and forwards it to another interface on the most optimal path to the packet's destination.

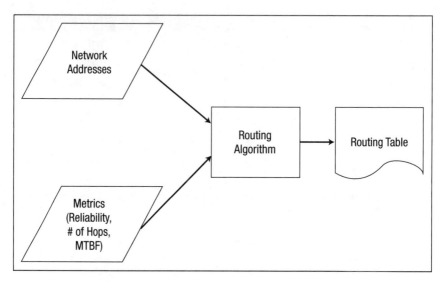

**Figure 4.2** Routing algorithm process.

# Data Link Layer

The data link layer is responsible for the transport of data across a physical me-dia. The data link layer packages data in the format of frames. This layer is di-vided into two sublayers: the LLC sublayer and the MAC sublayer. The LLC and MAC sublayers work together to perform all of the functions required of the data link layer. The data link layer performs these functions:

➤ Allows the upper layers of the OSI model to work independently of the type of media used at the physical layer.

➤ Provides optional flow control and frame sequencing.

➤ Provides error notification.

➤ Performs physical hardware addressing to ensure that all devices in an internetwork have a unique identification.

Different wide area network (WAN) and local area network (LAN) protocols have been developed for the data link layer. Figure 4.3 displays the topologies of a number of different LAN protocols. The difference between a WAN and a LAN protocol is the purpose of the link. *LAN protocols* are designed to provide efficient media access for a number of workstations, printers, and servers. *WAN protocols* are designed to provide data transport over some geographic distance. WAN links are typically slower than LAN protocols because of the physical dis-tance of their connections. This chapter does not describe any of the LAN or WAN protocols in detail. It is not necessary to have a detailed knowledge of each

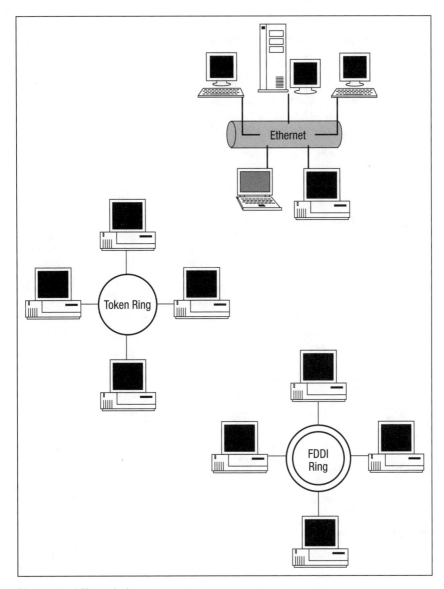

**Figure 4.3** LAN topologies.

of the LAN topologies and all of the functions that each performs for the exam. However, these are foundation skills that should be mastered before attempting to conquer some of the more difficult technologies.

## LAN Protocols

The three most popular LAN protocols used today are Ethernet, token ring, and fiber distributed data interface (FDDI). In the last few years, however, Ethernet has begun to dominate. LAN protocols operate at the data link layer and utilize the MAC address to allow computers and other devices to communicate with one another. A summary of these protocols follows:

➤ *Ethernet bus*—A LAN protocol that allows a number of devices to communicate with each other by competing for the use of a shared media. Ethernet uses the concept of carrier sense multiple access/collision detection (CSMA/CD) to govern when a device can send data. Basically, when a computer wants to send a message, it must listen to media (most often the media is category five cable). If it does not hear that another computer is sending a message, it sends its own message. The computer continues to listen to the media to ensure that its message did not collide with another computer's message. Ethernet typically runs at data rates of 10MB, 100MB, or 1,000MB.

➤ *Token ring*—IBM created the token ring protocol in 1970 to support its mainframe environments. Token ring is a LAN protocol that allows a number of devices to communicate by circulating a token around a ring and only allowing a computer to send a message if it has the token. After a computer has sent a message, it must release the token and wait for it to circulate the ring before sending another message. Token ring typically runs at data rates of 4MB and 16MB.

➤ *Fiber distributed data interface (FDDI)*—The FDDI topology is very similar to token ring except that it uses two rings that operate in a counter-rotating direction. Under normal operating conditions, only one ring is used to pass the token and user traffic. If part of the primary ring is broken, however, a secondary ring that moves in an opposing direction creates a self-healing LAN media, which means that traffic is transferred to the opposing ring, and the direction of traffic is reversed. In addition, FDDI utilizes fiber-optic cables to give it 100Mbps capacity.

## WAN Protocols

WAN protocols primarily function at the data link and physical layers. Chapters 11 and 12 are devoted to describing the more common WAN protocols (Frame Relay, ISDN, and PPP) in detail. The following is a brief synopsis of the main WAN protocols:

➤ *SDLC*—SDLC is primarily used for terminal-to-mainframe communication. SDLC requires that one device be labeled as the primary station and that all other devices be labeled as secondary stations. Communication can only occur between the primary and secondary stations.

➤ *HDLC*—HDLC provides for networks that require communication to occur between many different devices, as opposed to the central facility approach of

SDLC. HDLC provides for multipoint communication as well as point-to-point communication between two devices.

➤ *ISDN*—ISDN was developed to maximize the utilization of the current public switched telephone network (PSTN). ISDN calls for the use of digital facilities across the copper wiring used by current voice analog services.

➤ *Frame Relay*—Frame Relay provides digital communication for packet-switched networks. Frame Relay does not require a high level of error checking because of the use of digital facilities. In addition, it allows for the connection of multiple WAN sites via a single connection. This aggregation drastically reduces hardware and circuit costs.

➤ *PPP*—PPP provides communication between two networks, two nodes, or any combination of the two. It allows for encryption, multiple protocol support, and error control and is commonly used for WAN connections using leased lines.

# LLC Sublayer

The LLC sublayer performs more of the software functions of the data link layer. Its primary function is to allow the upper layers to communicate with other devices in connectionless or connection-oriented environments. Because confusion often occurs regarding the difference between connection-oriented and connectionless communication, an explanation of the difference between the two follows.

## Connection-Oriented Vs. Connectionless Communication

*Connection-oriented communication* involves using a nonpermanent path for data transfer. In order for two systems to communicate, they must establish a path that will be used for the duration of their connection. Connection-oriented communication involves three steps.

1. Establish the connection

2. Transfer the data

3. Terminate the connection

Connection-oriented services generally are able to reserve a guaranteed throughput rate. Data is sent sequentially over the established path for the duration of the connection. This is useful for transmitting data for services that don't tolerate delays and packet resequencing, such as many voice and video applications.

*Connectionless communication* involves using a permanently established link. Path selection and bandwidth allocation are done dynamically. Applications that can tolerate some delay or resequencing are typically based on connectionless service.

## Functions of the LLC Sublayer

The LLC sublayer performs the following functions:

➤ *Allows upper layers to perform independently of the LAN/WAN protocol or physical media*—The LLC sublayer allows upper-layer protocols like IP and IPX to act independently of the LAN topology or protocol. This is a major benefit because you can change the LAN protocols or media without affecting the upper layers. This autonomy is available because the LLC sublayer is not tied to a specific MAC protocol.

➤ *Provides SAPs for the lower MAC sublayer to communicate with the upper-layer functions*—The LLC sublayer provides a common set of SAPs so that the MAC sublayer can send information to the upper-layer services. The SAPs help the LLC sublayer to determine where to send the data received from the MAC sublayer.

➤ *Performs flow control for upper-layer protocols*—The data link layer is capable of using ready/not ready codes to indicate when it or its upper layers are capable of receiving more information. This allows communicating devices to throttle back on the communication data rate and minimizes the amount of data that has to be sent twice due to dropped packets.

➤ *Performs sequencing of frames*—The data link layer is capable of resequencing any frames that are received in the wrong order.

# Media Access Control Sublayer

The MAC sublayer interfaces with the physical layer and media. In comparison with the LLC sublayer, the MAC sublayer is responsible for performing more of the hardware functions of the data link layer.

The MAC sublayer maintains the physical address of a device. The physical address is also referred to as the *MAC address*. The MAC address is a 48-bit address expressed as 12 hexadecimal digits. The first six digits contain the unique identification of the manufacturer, and the last six digits are the serial number assigned by the manufacturer. Typically, a workstation has a piece of hardware called a *network interface card (NIC)* that has a MAC address burned into the read-only memory (ROM). The MAC address uniquely identifies this interface from any other interface in the world. The Institute of Electrical and Electronics Engineers (IEEE) developed a set of unique identification codes and distributes them to manufacturers. Each manufacturer is assigned a different identification code. An example of a MAC address is shown in Table 4.3.

The first column shows the entire physical address; it is typically shown in this format. The second column displays the first six digits; these identify the manufacturer code assigned by the IEEE. The last column displays the last six digits that are assigned by the manufacturer as a product serial number.

## Framing

The MAC sublayer is also responsible for framing data as it is received or transmitted onto the physical media. All WAN/LAN protocols implement specific frame formats; however, they all perform a subset of the following functions:

➤ Add a header and or trailer to the transmitted packet, indicating the protocol, frame length, and error-checking mechanism.

➤ Perform error checking on received frames.

➤ Strip the header off the received frame and pass the data to the LLC sublayer.

➤ Determine if any frames on the physical layer are destined for this device.

# Physical Layer

The physical layer performs the mechanical and electrical engineering functions of the OSI model. Because the physical layer specifies the conversion of 1s and 0s into an electrical current or pulse of light, it must communicate with its peer layers regarding the signals for activating, maintaining, and deactivating a physical circuit. Numerous standards are specified for the physical layer. The following is a list of three of the more common standards:

➤ *RS-232*—Used for serial data transmission for speeds of 19.2Kbps or less. RS-232 connects two devices that communicate over a serial link with either a 25-pin (DB-25) or a 9-pin (DB-9) serial interface.

➤ *V.35*—Used for serial data transmission for speeds up to 4Mbps. The V.35 standard was created by the International Telecommunication Union-Telecommunication Standardization Sector (ITU-T).

➤ *HSSI*—Designed for serial connections that require high data transmission rates. This standard allows for high-speed communication and runs at speeds up to 52Mbps.

| Table 4.3    MAC address example. | | |
|---|---|---|
| MAC Address | Manufacturer Code | Serial Number |
| FF34.2345.12AB | FF34.23 | 45.12AB |
| 45AB.2348.ABDD | 45AB.23 | 48.ABDD |

# Practice Questions

## Question 1

> Which two of the following are not physical layer standards? [Choose the two best answers]
>
> ❑ a. SDLC
>
> ❑ b. RS-232
>
> ❑ c. V.35
>
> ❑ d. HSSI
>
> ❑ e. ISDN

Answers a and e are correct. SDLC and ISDN are not physical layer standards; in fact, they are WAN protocols that function at the data link layer. RS-232 is a physical layer standard for data transmission speeds of 19.2Kbps or less; therefore, answer b is incorrect. V.35 is a physical layer standard for data transmission speeds up to 4Mbps; therefore, answer c is incorrect. HSSI is a physical layer standard desired for serial connections at very high data rates; therefore, answer d is incorrect.

## Question 2

> Which two answers are functions of the OSI model's network layer? [Choose the two best answers]
>
> ❑ a. Sequencing of frames
>
> ❑ b. Path determination
>
> ❑ c. Packet switching
>
> ❑ d. The electrical and mechanical functions required to send data

Answers b and c are correct. The network layer of the OSI model performs both path determination and packet switching. Path determination is the process of identifying the best path to a destination across an internetwork. Packet switching is the process of moving a packet from one network interface to another. Sequencing of frames is a function of the data link layer; therefore, answer a is incorrect. Typically, if the word "frame" is used in an OSI model question, the answer is going to have something to do with the data link layer. The electrical and mechanical functions required to send data refers to the functions performed by the physical layer of the OSI model; therefore, answer d is incorrect.

# Question 3

Which is an example of a physical (MAC) address?

- ○ a. AL45.5555.2334
- ○ b. 23CD4.23AB.F1
- ○ c. 00.FB12.0023.4512
- ○ d. A1B5.5AA4.FF21
- ○ e. 172.29.12.14

Answer d is correct. The physical (MAC) address is a 48-bit address represented as 12 hexadecimal digits. Answer a may appear to be correct; however, it contains a single character that makes it an invalid MAC address. AL45.5555.2334 has 12 digits; however, L is not a hexadecimal character, therefore, answer a is incorrect. 23CD4.23AB.F1 only has 11 chracters and is in the wrong format; therefore, answer b is incorrect. 00.FB12.0023.4512 has too many digits to represent a 48-bit address; therefore, answer c is incorrect. 172.29.12.14 is an IP address and not a MAC address; therefore, answer e is incorrect.

# Question 4

Which answer is not a characteristic of the data link layer?

- ○ a. Prepares data for transports across a physical link
- ○ b. Performs physical addressing
- ○ c. Determines the network topology
- ○ d. Performs flow control
- ○ e. Establishes, manages, and terminates sessions between end hosts

Answer e is correct. The session layer of the OSI model is responsible for establishing, managing, and terminating sessions between end hosts. The data link layer is responsible for the transport of data across a physical link; therefore, answer a is incorrect. The data link layer does perform physical addressing in the form of a MAC address; therefore, answer b is incorrect. The data link layer does determine the network topology with such protocols as Ethernet and token ring; therefore, answer c is incorrect. The data link layer does perform flow control with ready/not ready codes; therefore, answer d is incorrect.

## Question 5

> Which three protocols are examples of data link layer protocols? [Choose the three best answers]
>
> ❑ a. HDLC
>
> ❑ b. FTP
>
> ❑ c. SQL
>
> ❑ d. Token ring
>
> ❑ e. ISDN

Answers a, d, and e are correct. HDLC is a WAN protocol used in communication between stations; therefore, answer a is correct. Token ring is a LAN protocol/topology controlled by the data link layer; therefore, answer d is correct. ISDN is a layer 2 protocol that utilizes the existing copper wire of the PSTN to provide digital data services; therefore, answer e is correct. FTP is an application protocol that performs file transfers between an FTP server and an FTP host. FTP is not a data link layer protocol; therefore, answer b is incorrect. SQL is a session layer protocol that is used to make database calls; therefore, answer c is incorrect. This is a very typical question of the CCNA exam. It is necessary to know the protocols that exist at each layer of the OSI model.

## Question 6

> Given the following physical address, what is the vendor code of this address: BBD1.4822.53AA?
>
> ○ a. BBD148
>
> ○ b. 2253AA
>
> ○ c. BBD1
>
> ○ d. 53AA
>
> ○ e. 4822

Answer a is correct. The first six digits of the physical address represent the vendor code. The last six numbers of the physical address represent the serial number, not the vendor code; therefore, answer b is incorrect. Answers c, d, and e have no meaning on their own and are, therefore, incorrect.

# Question 7

Which answers are characteristics of connection-oriented communication? [Choose the two best answers]

❑ a.  Setup and maintenance procedures are performed to ensure delivery of messages.

❑ b.  A physical circuit exists between the two communicating devices.

❑ c.  It is a best-effort type of communication.

❑ d.  A virtual connection exists between the two devices.

Answers a and d are correct. Both virtual connection and setup and maintenance functions are performed during connection-oriented communication. A physical circuit is not necessary for connection-oriented communication; therefore, answer b is incorrect. Answer c is a characteristic of connectionless communication, not of connection-oriented communication, and is, therefore, incorrect.

# Question 8

Which of the following are examples of layer 3 addressing? [Choose the two best answers]

❑ a.  172.29.5.12

❑ b.  BB455467.0000.B333.A232

❑ c.  0000.B333.A232

❑ d.  S0:

Answers a and b are correct. 172.29.5.12 is an example of an IP logical address or a network layer address. BB455467.0000.B333.A232 is an example of an IPX logical address or a network layer address. 0000.B333.A232 is an example of a physical or layer 2 address, not a network or layer 3 address; therefore, answer c is incorrect. S0: has no meaning; therefore, answer d is incorrect.

# Question 9

> Which of the following are considered routing protocols? [Choose the two best answers]
>
> ❑ a. OSPF
>
> ❑ b. IPX
>
> ❑ c. IP
>
> ❑ d. EIGRP
>
> ❑ e. Token ring

Answers a and d are correct. Both OSPF and EIGRP are routing protocols. IPX and IP designate routed protocols; therefore, answers b and c are incorrect. Token ring is a layer 2 topology/protocol; therefore, answer e is incorrect.

# Question 10

> Which of the following are examples of a LAN protocol? [Choose the two best answers]
>
> ❑ a. Frame Relay
>
> ❑ b. Asynchronous transfer mode
>
> ❑ c. Ethernet
>
> ❑ d. FDDI
>
> ❑ e. ISDN

Answers c and d are correct. Both Ethernet and FDDI are examples of LAN protocols, not WAN protocols. While FDDI and Ethernet are layer 2 protocols, they are used for LANs instead of WANs. Frame Relay, asynchronous transfer mode, and ISDN are WAN protocols; therefore, answers a, b, and e are incorrect.

# Need to Know More?

 McNutt, Shawn, Mark Poplar, Jason Waters, and David Stabenaw. *CCNA Routing and Switching Exam Prep*. The Coriolis Group, Scottsdale, AZ, 2000. ISBN 1-57610-440-0. This book is a great complement to the CCNA Cram book. It has expanded coverage and detailed information about CCNS exam topics.

 Chappell, Laura. *Introduction to Cisco Router Configuration*. Cisco Systems Inc., Macmillan Publishing Company, Indianapolis, IN, 1998. ISBN 0-7645-3186-7. The first three chapters provide some great OSI material.

 Comer, Douglas E. *Internetworking with TCP/IP: Principles, Protocols, and Architectures*. Vol 1. Prentice Hall, Englewood Cliffs, NJ, 1995. ISBN 0-1321-6987-8.

 Syngress Media, with Richard D. Hornbaker, CCIE. *Cisco Certified Network Associate Study Guide*. Osborne/McGraw-Hill, Berkeley, CA, 1998. ISBN 0-07-882487-7. This book is a great study tool.

 The official Cisco documentation Web site at **www.cisco.com/public/ documentation.htm** provides valuable information on the following pages:

➤ www.cisco.com/univercd/cc/td/doc/cisintwk/ito_doc/55016.htm

➤ www.cisco.com/univercd/cc/td/doc/cisintwk/ito_doc/55771.htm

➤ www.cisco.com/univercd/cc/td/doc/cisintwk/ito_doc/55031.htm

➤ www.cisco.com/univercd/cc/td/doc/cisintwk/ito_doc/55773.htm

➤ www.cisco.com/univercd/cc/td/doc/cisintwk/ito_doc/55150.htm

➤ www.cisco.com/univercd/cc/td/doc/cisintwk/ito_doc/55780.htm

➤ www.cisco.com/univercd/cc/td/doc/cisintwk/ito_doc/55172.htm

# Working with Cisco Devices

**Terms you'll need to understand:**

✓ IOS Modes

✓ Console

✓ Interfaces

✓ EXEC

✓ Cisco Discovery Protocol (CDP)

✓ Telnet

✓ Ping

✓ Traceroute

**Techniques you'll need to master:**

✓ Logging into a router in both user and privileged modes

✓ Logging out of a router

✓ Understanding the help facility

✓ Utilizing the context-sensitive help facility

✓ Using the command history and editing features

✓ Explaining the command modes available on a router

✓ Understanding the CDP

✓ Accessing a router remotely

✓ Testing the network connectivity of a router

This chapter introduces the basics of working with and configuring Cisco devices. The topics covered include logging into a device, using the help facility, accessing the command history, and using editing features. This chapter also introduces discovering, accessing, and testing devices in a network.

# Cisco's Operating System

Cisco's Internetwork Operating System (IOS) is the software that is embedded into most Cisco device. This OS presents an administrator with a consistent user interface for configuring a wide variety of network devices.

The IOS presents the administrator with a command-line interface (CLI) that is used to enter commands and view device information. There are three ways to access the CLI:

➤ Console connection

➤ Modem connection

➤ Telnet

The most common way to configure a Cisco device initially is to attach a console cable (included with most Cisco products) between a personal computer's (PC's) serial port and the console port. Terminal emulation software (such as HyperTerminal in Windows NT) is then used to access the CLI.

If the device is located in a remote location, a modem is often attached to the device, allowing an administrator to dial into the device to access the CLI to configure or monitor it.

The third method of accessing the configuration interface on a Cisco device is to establish a Telnet connection directly through the network. Of course, for this to work, the device must have network connectivity functioning properly.

# Starting a Cisco Device

Although the exact startup procedure varies from device to device, there are a few commonalities shared by all Cisco devices. Whether a switch or router, every Cisco device goes through these basic steps when starting up:

1. Check hardware with a power-on-self-test (POST).

2. Load Cisco IOS software from an image file.

3. Apply device configuration from a configuration file.

# User Interface

This section provides background on the user interface of a router or switch. In addition, it describes the capabilities of the help facility, command history manipulation, and enhanced command-line editing features.

The CLI to Cisco's IOS is referred to as *EXEC*. This interface interprets the commands that are entered and performs the corresponding tasks. For security reasons, EXEC supports two types of access to its commands: user mode and privileged mode.

## User Mode

Upon logging in to a router or switch, you are placed into *user mode* automatically. EXEC commands in user mode allow information to be displayed, but router configuration settings cannot be changed. User mode commands are a subset of the privileged mode commands. Table 5.1 lists the commands available for a Cisco 2501 router while in EXEC user mode. The actual number and type of commands displayed varies based on the router configuration and Cisco IOS level. In addition, generating a list may require multiple screens of output. When that occurs, a "—More—" prompt is displayed as the last line of the screen to indicate that additional information is waiting to be displayed. To display the next line of information, press the Return or Enter key. To display the next screen of information, press the spacebar. Pressing any other key stops the listing (a few exceptions exist, such as the Shift key).

A greater than symbol (>) indicates that the router is in user mode. For example, if the hostname of the router is RouterA, the user mode prompt is RouterA>.

Use the **exit** or **logout** command to log out of the router.

## Privileged Mode

Typically, you must enter a password before you can place the router in EXEC privileged mode. *Privileged mode* allows all of the user mode commands to be executed, as well as the configuration parameters to be set, extensive testing to be performed, and other router modes to be accessed.

Table 5.2 lists the commands available while in EXEC privileged mode. The actual number and type of commands displayed varies based on the router configuration and Cisco IOS level.

| Table 5.1 | EXEC user mode commands. |
| --- | --- |
| **User command** | **Function** |
| access-enable | Creates a temporary access-list entry |
| clear | Resets functions |
| connect | Opens a terminal connection |
| disable | Turns off privileged commands |
| disconnect | Disconnects an existing network connection |
| enable | Turns on privileged commands |
| exit | Exits from EXEC |
| help | Views a description of the interactive help system |
| lat | Opens a lat connection |
| lock | Locks the terminal |
| login | Logs in as a particular user |
| logout | Exits from EXEC |
| mrinfo | Requests neighbor and version information from a multicast router |
| mstat | Shows statistics after multiple multicast traceroutes |
| mtrace | Traces a reverse multicast path from destination to source |
| name-connection | Names an existing network connection |
| pad | Opens an X.29 PAD connection |
| ping | Sends echo messages |
| ppp | Starts IETF Point-to-Point Protocol (PPP) |
| resume | Resumes an active network connection |
| rlogin | Opens an rlogin connection |
| show | Shows running system information |
| slip | Starts Serial Line Internet Protocol (SLIP) |
| systat | Displays information about terminal lines |
| telnet | Opens a Telnet connection |
| terminal | Sets terminal line parameters |
| tn3270 | Opens a tn3270 connection |
| traceroute | Traces a route to destination |
| tunnel | Opens a tunnel connection |
| where | Lists active connections |
| x3 | Sets X.3 parameters on PAD |
| xremote | Enters XRemote mode |

**Table 5.2    EXEC privileged mode commands.**

| EXEC Command | Function |
| --- | --- |
| access-enable | Creates a temporary Access-List entry |
| access-template | Creates a temporary Access-List entry |
| bfe | Action for manual emergency modes setting |
| clear | Resets functions |
| clock | Manages the system clock |
| configure | Enters configuration mode |
| connect | Opens a terminal connection |
| copy | Copies configuration or image data |
| debug | Accesses debugging functions (see also **undebug**) |
| disable | Turns off privileged commands |
| disconnect | Disconnects an existing network connection |
| enable | Turns on privileged commands |
| erase | Erases flash or configuration memory |
| exit | Exits from EXEC |
| help | Views a description of the interactive help system |
| lat | Opens a lat connection |
| lock | Locks the terminal |
| login | Logs in as a particular user |
| logout | Exits from EXEC |
| mrinfo | Requests neighbor and version information from a multicast router |
| mstat | Shows statistics after multiple multicast traceroutes |
| mtrace | Traces a reverse multicast path from destination to source |
| name-connection | Names an existing network connection |
| ncia | Starts/stops NCIA server |
| no | Disables debugging functions |
| pad | Opens an X.29 PAD connection |
| ping | Halts and performs a cold restart |
| resume | Resumes an active network connection |
| rlogin | Opens an rlogin connection |
| rsh | Executes a remote command |
| sdlc | Sends synchronous data link control (SDLC) test frames |
| send | Sends a message to other TTY lines |

*(continued)*

| Table 5.2    EXEC privileged mode commands *(continued)*. | |
| --- | --- |
| **EXEC Command** | **Function** |
| setup | Runs the **SETUP** command facility |
| show | Shows running system information |
| slip | Starts SLIP |
| start-chat | Starts a chat-script on a line |
| systat | Displays information about terminal lines |
| tarp | Accesses Target ID Resolution Protocol (TARP) commands |
| telnet | Opens a Telnet connection |
| terminal | Sets terminal line parameters |
| test | Tests subsystems, memory, and interfaces |
| tn3270 | Opens a tn3270 connection |
| traceroute | Traces a route to destination |
| tunnel | Opens a tunnel connection |
| undebug | Disables debugging functions (see also **debug**) |
| verify | Verifies checksum of a Flash file |
| where | Lists active connections |
| which-route | Performs an OSI route table lookup and displays the results |
| write | Writes running configuration to memory, network, or terminal |
| x3 | Sets X.3 parameters on PAD |
| xremote | Enters XRemote mode |

A pound sign (#) indicates that the router is in privileged mode. For example, if the hostname of the router is RouterA, the privileged mode prompt is RouterA#.

Use the **enable** command to enter privileged mode and the **disable** command to return to user mode.

## Context-Sensitive Help

Entering a question mark (?) at the command prompt generates a list of available commands for that EXEC mode. Context-sensitive help provides assistance while entering commands. Syntax checking, command prompting, and keyword completion are some of the context-sensitive help that is available within the Cisco IOS. Table 5.3 highlights several types of context-sensitive help.

The following information highlights the different types of context-sensitive help available to someone who would like to set the system clock on a router.

| Table 5.3 Context-sensitive help. | |
|---|---|
| **Command** | **Function** |
| ? | Displays a list of all commands available within a command mode |
| help | Displays a brief description of the help system for any command mode |
| <abbreviated command> ? | Displays a list of commands that begin with a specific character string |
| <abbreviated command> <**Tab**> | Completes a partial command name |
| <command> ? | Displays a list of the command's possible keywords |
| <command> <keyword> ? | Displays a list of the keyword's possible arguments |

```
r2#c
% Ambiguous command: "c"
```

This command abbreviation is not specific enough to be interpreted. Because several commands begin with the letter "c", the command interpreter does not know which command to execute.

```
r2#clok
Translating "clok"
% Unknown command or computer name, or unable to find computer
address
```

EXEC does not recognize the way this command is typed, or EXEC interprets the entry as a computer name and attempts to open a Telnet session, but is unable to resolve the name to an address.

```
r2#c?
clear clock configure connect copy
```

The abbreviated command followed by a question mark lists all commands in this router mode that begin with "c".

```
r2#clock ?
 set Set the time and date
```

The command followed by a space then a question mark lists all possible keywords for that command.

```
r2#clock set
% Incomplete command.
```

This command and keyword combination requires at least one argument to complete the command string.

```
r2#clock set ?
  hh:mm:ss Current Time
```

The command and keyword followed by a space and a question mark list the next possible arguments for the keyword.

```
r2#clock set 23:45:00
% Incomplete command.
```

Another incomplete command message is returned because another argument is required for this command and keyword combination.

```
r2#clock set 23:45:00 ?
  <1-31> Day of the month
  MONTH Month of the year
```

A space and a question mark at the end of the incomplete command string reveal additional arguments that are required for this command and keyword combination.

```
r2#clock set 23:45:00 31 12
                      ^
% Invalid input detected at '^' marker.
```

The caret (^) beneath a character indicates a syntax error. EXEC expected the word "December" to be entered instead of the number "12".

```
r2#clock set 23:45:00 31 December
% Incomplete command.
```

Another incomplete command message is returned because another argument is required for this command and keyword combination.

```
r2#clock set 23:45:00 31 december ?
  <1993-2035> Year
```

A space and a question mark at the end of the incomplete command string reveal additional arguments that are required for this command and keyword combination.

```
r2#clock set 23:45:00 31 december 1999 ?
  <cr>
```

Entering a space and a question mark after the command, keyword, and arguments returned a carriage return symbol. This indicates that the command line is syntactically correct, no additional values must be entered for this command, and pressing Return or Enter will execute the command string.

```
r2# clock set 23:45:00 31 december 1999
```

In the previous example, the command syntax is checked each time that a command is entered.

## Command History

EXEC also provides a record of recent commands that have been executed. The command history feature is available in many of the router modes. The commands are stored in a buffer as a list; the most recent commands are inserted at the bottom of the list, and older commands appear toward the top of the list. Table 5.4 lists the tasks that can be performed with this feature.

For example, pressing the Up Arrow key retrieves the most recent command executed. Repeatedly pressing the Up Arrow key scrolls through the command history from the most recent command to the oldest command. Pressing the Down Arrow key scrolls through the command history from the oldest command to the most recent command.

*Note: Command history is enabled by default. The default history size is 10 commands.*

## Editing Commands

EXEC includes an enhanced editing mode that supports several editing key functions. Used along with the command history, the editing commands prove quite handy. You can recall commands from the command history, edit them, then re-execute them without re-entering the entire command line. Table 5.5 describes the editing commands.

| Table 5.4 Command history. | |
|---|---|
| **Keystroke** | **Task** |
| Ctrl+P or Up Arrow | Recalls the last or previous command |
| Ctrl+N or Down Arrow | Recalls a more recent command |
| **show history** command | Displays the command history buffer |
| **terminal history size** <number of lines> | Sets the command history buffer size |

In addition, the enhanced editing command feature includes horizontal scrolling for long command lines. Should the cursor reach the right margin while you enter a command, the command line shifts 10 characters to the left. A dollar sign ($) at the beginning of the command line indicates that the line has been shifted. Each time the cursor reaches the right margin, the command line will be shifted. You can use the keystrokes listed in Table 5.5 to edit the line.

Enhanced editing is enabled by default. You can disable it with the **terminal no editing** command and reenable it with the **terminal editing** command.

Most laptop computers support functionality that can copy a previous command string and paste it on the command line so that it can be re-executed or edited.

# Cisco Discovery Protocol

The *Cisco Discovery Protocol (CDP)* is a proprietary protocol that enables network administrators to view summary information and to address information about other directly connected Cisco routers and switches. The CDP operates at the data link layer and connects physical media and network layer protocols. Any physical media supporting the Subnetwork Access Protocol (SNAP) can be used to connect CDP devices. Because the CDP resides at the data link layer, it enables two or more devices that support different network layer protocols to learn about each other.

Figure 5.1 provides an illustration of the CDP. Router A discovers router B via network 1 and router C via network 2 if the CDP is enabled on all three routers; however, router A will not discover router D, because routers A and D are not directly connected.

| Table 5.5 Editing commands. | |
| --- | --- |
| **Keystroke** | **Task** |
| Ctrl+A | Moves to the beginning of the command line |
| Ctrl+E | Moves to the end of the command line |
| Esc+F | Moves forward one word |
| Esc+B | Moves backward one word |
| Ctrl+F | Moves forward one character |
| Ctrl+B | Moves backward one character |

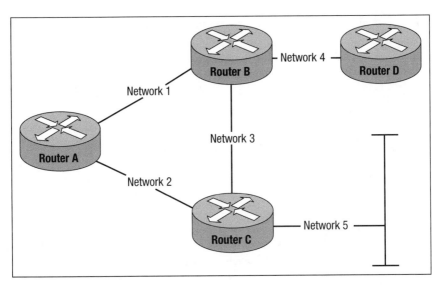

**Figure 5.1**  CDP.

## CDP Configuration

By default, CDP communication begins automatically on startup, but you can still enable or disable the CDP on a router's interface. The commands **cdp enable** and **no cdp enable** respectively enable and disable the CDP on an interface. If the CDP is enabled on an interface, that interface will advertise and discover its directly connected neighbors. This process involves exchanging frames at the data link layer, and the information discovered is stored in a router's cache memory. The **show cdp interface** command displays CDP configuration and status information.

## CDP Information

Because the router stores the CDP information discovered in its cache memory, you can retrieve the information with a **show** command. Two common commands exist for displaying CDP information: **show cdp neighbors** and **show cdp entry**. The **show cdp neighbors** command provides a summary of all of the CDP information from a router's directly connected neighbors.

The CDP neighbor information includes:

➤ Neighbor's device ID

➤ Local port type and number

➤ Holdtime value (in seconds)

➤ Neighbor's network device capability

➤ Neighbor's hardware platform

➤ Neighbor's remote port type and number

The following example lists the output generated from the **show cdp neighbors** command:

```
r2#show cdp neighbors
Capability Codes:R - Router, T - Trans Bridge, B - Source Route
Bridge
         S - Switch, H - Host, I - IGMP, r - Repeater

Device ID Local Intrfce Holdtme Capability Platform Port ID
r2      Eth 1   155     R     2500    Eth 0
r4      Eth 1   125     R     2500    Eth 0
r2#
```

The **show cdp entry** command provides additional detail about one device. As a result, the device ID (that is currently defined as a CDP neighbor) must be included as an argument in the **show cdp entry** command. The following example lists the output generated from the **show cdp entry <device id>** command:

```
r2#show cdp entry r4
- - - - - - - - - - - - - - - - - - - -
Device ID: r4
Entry address(es):
 IP address: 172.16.41.4
Platform: cisco 2500, Capabilities: Router
Interface: Ethernet1, Port ID (outgoing port): Ethernet0
Holdtime : 173 sec

Version :
Cisco Internetwork Operating System Software
IOS (tm) 2500 Software (C2500-JS-L), Version 11.2(15),
RELEASE SOFTWARE (fc1)
Copyright (c) 1986-1998 by cisco Systems, Inc.
Compiled Tue 07-Jul-98 22:22 by tmullins

r2#
```

The **show cdp entry** command output includes all of the layer 3 addresses configured on the neighboring router's directly connected interface.

*Note: The holdtime value indicates the age of the CDP information.*

# Testing Other Devices

Several methods exist for accessing and testing connectivity to other devices. The approach to testing and troubleshooting should follow the principles of the Open

Systems Interconnect (OSI) model. As discussed in Chapter 3, each layer depends on its lower layers for successful communication with its peer layers at the remote host. In other words, if layer 3 on one system can communicate with layer 3 on another system, then layers 1 and 2 of both systems are operating properly.

Several useful tools are available within the IOS to assist in testing and troubleshooting problems, including: **telnet, ping, traceroute,** and the **show interfaces** commands.

## Telnet

Telnet operates at the application layer and is an application that provides a virtual terminal. You can connect to a remote router that supports Transmission Control Protocol/Internet Protocol (TCP/IP). Telnet helps to answer the question, "Can I access the router remotely across the internetwork?" If a Telnet session can be established, all of the lower layers are operating properly. If not, one of the lower layers on the local or remote router is experiencing problems. The following example depicts the **telnet** command:

```
r2#telnet 172.16.41.4
Trying 172.16.41.4... Open
User Access Verification

Password:
r4>
```

## Ping

Ping operates at the network layer. It is a basic echo protocol that determines whether IP packets are being received by the remote hosts and the response time across the internetwork. Simply put, ping checks end-to-end connectivity. Ping sends a specific number echo request and waits a specified time for an equal number of echo replies. Ping helps to answer the question, "Are my packets being routed successfully?" If 100 percent of the echo replies are received, all of the lower layers are operating properly. If less than all of the replies are received, an internetwork routing problem or a problem with the lower layers may exist. The following is an example of a basic **ping** command output:

```
r2#ping 172.16.41.4

Type escape sequence to abort.
Sending 5, 100-byte ICMP Echos to 172.16.41.4, timeout is 2 seconds:
!!!!!
Success rate is 100 percent (5/5), round-trip min/avg/max = 4/4/4 ms
r2#
```

In this example, the exclamation points indicate that a successful echo reply was received. A period indicates a time-out condition and that the echo reply was not received.

## Traceroute

When you need to know where data is traveling in a network, **traceroute** is the perfect command. Like the **ping** command, traceroute sends packets to the remote destination host and awaits replies. Traceroute tests each step along the network path. It sets the time-to-live (TTL) value (which is a hop-count value) to one of the three packets it sends to the first hop. When an intermediate router receives these packets, it decreases each packet's TTL value by one. The packets now have a TTL value of zero, which generates an error message. The intermediate router sends an error message to the source device for each packet it received. The source device increases the TTL value to two and sends three more packets out.

The first intermediate router receives the packets, decreases the TTL value by one, and forwards the packets. This process continues with each router that receives traceroute packets sending error messages back to the source router as the TTL value reaches zero. Traceroute can then not only determine response times from the error messages it receives, but also identify the last router along the network path that was reached successfully. Traceroute helps to answer the question, "What route are my packets taking?" Like the **ping** command, if all of the error messages are received (including messages from the remote destination host), then the network layer and all of the lower layers are working well. If some of the error messages time out, you will be able to identify quickly where the problem is occurring. The following example lists output from the **traceroute** command:

*Note: The "msec" indicates a successful traceroute reply received. An asterisk (\*)*
*indicates a time-out condition.*

```
r2#traceroute 172.16.50.4

Type escape sequence to abort.
Tracing the route to 172.16.50.4

 1 172.16.41.4 4 msec 4 msec 4 msec
 2 172.16.50.4 4 msec 5 msec 4 msec
r2#
```

## Show Interfaces

The **show interfaces** command displays statistics for all of the interfaces on the router or switch. This command helps to answer the question, "Is my network link operating properly?" Two aspects exist for each interface: a physical aspect and a logical aspect. The physical aspect includes the interface hardware and operates at the physical layer. The logical aspect includes the interface software and operates at the data link layer. The hardware makes the actual network connection between devices, whereas the software transmits frames between devices. Therefore, two items must be verified when testing at the physical and data link layers: carrier detect signal and keepalive frames, respectively. A *carrier detect signal* triggers a line status that you can verify using the **show interfaces** command. The transmission of *keepalive frames* triggers the line protocol and can also be verified using the **show interfaces** command. The following demonstrates an example of the **show interfaces** command output:

```
r2#show interface ethernet 0
Ethernet0 is up, line protocol is up
 Hardware is Lance, address is 00e0.1e68.4011 (bia 00e0.1e68.4011)
—More—
r2#
```

In this example, the line status is "up" (the interface hardware is currently active), and the line protocol is "up" (the software processes that handle the line protocol believe the interface is usable). In other words, interface Ethernet0 is up/up, and the carrier detect signal and keepalive frames are being communicated. However, this status only verifies that layers 1 and 2 are working properly; it does not indicate that any of the layers above them are working properly. Table 5.6 lists the different line status/line protocol combinations you may encounter.

You will often seen an interface that reports *administratively down, line protocol is down* in the show interface output. This means that the interface was manually shut down or was disabled purposely.

| Table 5.6    Line status and line protocol combinations. | |
| --- | --- |
| Line Status/Line Protocol Combination | Description |
| Ethernet0 is up, line protocol is up | Interface is operational |
| Ethernet0 is up, line protocol is down | Network connection problem exists |
| Ethernet0 is down, line protocol is down | Physical interface problem exists |
| Ethernet0 is administratively down, line protocol is down | Interface has been disabled or shut down |

# Practice Questions

## Question 1

Which of the following prompts indicates that the router is in privileged EXEC mode?

○ a. Router>

○ b. Router#

○ c. Router(config)#

○ d. Router:

Answer b is correct. Router# is correct because a pound sign (#) immediately following the router's hostname (in this case "Router") indicates that the router is in privileged EXEC mode. A greater than symbol (>) after the hostname indicates that the router is in user mode; therefore, answer a is incorrect. The text "(config)#" after the hostname indicates that the router is in global configuration mode; therefore, answer c is incorrect. A colon (:) after the hostname is not a valid router mode indicator; therefore, answer d is incorrect.

## Question 2

The command **show cdp neighbors** does not display which of the following?

○ a. Neighbor's device ID

○ b. Neighbor's hardware platform

○ c. Neighbor's IOS version

○ d. Neighbor's port type and number

○ e. Local port type and number

Answer c is correct. The neighbor's IOS version is displayed by the **show cdp entry** command. Answers a, b, d, and e are displayed by the **show cdp neighbors** command and are, therefore, incorrect responses to the question.

# Question 3

> Which of the following router commands displays the keyword needed for the command **"clock"**?
>
> ○ a. **"cl?"**
>
> ○ b. **"cl ?"**
>
> ○ c. **"clock?"**
>
> ○ d. **"clock ?"**

Answer d is correct. **"clock ?"** will display the keyword needed to complete the command. The **"cl?"** and **"clock?"** keystrokes will display the commands beginning with the text "cl" and "clock", respectively; therefore, answers a and c are incorrect. The **"cl ?"** keystroke is an ambiguous command and returns an error; therefore, answer b is incorrect.

# Question 4

> The CDP operates at which layer?
>
> ○ a. Transport
>
> ○ b. Network
>
> ○ c. Data link
>
> ○ d. Physical

Answer c is correct. The CDP operates at the data link layer. Although the CDP can communicate over a variety of physical media, it does not operate at the physical layer; therefore, answer d is incorrect. The CDP allows a network device to exchange frames with other directly connected network devices. It enables those network devices (which may support different network layer protocols) to discover each other's protocol and address information and capabilities. But the CDP does not operate at the network layer; therefore, answer b is incorrect. Answer a is incorrect because the CDP does not operate at the transport layer and is not concerned with end-to-end connectivity like other transport layer protocols.

# Question 5

> Which command, when executed successfully, does not verify that two routers are routing packets between them successfully?
>
> ○ a.  **ping**
>
> ○ b.  **show interface**
>
> ○ c.  **trace**
>
> ○ d.  **telnet**

Answer b is correct. Although the **show interface** command displays the status of the interfaces on a router, it does not indicate whether packets are reaching their destination. The **ping** and **trace** commands verify routing by sending and receiving packets across the network; therefore, answers a and c are incorrect. In order for the **telnet** command to be successful, packets must be sent and received properly, so it also verifies routing; therefore, answer d is incorrect.

# Question 6

> In order to display the list of possible commands in privileged mode, which of the following sequence of keystrokes must be typed at the prompt?
>
> ○ a.  help
>
> ○ b.  h
>
> ○ c.  CTRL+H
>
> ○ d.  ?

Answer d is correct. The question mark (?) will display the list of possible commands when it is typed at the prompt, regardless of the router's current mode. The **help** and **h** commands display a brief description of the help system for any command mode; therefore, answers a and b are incorrect. The CTRL+H keystroke displays nothing; therefore, answer c is incorrect.

# Question 7

---

> Which of the following keystrokes will move your cursor to the beginning of the line in the Cisco IOS when enhanced editing is on?
>
> ○ a.  Ctrl+E
>
> ○ b.  Ctrl+F
>
> ○ c.  Ctrl+A
>
> ○ d.  Ctrl+B

Answer c is correct. The keystroke you would use to move the cursor to the beginning of the line is Ctrl+A. Answers a, b, and d all perform other editing functions. Ctrl+E moves the cursor to the end of the line. Ctrl+F moves the cursor forward one character. Ctrl+B moves the cursor backward one character.

# Question 8

---

> Which of the following indicate that Ethernet port 0 has been manually disabled?
>
> ○ a.  Ethernet0 is up, line protocol is up
>
> ○ b.  Ethernet 0 is up, line protocol is down
>
> ○ c.  Ethernet0 is down, line protocol is down
>
> ○ d.  Ethernet0 is administratively down, line protocol is down

Answer d is correct. Answers b, c, and d all indicate that the interface is not fully operational. However, answers b and c are incorrect because they both indicate connectivity problems, whereas the correct answer, d, indicates the interface is down on purpose. Answer a is incorrect because it states that the line is operational.

# Question 9

Which of the following keystrokes will complete a partially entered command in the Cisco IOS when enchanced editing is on?

○ a. Enter

○ b. Tab

○ c. Shift + Enter

○ d. Esc

Answer b is correct. The Tab key will complete a partially entered command in the Cisco IOS. You must only type enough of the command to make it unique. Enter will execute the command, so answer a is incorrect. Answers c and d are both incorrect because neither will produce the desired results.

# Need to Know More?

 McNutt, Shawn, Mark Poplar, Jason Waters, and David Stabenaw. *CCNA Routing and Switching Exam Prep.* The Coriolis Group, Scottsdale, AZ, 2000. ISBN 1-57610-440-0. This book is a great complement to the CCNA Cram book. It has expanded coverage and detailed information about CCNA exam topics.

 *Router Products Configuration Guide.* Cisco Internetwork Operating System, Release 11.0. Customer order number: DOC-RPCG 11.0. Text Part Number: 78-2032-01. Chapters 2 and 3 provide additional detail on the Cisco IOS user interface commands.

 Syngress Media, with Richard D. Hornbaker, CCIE. *Cisco Certified Network Associate Study Guide.* Osborne/McGraw-Hill, Berkeley, CA, 1998. ISBN 0-07-882487-7.

 With the Cisco's documentation CD-ROM, you can immediately access Cisco's entire library of end user documentation, selected product news, bug databases, and related information. The documentation CD-ROM is produced monthly.

 **www.cisco.com,** The official Cisco documentation Web site hosted by Cisco, contains helpful information. From the home page, search for "user exec mode" or "privileged exec mode", and you'll be presented with a choice of several pages of detailed information.

# LAN Switching

. . . . . . . . . . . . . . . . . . . . . . . . . . . . . . . . . . . . . . . . .

### Terms you'll need to understand:

✓ Switch

✓ Spanning tree protocol

✓ Cut-through switching

✓ Store-and-forward switching

✓ Frame tagging

### Techniques you'll need to master:

✓ Describing the advantages of local area network (LAN) segmentation

✓ Describing the operation of spanning tree protocol and its benefits

✓ Describing LAN segmentation using switches

✓ Distinguishing between cut-through and store-and-forward switching

✓ Describing the benefits of network segmentation with switches

Switching is a technology that has grown out of the demand for increased performance from existing network infrastructures. As applications such as email, Internet connectivity, client/server applications, and voice and video continue to demand more bandwidth, the need for switches is growing stronger. This increase in demand is also making switching technology more affordable. Switches are rapidly taking the place of hubs as the preferred method of connecting desktops in the wiring closet.

# Layer 2 Switching Technology

Remember from Chapter 2 that switches operate at layer 2 of the Open Systems Interconnect (OSI) model. The technology upon which layer 2 switches operate is the same as that provided by Ethernet bridges. The basic operation of a switch involves the following:

➤ Discovering media access control (MAC) addresses

➤ Filtering or forwarding frames

➤ Preventing loops

## Discovering MAC Addresses

Like a bridge, a switch monitors all frames that pass through it to learn the MAC addresses of each device connected to its ports. This information is stored in a database. The switch consults the database each time it receives a frame to determine whether to forward the frame to a different port or to drop it.

When the switch is initially booted up, the MAC address database is empty. Forwarding or filtering decisions cannot be made with an empty database, so, initially, each incoming packet is forwarded through all of the switch's ports. This is called *flooding* the frame. As flooding occurs, the switch begins to learn the MAC addresses and associate them with one of its ports.

This address learning process is a continual operation of the switch. Each MAC database entry is stored in memory and is only valid for a preset interval. If the entry is not refreshed by a new frame transmitting within the switch, it is discarded. So, as long as all stations have network activity within the MAC database entry lifetime, the switch builds a complete view of network devices.

## Filtering and Forwarding

Each time the switch receives a frame, it examines the destination MAC address. If this address exists in the MAC database, the frame is forwarded only through the switch port associated to the address. This process frees all of the segments connected to different ports of the excess bandwidth taken by the frame. This is known as *frame filtering*.

Whenever the destination MAC address is unknown, the frame is flooded to all switch ports. This is undesirable because it wastes bandwidth.

## Preventing Loops

Bridges introduce the possibility of creating a bridged network with multiple paths to a single destination. Typically, this type of redundancy is considered favorable, but for bridges it can cause problems in the form of *bridging loops*. These occur when circular connections exist in a bridged network. Figure 6.1 illustrates a bridged network with bridging loops.

Figure 6.1 shows that a loop can exist in a network. For example, if someone sends a broadcast message from segment 2, the message would be forwarded to physical segment 3 by bridges B and C. Bridge A would then receive two broadcasts and forward both broadcasts to physical segment 1. Bridge D would have forwarded this broadcast to physical segment 1 as well. Subsequently, bridge D will receive the two broadcasts forwarded by bridge A and forward these packets to physical segment 2. This continuous forwarding of broadcast packets wastes bandwidth. With more complex bridged networks, the broadcast packets can be forwarded exponentially, leading to what is termed a *broadcast storm*. This occurs when so many broadcasts are being continuously forwarded that they consume all of the available bandwidth. The *spanning tree protocol*, which implements an algorithm that removes all circular connections in a bridged network, eliminates bridging loops.

## Spanning Tree Protocol

The spanning tree protocol creates a loop-free network topology by placing connections that create loops in a blocking state. It is important to note that this protocol does not eliminate loops, but only blocks the connections that create the loops. Loops in a network often provide needed redundancy in case of a physical connection being disconnected. The spanning tree protocol maintains the benefits of redundancy, while eliminating the disadvantages of looping. To illustrate how the spanning tree protocol functions, we will use our bridged network in Figure 6.1.

The spanning tree protocol selects a root bridge in the network (in this case, bridge A). Next, every other bridge selects one of its ports with the least *path cost* to the root bridge. The least path cost is the sum of the cost to traverse every network between the indicated bridge and the root bridge. The root path cost can be determined in multiple ways; in this case, we have arbitrarily assigned costs to each path. Next, *designated bridges* are determined. These consist of the bridge on each LAN with the lowest aggregate root path cost. The designated bridge is the only bridge on a LAN allowed to forward frames. Table 6.1 details the bridge identifier and its root path cost to reach the root bridge. Figure 6.2 illustrates our network with the root path cost assigned to each bridge interface.

| Table 6.1 Spanning tree protocol. | |
|---|---|
| **Bridge Number** | **Aggregate Root Path Cost** |
| Bridge A | 0 |
| Bridge B | 10 |
| Bridge C | 30 |
| Bridge D | 20 |

By applying the spanning tree protocol, we block the connection between bridge C and physical segments 2 and 3, because bridge D and bridge B both have lower aggregate root path costs to the root bridge (bridge A). We also block the connection between bridge D and physical segment 2, because bridge B has a lower root path cost than bridge D. In Figure 6.3, we illustrate our bridged network after the spanning tree protocol has been applied. Note that the connections between bridge C and physical segments 2 and 3 are blocked, as well as the connection between bridge D and physical segment 2.

We now have no circular routes in our network, but we maintain redundancy, because the spanning tree protocol is applied whenever a bridge is powered up or a topology change occurs. Therefore, if the connection between bridge B and physical segment B was broken, the spanning tree protocol would run and the connection between bridge D and physical segment 2 would no longer be blocked.

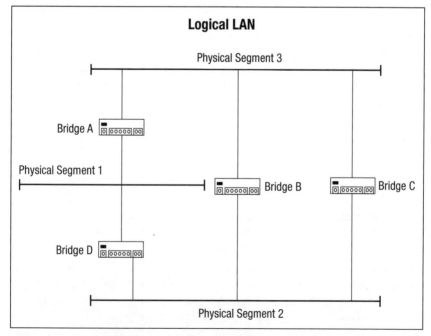

**Figure 6.1** Bridged network with bridging loops.

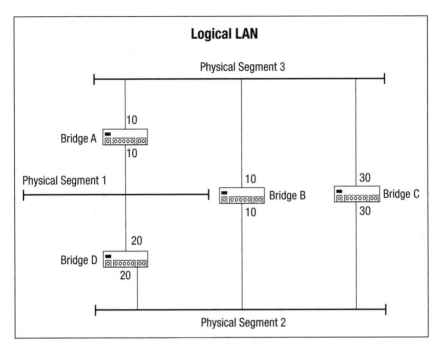

**Figure 6.2**    Spanning tree protocol root path cost illustration.

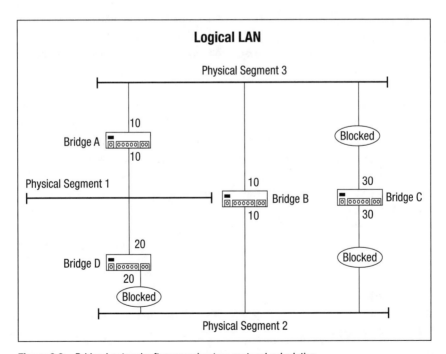

**Figure 6.3**    Bridged network after spanning tree protocol calculation.

# Cisco Switching Methods

All of the switching methods used by Cisco switches provide increased through-put in comparison to bridges. The hardware-based architectures of switches allow them to make decisions at wire speed. The primary difference between the various methods is the process each uses to switch frames.

*Note: We have consistently used frames to represent layer 2 data messages in this chapter. The term cell can also be used to identify layer 2 data messages. This term is used when referring to data traffic using the asynchronous transfer mode (ATM) technology. The CCNA exam does not cover this technology, so we have only presented frames in this chapter to simplify the concepts.*

## Store-and-Forward

In *store-and-forward switching* mode, the switch reads the entire incoming frame and copies the frame into its buffers. After the frame has been completely read, the switch performs the layer 2 cyclical redundancy check to determine if an error occurred during transmission. If the frame has an error, the switch drops the frame. If no error is identified, the switch checks its forwarding table to determine the proper port (in the case of a unicast) or ports (in the case of a multicast) to which the frame must be forwarded.

Store-and-forward switches have the highest latency of any switching mode, because the switch must read the entire frame before making a forwarding decision. The added error checking of store-and-forward, however, reduces the number of erred frames that are forwarded.

## Cut-Through

Cut-through switches introduce a lower level of latency during the switching process than do store-and-forward switches. They achieve increased performance by eliminating the error checking and making forwarding decisions based only on the first six bytes of the incoming frame. (These first six bytes contain the destination MAC address of the frame.) Cut-through switches read the destination address of the incoming frame and immediately check the forwarding table to determine the proper destination ports. This increased performance does, however, allow erred frames to be forwarded more often than store-and-forward switches do.

## Fragment-Free

Fragment-free switching is a modification to the cut-through switching method. Like cut-through, fragment-free switches read only a portion of the frame before beginning the forwarding process. The difference is that fragment-free switches read the first 64 bytes, which is enough to check the frame for collisions. This allows for better error checking than with cut-through switches with a minimal loss in latency.

 Fragment-free switching is the default method used by Catalyst 1900 switches.

# Cisco Switches

Cisco produces a wide variety of switching products to meet almost any business need. At the high end, there are products such as the Catalyst 5000 through 8500 series, designed as high-performance multilayer switches for large network backbones. At the other end of the spectrum are products such as the 1900 and 2820 series, which are affordable solutions for workgroups and desktop connectivity.

As a CCNA candidate, you should be very familiar with the latter group of switches. You will need to be able to implement these switches as high-speed hub replacements or as backbones to small or midsize LANs.

In addition, you will need to be able to implement virtual local area networks (VLANs) and connect multiple switches using some type of trunk connection. These tasks are covered in Chapter 7.

In the following sections, you will be examining the functionality and configuration of the Catalyst 1900 series switch. This is an extremely popular switch, because it provides low-cost switched connectivity for desktops or 10BaseT hubs, and Fast Ethernet connectivity for servers or backbones. It is also an excellent starting point for learning switching technology. Figure 6.4 shows a Catalyst 1900 switch in a typical environment.

# Switch Startup

The startup process for a Cisco switch can be monitored in the following ways:

➤ Observing the light-emitting diodes (LEDs) on the switch chassis

➤ Examining the Cisco Internetwork Operating System (IOS) output by connecting a terminal to the switch's console port

Cisco catalyst switches have several LEDs that give a convenient visual indicator of the switch's operational status. These LEDs are green when the switch is functioning properly and amber when there's any sort of problem.

The Catalyst 1900 series switch executes a power-on-self-test (POST) each time the switch is powered on and can be monitored by watching the LEDs on the switch chassis. The typical sequence is as follows:

**Figure 6.4** Catalyst 1900 switch environment.

1. Initially, all LEDs are green.

2. Each LED is associated with a specific POST. Each LED turns off after its task is complete or turns amber if there's a problem.

3. The system LED turns amber if any test fails.

4. When the POST is complete, the LEDs blink, then turn off.

In addition to monitoring LEDs, any errors encountered during startup can be checked by attaching a terminal to the console port of the switch and observing the text output. The initial output from a Catalyst 1900 switch with no errors looks similar to the following:

```
Catalyst 1900 Management Console
Copyright (c) Cisco Systems, Inc.1993-1999
All rights reserved.

Standard Edition Software
Ethernet address:    00-E0-1E-7E-B4-40
```

```
PCA Number: 73-2239-01
PCA Serial Number: SAD01200001
Model Number: WS-C1924-A
System Serial Number: FAA01200001
--------------------------------

User Interface Menu

[M] Menus
[I] IP Address
[P] Console Password

Enter Selection:
```

# Configuring the Switch

There are three different options for configuring a new Catalyst 1900 switch:

➤ Menu-driven interface

➤ Command-line interface (CLI) (only available on Enterprise Edition IOS software)

➤ Web-based interface

These configuration options may vary depending on which model switch you have and which version of software it is running. Using the menu-driven interface may seem like the easiest and quickest way to get your switch running. It is important, however, that you learn how to configure the switch through the CLI as well.

*Note: The CLI is the standard interface used to configure any Cisco device running the IOS, Cisco's proprietary OS.*

The Web-based interface is another easy visual way to monitor and configure the switch. It is important to note, however, that before you can use the Web-based interface, the switch must have a valid Internet Protocol (IP) address. For this reason, you must first configure at least an IP address using one of the other two configuration methods.

## Default Configuration

Cisco switches come with a default configuration that is actually usable in many cases without any additional customization. Table 6.2 shows the default configuration settings of a Catalyst 1900 switch. For most situations, you will want to configure at least some basic options on the switch, such as an IP address, default gateway, and duplex options.

| Table 6.2 Catalyst 1900 default configuration. | |
|---|---|
| **Option** | **Default Value** |
| IP Address | 0.0.0.0 |
| CDP | Enabled |
| Switching mode | Fragment-free |
| 100BaseT port | Auto-negotiate duplex mode |
| 10BaseT port | Half duplex |
| Spanning tree protocol | Enabled |
| Console password | None |

# Using the Menu-Driven Interface

Using the menu-driven interface to configure a Catalyst 1900 switch is a simple and straightforward process. You must first connect to the switch through the console port using a PC with terminal emulation software or Telnet into the switch. As soon as the switch starts up, a menu that you use to select the option to configure appears. The initial management console logon screen looks like this:

```
User Interface Menu

[M] Menus
[K] Command Line
[I] IP Address
[P] Console Password


Enter Selection:
```

You may want to give the switch a password by pressing P and following the instructions about setting the console password. You can enter the IP Configuration menu by pressing I:

```
Catalyst 1900 - IP Configuration

Ethernet Address:00-E0-1E-7E-B4-40

----------Settings----------
[I] IP address                0.0.0.0
[S] Subnet mask               0.0.0.0
[G] Default gateway             0.0.0.0
[B] Management Bridge Group1 (fixed)
[M] IP address of DNS server 1      0.0.0.0
[N] IP address of DNS server 2      0.0.0.0
[D] Domain name
[R] Use Routing Information Protocol    Enabled
```

```
----------Actions----------
[P] Ping
[C] Clear cached DNS entries
[X] Exit to previous menu

Enter Selection:
```

You can access the Management Console Main Menu by pressing M:

```
Catalyst 1900 - Main Menu

[C] Console Settings
[S] System
[N] Network Management
[P] Port Configuration
[A] Port Addressing
[D] Port Statistics Detail
[M] Monitoring
[B] Bridge Group
[R] Multicast Registration
[F] Firmware
[I] RS-232 Interface
[U] Usage Summaries
[H] Help

[X] Exit Management Console

Enter Selection:
```

Almost every option that you may need to configure for a Catalyst switch has an associated menu command.

# Using the CLI

The CLI, while slightly more difficult to learn than the menu-driven interface, is important to know because it is used for configuration across the entire Cisco product line. The CLI is available on switches that are running the Enterprise Edition of Cisco's IOS. From the initial management console logon screen, press K to enter the CLI. You will get a prompt that looks similar to the following:

```
1900>
```

Enter privileged mode by using the **enable** command. Then, enter configuration mode by using the **config terminal** command.

```
1900>enable
Enter Password: <enable password>
1900#config terminal
1900(config)#
```

## Configuring TCP/IP Options

Giving the switch an IP address is one of the first things that should be done. The command used to do so is **ip address {ip address} {subnet mask}**. The default gateway should also be specified by using the **ip default-gateway {ip address}** command. The following is an example:

```
ip address 192.168.1.10 255.255.255.0
ip default-gateway 192.168.1.1
```

You may also need to configure a domain name for the switch and tell it how to resolve names by giving it a name-server address.

```
ip domain-name cisco.com
ip name-server 192.168.1.20
```

Now, we can view the TCP/IP information by using the **show ip** command:

```
hostname# show ip

IP Address:192.168.1.10
Subnet Mask:255.255.255.0
Default Gateway:192.168.1.1
Management VLAN: 1
Domain name: cisco.com
Name server 1:192.168.1.20
Name server 2:198.92.30.32
HTTP server :Enabled
HTTP port : 80
RIP :Enabled
```

## Using the Web Interface

Catalyst 1900 and 2820 switches come with a built-in web server that can be used for monitoring and configuring the switch. It is very visually oriented and allows you to change configuration options in a point-and-click environment. All you have to know is the IP address of the switch, and you can point your Web browser to the switch's IP address. If the switch has been configured with a password, you will have to enter it to use the Web interface.

# Practice Questions

## Question 1

What is maintained in a bridge's forwarding table?

○ a. A device's IP address and the IP network on which the device resides.

○ b. A device's MAC address and the physical segment on which that device resides.

○ c. The MAC addresses and the best interfaces to use to forward a frame to a destination MAC address.

○ d. The IP network and MAC address of devices.

Answer c is correct. Forwarding tables maintain MAC addresses. In addition, forwarding tables maintain the best interfaces to use to forward a frame to a destination MAC address. Answer a is incorrect because a bridge does not maintain IP addresses in its forwarding table. IP is a layer 3 protocol and is used by routers, not bridges. Answer b is a trick answer because it is partially correct. However, bridges do not maintain the physical segment on which a device resides. Bridges only maintain the next physical segment to forward a frame en route to the device's physical segment. In some cases, the device will exist on this physical segment, but not in all cases. Answer d is incorrect because bridges do not maintain IP network information.

## Question 2

What is the name of the protocol used to eliminate bridging loops?

○ a. Switching

○ b. ISL

○ c. Frame tagging

○ d. Spanning tree protocol

Answer d is correct. The spanning tree protocol is used to remove circular routes in bridged and switched networks. Answer a is incorrect because switching is a layer 2 technology, not a protocol. Answer b is incorrect because inter-switch link (ISL) is used to allow VLANs to span multiple physical switches. Answer c is incorrect because frame tagging is a process used to identify the VLAN of a frame between switches.

## Question 3

> Switches provide higher port densities than bridges.
>
> ○ a. True
> ○ b. False

Answer a is correct, True. Switches provide higher port densities than bridges. The increased port density is one of the main factors that allow switches to provide a higher throughput than bridges.

## Question 4

> Which of the following switching methods provides the greatest frame throughput?
>
> ○ a. Store-and-forward switching
> ○ b. Frame-tag switching
> ○ c. Cut-through switching
> ○ d. ISL switching

Answer c is correct. Cut-through switching provides high throughput frame switching because it reads only a portion of the frame before making the forwarding decision. Cut-through switching does not provide error checking. Answer a is incorrect because store-and-forward switching has slower frame throughput rates than cut-through switching because of its error-checking capabilities and because it reads the entire frame before making a forwarding decision. Answer b is incorrect because frame-tag switching does not exist; frame tagging is a process used to identify a frame's VLAN between switches. Answer d is incorrect because it is used to allow VLANs to span multiple switches as well.

## Question 5

> Which of the following are valid ways to configure a Catalyst 1900 switch? [Choose all that apply]
>
> ❑ a. From a configuration file
> ❑ b. From the switch's built-in menu interface
> ❑ c. From the switch's CLI
> ❑ d. From your Web browser

Answers a, b, c, and d are correct. Each of these answers is a valid method to configure a Catalyst 1900 switch.

# Question 6

> Which of the following commands could be used to assign an IP address to a Catalyst 1900 switch?
>
> ○ a.  **ip-address** 10.1.1.10 255.0.0.0
>
> ○ b.  **ip address** 10.1.1.10 and **subnet-mask** 255.0.0.0
>
> ○ c.  **ip** 10.1.1.10/255.0.0.0
>
> ○ d.  **ip address** 10.1.1.10 255.0.0.0

The correct answer is d. The command for assigning an IP address to a switch from the command prompt is **ip address** *{address}{subnet-mask}*. Answers a and c are incorrect because these are invalid commands. Answer b is incorrect because subnet-mask is not a valid command.

# Question 7

> What command can be used on a Catalyst 1900 switch to view it's TCP/IP configuration information?
>
> ○ a.  **show tcp/ip**
>
> ○ b.  **show ip**
>
> ○ c.  **show network**
>
> ○ d.  **display network**

The correct answer is b. The **show ip** command will display information about the TCP/IP settings the switch is using. Answers a, c, and d are all invalid commands.

# Need to Know More?

McNutt, Shawn, Mark Poplar, Jason Waters, and David Stabenaw: *CCNA Routing and Switching Exam Prep.* The Coriolis Group, Scottsdale, AZ, 2000. ISBN 1-57610-440-0. This book is a great complement to the CCNA Cram book. The switching chapters expand on the information presented here.

Chappell, Laura: *Introduction to Cisco Router Configuration.* Cisco Systems Inc., Macmillan Publishing Company, Indianapolis, IN, 1998. ISBN 0-7645-3186-7. This book provides a great overview of the concepts tested on the CCNA exam.

Ford, Merilee, H. Kim Lew, Steve Spanier, and Kevin Downes: *Internetworking Technologies Handbook 2nd Edition.* Macmillan Publishing Company, Indianapolis, IN, 1998. ISBN 1-56205-102-3. This book is full of resourceful information on internetworking technologies.

Lammle, Todd, Donald Porter, and James Chellis: *CCNA Cisco Certified Network Associate.* Sybex Network Press, Alameda, CA, 1999. ISBN 0-7821-2381-3. This book is a great supplement for learning the technologies tested on the CCNA exam.

Syngress Media, with Richard D. Hornbaker, CCIE: *Cisco Certified Network Associate Study Guide.* Osborne/McGraw-Hill, Berkeley, CA, 1998. ISBN 0-07882-487-7. Another great book for review before taking the CCNA exam.

Visit **www.cisco.com/univercd/cc/td/doc/product/software/ios113ed/113ed_cr/switch_c/xcisl.htm** for a great article titled *Configuring Routing between VLANs with ISL Encapsulation.*

# Extending
# Switch Functionality

**Terms you'll need to understand:**

✓ Virtual local area network (VLAN)

✓ Trunking

✓ Inter-switch link (ISL)

✓ VLAN Trunking Protocol (VTP)

**Techniques you'll need to master:**

✓ Describing VLAN operation

✓ Creating VLANs

✓ Establishing a trunk connection between switches

✓ Understanding VTP

In this chapter, you will be introduced to some of the advanced features available on Cisco switches. You will learn to interconnect switches through trunk connections. You will also learn how to configure and manage VLANs.

# VLANs

A VLAN is a group of switched ports that acts as a separate, isolated LAN. There can be several VLANs defined on a single switch. A VLAN can also span multiple switches. Workstations in separate VLANs will never encounter traffic or share bandwidth from other VLANs unless the data is routed. In other words, a router or switch with routing capabilities is required if devices on different VLANs need to communicate.

Remember from Chapter 2 that one of the main benefits to switches is that they segment a network into many collision domains. Each port represents a single collision domain, and devices share bandwidth only with other devices on the same switch port. Unless a switch is segmented into VLANs, however, all of the devices on the switch are still in the same broadcast domain; that is, all broadcasts (and multicasts) are sent to each port throughout the switching fabric.

VLANs introduce a way to limit the broadcast traffic in a switched network (a job normally associated with routers). When you create a VLAN by defining which ports belong to it, you are really just creating a boundary for broadcast traffic. This has the effect of creating multiple, isolated LANs on a single switch.

Figure 7.1 shows a 12-port switch that has been divided into two VLANs. Ports 1 through 6 are VLAN 1, and ports 7 through 12 are VLAN 2.

 It is important to understand the need for routers in a switched network. If devices on different VLANs need to communicate, routing is required to facilitate this exchange of data.

What happens when a device on one VLAN needs to communicate with a device on another VLAN? Because a VLAN is a closed layer 2 network, traffic must cross a layer 3 device to communicate with other VLANs. This means that a router is required to facilitate the exchange of packets between VLANs.

*Note: The behavior we're describing here is that of layer 2 switching. There are layer 3 switches on the market that perform routing, but these are beyond the scope of this book.*

It is possible for a device to participate in more than one VLAN by using a special type of network card that performs ISL. ISL is discussed later in this chapter.

The real benefit to using VLANs is that they can span multiple switches. Figure 7.2 shows two switches that are configured to share VLAN information.

**Figure 7.1**   Simple VLAN.

**Figure 7.2**   VLANs spanning multiple switches.

A large campus network may have hundreds of switches spread throughout several buildings. A user can be put on the appropriate VLAN easily, no matter where he or she is physically located. Users on the same VLAN do not have to be connected to the same device. Therefore, LANs are no longer tied to the physical location of users, but can be assigned based on department, functional area, or security level. By isolating users according to department or functional area, network administrators can keep the majority of data traffic within one VLAN, thereby maximizing the amount of traffic switched at hardware speeds versus what is routed at slower software speeds.

The ability to assign a user to a VLAN on a port-by-port basis makes adding, moving, or deleting users simple. For example, let's say a user changes from the accounting to the marketing department. If the network administrator designed the network and VLANs by functional department, this user would have changed VLANs. To accommodate this change, the administrator only has to make a software configuration change in the switch by assigning that user's port to the new VLAN.

In addition, VLANs provide the flexibility necessary to group users by security level. This can greatly simplify applying a security policy to a network. In summary, the benefits of VLANs are that they:

➤ Simplify security administration.

➤ Allow users to be grouped by functional area versus physical location.

➤ Simplify moving and adding users.

# Frame Tagging

Frame tagging is the method used by Cisco Catalyst switches to identify to which VLAN a frame belongs. As a frame enters the switch, the switch encapsulates the frame with a header that "tags" the frame with a VLAN ID. Any time a frame needs to leave one switch for another, the tagged frame is sent throughout the switching fabric. When the frame arrives at the destination switch, the tag tells the switch to which VLAN the frame belongs. This process is illustrated in Figure 7.3 using the VLAN IDs 10, 20, and 30. The tag is stripped off of the frame before the frame is sent out to the destination device. This process gives the illusion that all ports are physically connected to the same switch.

 Be sure to understand the function of frame tagging, which "tags" a frame with a user-defined VLAN ID.

# Trunk Connections

Under normal circumstances, a switch port can carry traffic for a single VLAN only. For VLANs to span multiple switches, a trunk connection must be created. This trunk connection transports data from multiple VLANs. Trunk connections allow VLANs to be used throughout the switching fabric of large networks.

Any FastEthernet or asynchronous transfer mode (ATM) port on a Catalyst switch can be designated as a trunk port. This port typically connects to another switch via a cross-over 100BaseT cable in the case of a Fast Ethernet trunk.

For the trunked port to transport multiple VLANs, it must understand frame tags.

## ISL

ISL is a technology developed by Cisco that allows a single Ethernet interface to participate in multiple VLANs. When a trunk connection is made on a Catalyst switch's Ethernet port, it utilizes ISL. ISL is also available on Ethernet cards that can be used in servers or routers.

A device utilizing an ISL Ethernet card will appear to have many physical cards, each connected to a different segment. ISL allows this single Ethernet card to have many logical (virtual) addresses. The user must configure each logical interface with an address that reflects the VLAN to which it belongs.

ISL works by allowing the frame-tagging information to be passed along to the Ethernet card. The Ethernet card then reads the frame tag, which identifies the VLAN to which the frame belongs. Conversely, the ISL Ethernet card creates the frame tags when transmitting frames.

*Note: ISL is a technology proprietary to Cisco and, therefore, is not supported on equipment made by other vendors. However, in mid-1998, the Institute of Electrical and Electronics Engineers (IEEE) standardized a frame-tagging process similar to*

**Figure 7.3**    ISL and frame tagging.

*Cisco's ISL. The new standard is a protocol called 802.1Q. With 802.1Q, switches from multiple vendors can co-exist in the same switching fabric.*

# VTP

VTP is a protocol used between switches to simplify the management of VLANS. Configuration changes that are made to a VTP server are propagated across trunks to all connected switches.

All switches that are to be managed in this way must be members of the same *management domain.* A VTP management domain is the entire group of switches that share configuration information.

For example, when you add a new VLAN to a member switch, the VLAN is available in all of the network switches automatically. VTP allows switched net-works to scale to larger environments; otherwise, VLAN configuration would have to be maintained manually on individual switches.

By default, Catalyst switches are set to a no-management-domain state. The switches remain in a no-management state until a user configures the management domain or they receive an advertisement for a domain over a trunk link. The default VTP configuration parameters are shown in Table 7.1

## VTP Modes

When it has a management domain, a switch operates in one of three VTP modes: server, client, or transparent. The default mode is server.

In VTP server mode, a switch can create, modify, or delete VLAN and other configuration parameters for the entire VTP domain. VTP messages are sent

| Table 7.1    Default VTP configuration. | |
|---|---|
| Option | Default Value |
| VTP Domain Name | None |
| VTP Mode | Server |
| VTP Password | None |
| VTP Pruning | Disabled |
| VTP Trap | Enabled |

over all trunk links, and configuration changes are propagated to all switches in the management domain.

In VTP client mode, the switch receives VTP messages and applies configuration changes made from any VTP server. However, a client cannot create, change, or delete VLAN information.

In VTP transparent mode, the switch forwards all VTP messages to other switches in the domain, but does not use the configuration from VTP advertisements. A VTP transparent switch can create, modify, or delete VLANs, but the changes apply only locally and are not transmitted to other switches.

### VTP Pruning

VTP can detect if a trunk connection is carrying unnecessary traffic. By default, all trunk connections carry traffic from all VLANs in the management domain. In many cases, however, a switch does not need a local port configured for each VLAN. In this event, it is not necessary to flood traffic from VLANs other than the ones supported by that switch. VTP pruning enables the switching fabric to prevent flooding traffic on trunk ports that do not need it. This is illustrated in Figure 7.4.

# Configuring VLANs

In the rest of this chapter, we will look at the Cisco commands used to configure, monitor, and maintain VLANs and trunk connections.

Before you begin creating VLANs, you must determine whether the switch will participate in a VTP domain that will synchronize VLAN configuration with the rest of the network. Also, if you want to use VLANs across multiple switches, a trunk connection must be made to interconnect the switches.

The steps required to configure VLANs are as follows:

1. Enable VTP (optional).

2. Enable trunking (optional).

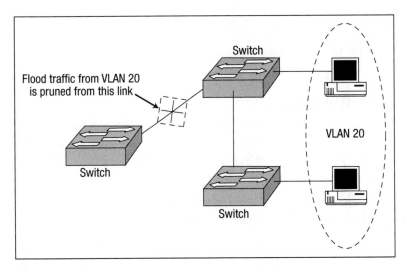

**Figure 7.4** VTP pruning.

3. Create VLANs.

4. Assign VLANs to ports.

# Enabling VTP

When adding a new switch to an existing domain, it is good practice to add it in VTP client mode initially. This way, you can prevent the switch from propagating incorrect VLAN information to other switches. In the following example, however, we are setting up a new VTP domain and will place the switch into server mode. The commands to do so are as follows:

```
1900#conf terminal
Enter configuration commands, one per line. End with CNTL/Z
1900(config)#vtp server
1900(config)#vtp domain ccnalab
```

To verify VTP information, use the **show vtp** command from EXEC privileged mode:

```
hostname# show vtp

VTP version: 1
    Configuration revision: 3
    Maximum VLANs supported locally: 1005
    Number of existing VLANs: 5
    VTP domain name     : ccnalab
    VTP password        : vtp_server
    VTP operating mode  : Server
```

```
VTP pruning mode     : Enabled
VTP traps generation : Enabled
Configuration last modified by: 0.0.0.0 at 00-00-0000 00:00:00
```

## Enabling Trunking

The next step is to create a trunk connection to other switches that will be sharing VLAN information. In the following example, assume that we are connecting two Catalyst 1900 switches via their 100BaseT ports using a crossover category 5 Ethernet cable. We are using the FastEthernet ports known in the IOS as f0/26.

The **trunk** command has five options: on, off, desirable, auto, and negotiate. Table 7.2 shows the function of each trunk mode.

To enable trunking on a port, enter interface configuration mode for the desired port first, and then use the **trunk** command with the appropriate option, as below:

```
1900#conf terminal
Enter configuration commands, one per line. End with CNTL/Z
1900(config)#interface f0/26
1900(config-if)#trunk on
```

The same configuration must be executed for the appropriate port on the connected device. Because we set the trunk to on mode in the previous example, the corresponding port must be set to on, auto, or desirable for the trunk connection to be established.

To verify the trunk operation, use the **show trunk** command. Its syntax is as follows:

```
show trunk [a | b]
```

A Catalyst 1900 switch has two FastEthernet ports that can act as trunk connections. They are known as interfaces f0/26 and f0/27. When using the **show trunk** command, option A refers to the first trunk port (in this case, f0/26). Option B is for port f0/27. So, to see the trunking status for FastEthernet port A (f0/26), use the following command:

```
1900#show trunk a
DISL state: On, Trunking: On, Encapsulation type: ISL
```

## Creating VLANs

To create a new VLAN, use the **vlan** command from global configuration mode. This command has several options that can be specified, but for our purposes, all we need to have is a four-digit number to identify the VLAN and a name for it.

| Table 7.2 | Trunk command options. |
|-----------|------------------------|
| **Option** | **Function** |
| On | Port goes into permanent ISL trunk mode. Negotiates with the connected device to convert the link to a trunk. |
| Off | Disables trunking on this port. Negotiates with the connected device to convert the link to non-trunk. |
| Desirable | Port will enter trunk mode if the connected device is set to on, desirable, or auto; otherwise, port is a non-trunk. |
| Auto | Port will enter trunk mode if the connected device is set to on or desirable; otherwise, port is a non-trunk. |
| Negotiate | Port goes into permanent ISL trunk mode, but no negotiation takes place with the connected device. |

Each VLAN must have a unique numeric ID, which can be any number from 1 to 1005.

We will create a VLAN called Engineering and make it VLAN 2:

```
hostname(config)# vlan 2 name Engineering
```

To verify the configuration of the VLAN, use the **show vlan** *vlan#* command:

```
1900#show vlan 2

VLAN Name        Status     Ports
---------        ------     -----
2 Engineering    Enabled
-------------    -------


VLAN Type     SAID    MTU   Parent RingNo BridgeNo Stp  Trans1 Trans2
---------     ----    ---   ------ ------ -------- ---  ------ ------
2 Ethernet    100009  1500  0      1      1        Unkn 0      0
```

## Assigning VLAN to Ports

Now that the VLAN has been created, you can statically assign which ports will be members of the VLAN. A port can belong to only one VLAN at a time. By default, all ports are members of VLAN 1.

To assign a VLAN to a port, enter interface configuration mode for the appropriate port, then use the **vlan-membership** command:

```
1900#conf terminal
Enter configuration commands, one per line. End with CNTL/Z
```

```
1900(config)#interface ethernet 0/8
1900(config-if)#vlan-membership static 2
```

To verify VLAN membership and to see which ports belong to what VLAN, use the **show vlan-membership** command:

```
hostname# show vlan-membership
Port  VLAN Membership Type   Port VLAN Membership Type
----  ---- ----------------   ---- ---- ----------------
 1     1   Static             14    2   Static
 2     1   Static             15    2   Static
 3     1   Static             16    2   Static
 4     1   Static             17    2   Static
 5     1   Static             18    2   Static
 6     1   Static             19    2   Static
 7     1   Dynamic            20    2   Static
 8     1   Dynamic            21    2   Static
 9     1   Dynamic            22    2   Static
10     1   Dynamic            23    2   Static
11     1   Dynamic            24    2   Static
12     1   Dynamic            AUI   2   Static
13     1   Dynamic
 A     1   Static
 B     2   Static
```

# Practice Questions

## Question 1

Which of the following are advantages of VLANs? [Choose the two best answers]

❑ a.  Reduces switching overhead

❑ b.  Increases switching throughput

❑ c.  Simplifies adding, moving, and changing users

❑ d.  Allows users to be grouped by functional area, not physical location

Answers c and d are correct. VLANs increase the flexibility of assigning users to LANs. This increased simplicity allows users to be grouped by functional area rather than physical location, because VLANs can span multiple switches. Answer a is incorrect because VLANs do not reduce the amount of overhead required to switch a frame. Answer b is incorrect because VLANs do not provide any increased switching throughput.

## Question 2

What must be done to allow a VLAN to span two or more switches?

◯ a.  Set up a VTP domain

◯ b.  Set up a trunk connection

◯ c.  Configure the duplex setting on the ports

◯ d.  Configure port security on the switch

Answer b is correct. A trunk connection must be established in order for a VLAN to span multiple switches. Trunk ports recognize frame tags and are, therefore, able to carry information on multiple VLANs. Answer a is incorrect because a VTP domain is not necessary for switches to share VLAN information. Answer c is incorrect because the duplex setting does not have to be configured manually to connect two switches. Answer d is incorrect because port security is not necessary for a VLAN to span switches.

## Question 3

What are the advantages of using VTP in a switching environment? [Choose the two best answers]

❑ a.  Enables VLANs to span multiple switches

❑ b.  Simplifies the management of VLANs

❑ c.  Simplifies the scalability of the switched network

❑ d.  Allows switches to read frame tags

Answers b and c are correct. VTP simplifies the management of VLANs because configuration information is propagated automatically throughout the switching fabric when changes are made. Without VTP, each switch would have to be configured manually; therefore, VTP makes it easier to scale to a larger switched environment. Answer a is incorrect because VTP is not necessary for VLANs to span multiple switches. Answer d is incorrect because the VTP does not allow the switch to read frame tags.

## Question 4

What is ISL used for?

○ a.  To allow an Ethernet interface to understand frame tags

○ b.  To make two Ethernet interfaces appear as one

○ c.  To connect an Ethernet switch with a high-speed core switch such as ATM

○ d.  To allow simultaneous routing and switching

The correct answer is a. ISL allows an Ethernet interface to understand frame tags, which identify the VLAN to which a packet belongs. For this reason, an ISL interface can participate in multiple VLANs, which is necessary for a trunk connection. Answer b is incorrect because ISL can actually have the opposite effect of this—a single Ethernet interface may appear to be several by having multiple layer 3 addresses. Answers c and d are incorrect because these are not functions of ISL.

## Question 5

> What is the purpose of VTP pruning?
>
> ○ a.  To detect loops in the switching fabric
>
> ○ b.  To disable a trunk connection that creates a bridging loop
>
> ○ c.  To simplify the management of VLANs
>
> ○ d.  To prevent flooding unnecessary traffic across trunk connections

The correct answer is d. VTP pruning is used to prevent flooding of unnecessary traffic across trunk connections. Answer a is incorrect because this is a function of the spanning tree protocol. Answer b is incorrect because this is not the purpose of VTP pruning. Answer c is incorrect because this is the purpose of the VTP, not VTP pruning.

## Question 6

> Which of the following is a valid command to create a VLAN on a Catalyst 1900 switch and name it Accounting?
>
> ○ a.  **switch(config)#create vlan 10 name Accounting**
>
> ○ b.  **switch#create vlan 10 name Accounting**
>
> ○ c.  **switch(config)#vlan 10 name Accounting**
>
> ○ d.  **switch#vlan 10 name Accounting**

The correct answer is c. The correct syntax to create a VLAN in command mode is **vlan** *{number}* **name** *{name}* from global configuration mode. Answer d has the correct syntax for the command, however, the switch is not in configuration mode; therefore, answer d is incorrect. Answers a and b are incorrect because the word 'create' is not a part of this command.

## Question 7

Which of the following commands will assign Ethernet port 9 on a Catalyst 1900 to VLAN 20?

- ○ a. **interface Ethernet 0/9** and **vlan-membership static 20**
- ○ b. **vlan-membership interface Ethernet 0/9 static 20**
- ○ c. **interface Ethernet 0/9** and **vlan 20**
- ○ d. **vlan 20 interface Ethernet 0/9**

The correct answer is a. To assign an interface to a VLAN, you must first enter port configuration mode by using the **interface Ethernet 0/9** command from global configuration mode. Then, use the **vlan-membership** command to assign a VLAN to the port. Answers b, c, and d are all invalid syntax.

# Need to Know More?

 McNutt, Shawn, Mark Poplar, Jason Waters, and David Stabenaw: *CCNA Routing and Switching Exam Prep.* The Coriolis Group, Scottsdale, AZ, 2000. ISBN 1-57610-440-0. This book is a great complement to the CCNA Cram book. The switching chapters expand on the information presented here.

 Chappell, Laura: *Introduction to Cisco Router Configuration.* Cisco Systems Inc., Macmillan Publishing Company, Indianapolis, IN, 1998. ISBN 0-7645-3186-7. This book provides a great overview of the concepts tested on the CCNA exam.

 Ford, Merilee, H. Kim Lew, Steve Spanier, and Kevin Downes: *Internetworking Technologies Handbook 2nd Edition.* Macmillan Publishing Company, Indianapolis, IN, 1998. ISBN 1-56205-102-3. This book is full of resourceful information on Internetworking Technologies.

 Lammle, Todd, Donald Porter, and James Chellis: *CCNA Cisco Certified Network Associate.* Sybex Network Press, Alameda, CA, 1999. ISBN 0-7821-2381-3. This book is a great supplement for learning the technologies tested on the CCNA exam.

 Syngress Media, with Richard D. Hornbaker, CCIE: *Cisco Certified Network Associate Study Guide.* Osborne/McGraw-Hill, Berkeley, CA, 1998. ISBN 0-07882-487-7. Another great book for review before taking the CCNA exam.

 Visit **www.cisco.com/univercd/cc/td/doc/product/software/ ios113ed/113ed_cr/switch_c/xcisl.htm** for a great article titled *Configuring Routing between VLANs with ISL Encapsulation.*

# Router Configuration and Software Management

· · · · · · · · · · · · · · · · · · · · · · · · · · · · · · · · · · · · · · · · · · · · ·

### Terms you'll need to understand:

✓ Running configuration file

✓ Startup configuration file

✓ Trivial File Transfer Protocol (TFTP)

✓ **enable secret** password command

✓ **service password-encryption** command

✓ Boot field

✓ Configuration register

### Techniques you'll need to master:

✓ Managing configuration files from the EXEC privileged mode

✓ Copying and moving configuration files

✓ Setting up the router passwords, identification, and banner

✓ Identifying the main Cisco Internetwork Operating System (IOS) commands for router startup

✓ Performing the initial configuration using the **setup** command

✓ Loading software from various sources on Cisco routers

✓ Backing up and upgrading software on Cisco routers

✓ Configuring a router via the initial setup sequence

This chapter focuses on a number of very important and often applied skills in networking. The ability to manage configuration files, to load and copy Cisco software, and to understand the impact of these types of commands is vital for success. More importantly, you need to master these crucial skills to avoid causing a disaster in your company's network. Understanding the many password types and security levels used on Cisco routers is important. Finally, this chapter describes and illustrates the steps required to set up a router via the initial setup sequence.

# Router Elements

This section describes the various interface modes in which you may work on a router. It also provides an overview of the different components within a router and explains how to examine the status of each of those components.

## Router Modes

Regardless of how you access a router (through the console port, a modem connection, or a router interface), you can place it in one of several modes. Other router modes exist beyond the user and privileged modes discussed previously. Each router mode enables specific functions to be performed. The different types of router modes include user, privileged, setup, RXBOOT, global configuration, and other configuration modes, as shown in Table 8.1.

### User Mode

As stated earlier, *user mode* provides a display-only environment. You can view limited information about the router, but cannot change the configuration.

### Privileged Mode

*Privileged mode* enables you to perform an extensive review of the router. This mode supports testing commands, debugging commands, and commands to manage the router configuration files.

### Setup Mode

*Setup mode* is triggered on router startup when no configuration file resides in non-volatile random access memory (NVRAM). This mode executes an interactive prompted dialog to assist in creating an initial router configuration.

### RXBOOT Mode

A router's maintenance mode is called *RXBOOT mode* or *ROM monitor mode*. This mode facilitates recovery functions when the router password is lost or the IOS file stored in Flash memory has been erased or is corrupt. Pressing the Break key (from a console terminal directly connected to the router) within the first 60 seconds of startup also allows you to place the router in this mode.

| Table 8.1 | Router modes. | | |
|---|---|---|---|
| **Mode** | **Function** | **How Accessed** | **Prompt** |
| User | Limited display | Log in to the router | Router> |
| Privileged | Display, testing, debugging, configuration file manipulation | From user mode, enter the **enable** command | Router# |
| Setup | Create initial router configuration | During router startup, if the configuration file is missing from NVRAM (console access only) | Interactive dialog prompts |
| RXBOOT | Perform router recovery | Press the Break key during router startup (console access only) | > |
| Global | Perform simple configuration | From EXEC privileged mode, enter the **configure** command | Router (config)# |
| Others | Perform complex and multiline configuration | From within global configuration mode, the command entered varies | Router (config-<mode>)# |

## Global Configuration Mode

You perform simple configuration tasks in *global configuration mode*. For example, router names, router passwords, and router banners are configured in this mode.

## Other Configuration Modes

You perform complex router configuration tasks in several other configuration modes. You enter interface, subinterface, controller, and routing protocol configurations from within these other modes.

# Router Components

Every router contains several components that compose its configuration. These components are random access memory (RAM), NVRAM, Flash memory, ROM, and interfaces.

## RAM

*RAM* serves as a working storage area for the router. RAM contains data such as routing tables, various types of cache and buffers, as well as input and output queues. RAM also provides storage for temporary memory for the router's active IOS and configuration file (the *running configuration file*). However, the entire content of RAM is lost if the router is powered down or restarted.

## NVRAM

Conversely, *NVRAM* retains its content when the router is powered down or restarted. NVRAM stores permanent information, such as the router's backup configuration file. The startup configuration file is retrieved from NVRAM during startup and loaded into RAM.

## Flash

*Flash memory* stores the Cisco IOS image and associated microcode. Flash memory is erasable, electronically reprogrammable *ROM* that retains its content when the router is powered down or restarted. Several copies or versions of an IOS image can be contained in Flash memory. It is Flash memory that allows software to be upgraded without adding, removing, or replacing chips on the processor.

## ROM

Like Flash memory, ROM contains a version of IOS—usually an older version with minimal functionality. It also stores the bootstrap program and power-on diagnostic programs. However, software upgrades can be performed only by replacing chips on the central processing unit (CPU).

## Interfaces

*Interfaces* provide the network connections where packets move in and out of the router. Depending on the model of router, interfaces exist either on the motherboard or on separate, modular interface cards. Figure 8.1 shows the various router components and the router elements they contain.

# Router Status

Routine administration of a router involves examining the status of the router. The **show** command enables you to view the status of the router's components. You can execute **show** from either user or privileged mode. However, the

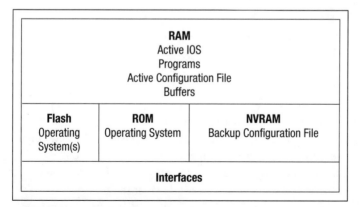

**Figure 8.1**   The router components.

**Figure 8.2** The **show** command keywords.

keywords used with the **show** command are different in user and privileged mode. Figure 8.2 illustrates some of the more common **show** command keywords and the router components with which they are associated.

The **show version** command displays the hardware configuration, software version, boot images, and names and sources of configuration files, as shown below:

```
r2#show version
Cisco Internetwork Operating System Software
IOS (tm) 2500 Software (C2500-IS-L), Version 11.3(7)T,
RELEASE SOFTWARE (fc1)
Copyright (c) 1986-1998 by cisco Systems, Inc.
Compiled Tue 01-Dec-98 12:21 by ccai
Image text-base: 0x0303A9D8, data-base: 0x00001000

ROM: System Bootstrap, Version 11.0(10c)XB1, PLATFORM SPECIFIC
RELEASE SOFTWARE
(fc1)
BOOTFLASH: 3000 Bootstrap Software (IGS-BOOT-R),
Version 11.0(10c)XB1, PLATFORM
SPECIFIC RELEASE SOFTWARE (fc1)

r2 uptime is 2 days, 7 hours, 17 minutes
System restarted by reload
System image file is "flash:c2500-is-l_113-7_T",
```

```
booted via flash

cisco 2500 (68030) processor (revision M) with
6144K/2048K bytes of memory.
Processor board ID 06972781, with hardware revision 00000000
Bridging software.
X.25 software, Version 3.0.0.
1 Ethernet/IEEE 802.3 interface(s)
1 Token Ring/IEEE 802.5 interface(s)
2 Serial network interface(s)
32K bytes of non-volatile configuration memory.
8192K bytes of processor board System flash (Read ONLY)

Configuration register is 0x2102

r2#
```

The **show memory** command displays statistics about the router's memory, as shown below:

```
r2#show memory
              Head Total(b) Used(b)  Free(b) Lowest(b) Largest(b)
Processor  87510 5733104  809476 4923628  4872780   4890708
     I/O 600000 2097152  488444 1608708  1476032   1532904


     Processor memory

Address Bytes Prev. Next Ref PrevF NextF Alloc PC What
87510  1068  0     87968 1         31A0B86 List Elements
87968  2868  87510 884C8 1         31A0B86 List Headers
884C8  3884  87968 89420 1         314B0E0 TTY data
89420  2000  884C8 89C1C 1         314D52E TTY Input Buf
89C1C   512  89420 89E48 1         314D55E TTY Output Buf
89E48  3000  89C1C 8AA2C 1         31B31BA Interrupt Stack
8AA2C    44  89E48 8AA84 1         36C16D8 *Init*
8AA84  1068  8AA2C 8AEDC 1         31A0B86 messages
8AEDC    88  8AA84 8AF60 1         31AFBAC Watched Boolean
8AF60    88  8AEDC 8AFE4 1         31AFBAC Watched Boolean
8AFE4    88  8AF60 8B068 1         31AFBAC Watched Boolean
8B068    88  8AFE4 8B0EC 1         31AFBAC Watched Boolean
8B0EC  1032  8B068 8B520 1         31B796A Process Array
8B520  1000  8B0EC 8B934 1         31B7D1C Process Stack
8B934   480  8B520 8BB40 1         31B7D2E Process
8BB40   128  8B934 8BBEC 1         31AFDBC Process Events
8BBEC    44  8BB40 8BC44 1         36C16D8 *Init*
8BC44  1068  8BBEC 8C09C 1         31A0B86 List Elements
 —More—
```

The **show protocols** command displays the network layer protocols and addresses that are configured on the router, as shown below:

```
r2#show protocols
Global values:
 Internet Protocol routing is enabled
Ethernet0 is up, line protocol is up
 Internet address is 172.16.57.1/24
Serial0 is administratively down, line protocol is down
Serial1 is administratively down, line protocol is down
TokenRing0 is administratively down, line protocol is down
r2#
```

The **show running-config** command displays the active configuration file. Use the **write terminal** command if the router's IOS version is 10.3 or earlier. The **write terminal** command is also supported in later versions of the IOS, as shown below:

```
r2#show running-config
Building configuration...
Current configuration:
!
version 11.3
service timestamps debug uptime
service timestamps log uptime
no service password-encryption
!
hostname r2
!
interface Ethernet0
 description Engineering LAN Segment
 ip address 172.16.57.1 255.255.255.0
!
interface Serial0
 no ip address
 no ip mroute-cache
 shutdown
 no fair-queue
!
interface Serial1
 no ip address
 shutdown
!
interface TokenRing0
 no ip address
 shutdown
!
```

```
ip classless
!
!
line con 0
line aux 0
line vty 0 4
 login
!
end

r2#
```

The **show startup-config** command displays the backup configuration file. Use the **show configuration** command if the router's IOS version is 10.3 or earlier. The **show configuration** command is also supported in later versions of the IOS, as shown below:

```
r2#show startup-config
Using 424 out of 32762 bytes
!
version 11.3
service timestamps debug uptime
service timestamps log uptime
no service password-encryption
!
hostname r2
!
interface Ethernet0
 description Engineering LAN Segment
 ip address 172.16.57.1 255.255.255.0
!
interface Serial0
 no ip address
 no ip mroute-cache
 shutdown
 no fair-queue
!
interface Serial1
 no ip address
 shutdown
!
interface TokenRing0
 no ip address
 shutdown
!
ip classless
!
```

```
!
line con 0
line aux 0
line vty 0 4
 login
!
end

r2#
```

The **show interfaces** command displays statistics for all of the interfaces on the router or a specific interface, as shown below:

```
r2#show interface ethernet 0
Ethernet0 is up, line protocol is up
 Hardware is Lance, address is 00e0.1e60.9d9f (bia 00e0.1e60.9d9f)
 Description: Engineering LAN Segment
 Internet address is 172.16.57.1/24
 MTU 1500 bytes, BW 10000 Kbit, DLY 1000 usec,
    reliability 255/255, txload 1/255, rxload 1/255
 Encapsulation ARPA, loopback not set, keepalive set (10 sec)
 ARP type: ARPA, ARP Timeout 04:00:00
 Last input 00:00:01, output 00:00:03, output hang never
 Last clearing of "show interface" counters never
 Queueing strategy: fifo
 Output queue 0/40, 0 drops; input queue 0/75, 0 drops
 5 minute input rate 0 bits/sec, 0 packets/sec
 5 minute output rate 0 bits/sec, 0 packets/sec
    42 packets input, 9697 bytes, 0 no buffer
    Received 42 broadcasts, 0 runts, 0 giants, 0 throttles
    0 input errors, 0 CRC, 0 frame, 0 overrun, 0 ignored, 0 abort
    0 input packets with dribble condition detected
    80 packets output, 16167 bytes, 0 underruns
    0 output errors, 0 collisions, 2 interface resets
    0 babbles, 0 late collision, 0 deferred
    0 lost carrier, 0 no carrier
    0 output buffer failures, 0 output buffers swapped out
r2#
```

The **show flash** command displays information about the Flash memory device, as shown below:

```
r2#show flash

System flash directory:
File Length  Name/status
 1  7181580 c2500-is-l_113-7_T
```

```
[7181644 bytes used, 1206964 available, 8388608 total]
8192K bytes of processor board System flash (Read ONLY)

r2#
```

# Managing Configuration Files

The process of managing configuration files is straightforward; however, it has been made difficult by the many different versions of Cisco software and the wide variety of architectures used in Cisco hardware. This section will bring light to these subjects; present an overview of the different types of configuration files and the commands used to move, display, and copy these files; and highlight some of the areas that can cause confusion when managing configuration files.

 The material presented in this chapter assumes the implementation of Cisco IOS release 11.0 or later. Don't worry, the CCNA exam uses this assumption as well.

## Types of Configuration Files

Cisco IOS software uses and requires a configuration file to determine how a router is to function. Typically, a network administrator enters the commands necessary for his or her environment into a router configuration file. Only two types of configuration files exist for the context of the CCNA exam:

➤ The running configuration file exists in RAM and contains the commands that Cisco IOS uses to drive the actions of the router.

*Note: RAM is erased during power cycles or software reloads. Therefore, the running configuration file is erased as well.*

➤ The startup configuration file exists in NVRAM and is the backup for the running configuration file.

 Startup configuration files reside in NVRAM, and running configuration files exist in RAM.

The router will always use the running configuration file to execute. However, any time a router is restarted (cycling power or reloading the software), the running configuration file is erased and the startup configuration file is the only remaining configuration file. Therefore, during the boot sequence of a router, the router copies the startup configuration file to the running configuration file (NVRAM to RAM). Thus, it is paramount that any time a change is made to a running configuration the change is also copied to the startup configuration. The many ways of preventing the loss of changes made are discussed in this chapter.

## Displaying the Running and Startup Configuration

The purpose of displaying a running or startup configuration file is to determine the configuration commands being executed on a router. Use the **show running-config** or **show startup-config** command to show the running configuration and startup configuration files, respectively. Displaying the running configuration file shows the commands being executed at the time that the **show** command is executed, as shown below:

```
Router#show running-config
Building configuration...
Current configuration:
Last configuration change at 03:25:38 UTC Sat Jan 1 2000
version 11.2
no service password-encryption
no service udp-small-servers
no service tcp-small-servers
hostname Router
enable secret 5 $1$2uUP$2I.LOxxD3wnX.7WDMHzb60
enable password cisco
no ip domain-lookup

interface Serial0
  ip address 138.144.2.2 255.255.255.0
  encapsulation frame-relay
  bandwidth 2000
  frame-relay lmi-type cisco

interface Serial1
  no ip address
  shutdown
!
interface TokenRing0
  ip address 138.144.3.1 255.255.255.0
  ring-speed 16
!
interface TokenRing1
  ip address 138.144.4.1 255.255.255.0
  ring-speed 16
```

```
!
router igrp 1
 network 138.144.0.0
 !
no ip classless
 !
snmp-server community public RO
 !
line con 0
line aux 0
line vty 0 4
password cisco
login
 !
end
```

*Note: The Router# prompt indicates that the command is initiated from the EXEC privileged (enable) command line. It is important to know in what mode a command should be executed.*

## Configuring the Running and Startup Configuration Files

The running configuration file often requires changes while the router is functioning. Cisco IOS is designed to accept changes to a running or startup configuration file without restarting (reloading) or cycling the power of the router. The following commands are used to manipulate the configuration files:

➤ *Router# configure terminal*—Allows a user to add, change, or delete commands in the running configuration file while the router is executing.

➤ *Router# configure memory*—Allows a user to add, change, or delete commands in the startup configuration file.

Making changes to the running configuration file will immediately affect the behavior of a router.

## Backing Up and Restoring Configuration Files

Configuration files are copied and moved constantly in most networks. One common method of copying files is with the use of a *Trivial File Transfer Protocol* (*TFTP*) server. Most Unix machines have built-in TFTP support. There are also TFTP server programs available for Windows based PCs. Cisco makes a TFTP server program that is available on their Web site. Cisco routers use a TFTP server to load IOS and to copy software and configuration files. To copy a file using the TFTP, one device needs to be executing TFTP server software and the other device needs to be executing the client software. Cisco routers are equipped with both functions. Network administrators often need to back up a running or startup configuration file on a central server. The following command sequence accomplishes this goal:

```
Router# copy running-config TFTP
Remote host []? 172.15.12.2 (IP Address of TFTP Server)
Name of configuration file to write [router-confg]? <Return>
Write file Router-confg on host 172.15.12.2? [confirm] <Return>
Building configuration…
Writing Router-confg !!!!!!!!!!!!!!!!!![OK]
```

*Note: Pay attention to the order and syntax of commands during the test. The function of a command can completely change, depending on the syntax.*

The reverse process occurs when a configuration file is copied from a central server to an executing router. This process is most often used when a router has gone dead or someone has accidentally deleted the configuration file on the router. If the running configuration was backed up on a TFTP server, it is really simple to restore the configuration file. The first step for restoring the configuration file on a router is to determine Internet Protocol (IP) connectivity from the central server to the router. This might require the use of a ping test and/or the configuration of an IP address on the router. The following command sequence is used for restoring a running configuration file:

```
Router# copy TFTP running-config
Host or network configuration file [host]? <Return>
Address of remote host [255.255.255.255]? 172.15.12.2 (TFTP
Server)
Name of configuration file [Router-confg]?Router-confg (File name)
Configure using Router-confg from 172.15.12.2? [confirm] <Return>
Loading Router-confg from 172.15.12.2 (via serial 1): !!!!!
[OK - 875/32723]
Router#
```

Exercise caution when performing configuration file changes across networks, especially to remote sites. Visit Cisco's Web site and utilize the search engine to identify anything that you might need to be aware of while performing configuration file backups or restores in your network. Always be sure to find hardware-specific features before changing configuration files or Cisco IOS software.

Another method of backing up a running configuration is to save it to NVRAM. You should complete this process after every change to the running configuration file, unless a good reason exists to keep the startup configuration different. By copying the running configuration to NVRAM, you are ensuring that if the router is reloaded or the power is cycled, it will boot with the same configuration that you are currently executing. The following command sequence is required for this process:

```
Router#copy running-config startup-config
Building configuration...
[OK]
```

The startup configuration file can also be copied into RAM, thereby overwriting the running configuration file, by performing the following command:

```
Router# Copy startup-config running-config
```

*Note: It is necessary to know all of the backup and restore commands for the CCNA exam. Be sure to pay special attention to the syntax of these commands. It is easy to forget the sequence of words for the different commands.*

Finally, the startup configuration file can be completely erased. When this occurs, the router boots into setup mode the next time it is reloaded:

```
Router#erase startup-config
```

# Router Passwords

The router passwords on the Cisco router provide security against snooping users; Cisco IOS passwords were never intended to resist a determined, intelligent attack. Many programs exist (Cisco is aware of these programs) that can crack the MD5 encryption algorithm Cisco IOS employs. Cisco always recommends that some type of user authentication protocol be used to enhance the security of Cisco routers. RADIUS and TACACS are two of the more popular authentication methods that major corporations use today. Cisco routers utilize five different password types to provide security.

## enable password and enable secret Password Commands

The **enable password** and **enable secret** password commands are designed to provide an additional layer of security for passwords. Both commands allow you to establish an encrypted password that requires users to enter access enable mode.

The **enable secret** command was developed to use an improved encryption algorithm. The **enable secret** password overrides the **enable password** when it is present. An **enable secret** password can be entered by performing the following command:

```
Router(config)#enable secret phoenix
Router#
```

The **enable password** and **enable secret** commands also provide for security levels. These options are not part of the objectives set by the CCNA exam and are not, therefore, presented in this book.

## console and auxiliary Password Commands

The **console** and **auxiliary** password commands restrict user mode access via the console or auxiliary ports on the router:

```
Router(config)#line aux 0
Router(config-line)#login
Router(config-line)#password phoenix
```

The **login** command designates that you want a user to have to enter a password every time he or she connects to the router via the auxiliary port. The **login** command can be added to the console port to require a password login as well. The console password is set with the same command format as the "aux" password, except that the keyword "aux" is changed to "con."

## virtual terminal Password Command

The **virtual terminal** or **vty** password restricts user mode accessed via a Telnet session. The **virtual terminal** password must be set or a user will not be able to log into the router with a Telnet session. Multiple virtual terminal sessions can be engaged at one time. A separate password can be additionally specified for each virtual terminal session:

```
Router(config-line)#line vty 0 4
Router(config-line)#login
Router(config-line)#password phoenix
```

The Cisco IOS allows 5 simultaneous telnet connections. Notice that the syntax is '*line*' then '*line type*', and '*line number*'. Cisco interface numbers always start with '0'. For this example, we are specifying all 5 ports, numbers 0 through 4 to designate five virtual terminals that all use the password "phoenix."

Of the five different types of passwords, only the **enable secret** password is encrypted by default. For the remaining passwords, you must use the **service password-encryption** command. This command encrypts the enable, console, auxiliary, and virtual terminal passwords:

```
Router(config)#service password-encryption
```

Passwords that have already been set in the configuration file will not become encrypted; only passwords that are entered after the **service password-encryption** command has been entered will be encrypted. The **service password-encryption** command does not provide a high level of network security, but helps to keep unauthorized individuals from viewing a password in a configuration file.

# Router Identification and Banner

A router's name is referred to as the *hostname*. The default hostname for all Cisco routers is "Router." You can change the hostname of a router in global configuration mode by entering the **hostname** command. The hostname is changed with the following commands:

```
Router(config)#hostname Phoenix
Phoenix(config)#
```

Notice that the hostname changed from "Router" to "Phoenix" immediately after executing the command.

The **banner motd** command allows you to display a message-of-the-day (MOTD) banner every time you log into the router. Even though the banner message was designed to convey day-to-day messages, it is typically used for displaying security messages for legal reasons:

```
Phoenix(config)#banner motd * Authorized Access Only,
 All Violations Will Be Prosecuted *
Phoenix(config)#
```

*Note: The asterisk (*) before the word "Authorized" and after the word "Only" represents the start and finish of the text to be displayed as the banner.*

In this scenario, the next time you Telnet into the router, the MOTD banner will display the following message:

```
Authorized Access Only, All Violations Will Be Prosecuted.
User Access Verification
Password:
```

A description can be added to every interface using the **description** command. Typically, an interface description, which is limited to 80 characters, is used to describe the function of the interface:

```
Phoenix(config)#interface s0
Phoenix(config-line)#description 56K between Phoenix and San Diego
Phoenix(config-line)#
```

The next time someone views the running configuration file, they will see the following description:

```
interface Serial0
description 56K connection between Phoenix and San Diego
ip address 138.144.2.2 255.255.255.0
encapsulation frame-relay
bandwidth 2000
frame-relay lmi-type cisco
```

# Initial Configuration of a Cisco Router

The first time a Cisco router is powered on, the startup configuration file is blank, so it will boot into the initial configuration dialog. This dialog is designed to walk a novice through the basic steps and requirements of configuring a Cisco router. The *initial configuration dialog* is a menu-driven command-and-response query designed to configure a router with a bare-bones configuration. The dialog will start anytime a configuration file is not found in NVRAM during the boot sequence, as described previously. The two instances when a configuration file will not exist in NVRAM are the first time the router is powered on or if the router was reloaded subsequent to erasing the startup configuration file.

```
Would you like to enter the initial configuration
dialog? [yes] <Return>
First, would you like to see the current interface
summary? [yes] <Return>
Any interface listed with OK? Value "NO" does not have a
valid configuration
Interface    IP-Address    OK?    Method    Status    Protocol
Serial 0     unassigned    NO     not set   up        down
Serial 1     unassigned    NO     not set   up        down
Ethernet 1   unassigned    NO     not set   up        down
Ethernet 2   unassigned    NO     not set   up        down
Configuring global parameters:
```

Notice that in the configuration dialog, many of the questions have answers in brackets following the question. This is the default value or answer for the question. To accept the default, simply press Enter and move on to the next question. If you don't want to use the default value, simply enter your own answer.

The previous interface summary indicates that the router has two serial and two Ethernet interfaces. In this example, we will configure both serial interfaces and neither of the Ethernet interfaces. None of the four interfaces have been assigned IP addresses, which is indicated by the "unassigned" listed under the IP-Address column. The status of the interface is set to "up" because this is the default value. We must manually shut down the interface to turn it off. However, the protocol is listed as "down" because no active connections are on the interface. After the interface summary is displayed, the next step in the initial configuration dialog is to configure the hostname, passwords, routing protocols, and IP addressing. An example is shown below:

```
Enter host name [Router] Phoenix
The enable secret is a one-way cryptographic secret used instead
 of the enable password when it exists.
Enter enable secret: Phoenix
The enable password is used when no enable secret exists and when
Using older software and some boot images.
Enter enable password: Cisco
Enter the virtual terminal password: Telnet
Configure SNMP Network Management? [yes]: no
Configure IP? [yes]<Return>
        Configure IGRP Routing? [yes]: no
        Configure RIP Routing? [yes]: no
Configure Interfaces:
        Configuring interface Ethernet 0:
        Is this interface in use? [yes] no
        Configuring interface Ethernet 1:
        Is this interface in use? [yes] no
        Configuring interface Serial 0:
        Is this interface in use? [yes] <Return>
        Configure IP on this interface? [yes] <Return>
        Configure IP unnumbered on this interface? [no] : <Return>
        IP Address for this interface: 172.29.3.4
        Number of bits in subnet field [8]: <Return>
        Class B network is 172.29.0.0, 8 subnet bits; mask is
255.255.255.0
        Configuring interface Serial 1:
        Is this interface in use? [yes] <Return>
```

```
Configure IP on this interface? [yes] <Return>
Configure IP unnumbered on interface? [no] : <Return>
IP Address for this interface: 172.29.4.3
Number of bits in subnet field [8]: <Return>
    Class B network is 172.29.0.0, 8 subnet bits; mask is
255.255.255.0
```

Now we have configured the two serial interfaces, set up our passwords, and chosen any routing protocols that we wanted to utilize. For the sake of simplicity, however, we did not turn on either the Routing Information Protocol (RIP) or the Interior Gateway Routing Protocol (IGRP) in this example. The router will then show us the configuration that we created:

```
The following configuration command script was created:
Hostname Phoenix
Enable secret 5 09371034073401823
Enable password Cisco
Line vty 0 4
Password Telnet
No snmp-server
!
ip routing
!
interface Ethernet 0
Shutdown
No ip address
Interface Ethernet 1
Shutdown
No ip address
Interface Serial 0
Ip address 172.29.3.4 255.255.255.0
Interface Serial 1
Ip address 172.29.4.3 255.255.255.0
!
end
Use this configuration? [yes/no]: yes
```

We have now completed the initial configuration dialog and successfully configured the Phoenix router with IP addressing.

# Upgrading Cisco IOS Software

Cisco IOS is constantly being revised to add new features or to fix bugs in previous versions. The process of upgrading software on a Cisco router can be broken down into three main steps:

1. Back up the current Cisco IOS.

2. Copy the new Cisco IOS to the router.

3. Reload the Cisco router and verify the new IOS.

## Back Up Current IOS

The first part of backing up the current IOS involves determining what version of IOS is running on the router and the file name of the software image. It is also necessary to note the size available in Flash memory. The new version of IOS must not be larger than the total Flash memory on the router. The **show version** command displays this information, as shown below:

```
Phoenix#sh vers
Cisco Internetwork Operating System Software
IOS (tm) 2500 Software (C2500-J-L), Version 11.2(13),
RELEASE SOFTWARE (fc1)
Copyright (c) 1986-1998 by cisco Systems, Inc.
Compiled Tue 31-Mar-98 12:27 by tlane
Image text-base: 0x0303F1E4, data-base: 0x00001000
ROM: System Bootstrap, Version 11.0(10c)XB1,
PLATFORM SPECIFIC RELEASE SOFTWARE (fc1)
BOOTFLASH: 3000 Bootstrap Software (IGS-BOOT-R), Version 11.0(10c)XB1,
PLATFORM SPECIFIC RELEASE SOFTWARE (fc1)

Phoenix uptime is 7 minutes
System restarted by reload
System image file is "flash:11-2-13.img", booted via flash

cisco 2500 (68030) processor (revision L)
with 2048K/2048K bytes of memory.
Processor board ID 07112268, with hardware revision 00000000
Bridging software.
SuperLAT software copyright 1990 by Meridian Technology Corp.
X.25 software, Version 2.0, NET2, BFE and GOSIP compliant.
TN3270 Emulation software.
2 Ethernet/IEEE 802.3 interface(s)
2 Serial network interface(s)
32K bytes of non-volatile configuration memory.
16384K bytes of processor board System flash (Read ONLY)
Configuration register is 0x2102
```

From the previous command listing, we can determine that we have 16,384KB of Flash memory available. Therefore, we can copy any software image less than or equal to 16,384KB to this device. The name of the file name is provided as

"11-2-13.img." After the memory requirements and the file name have been determined, copy the old image to a TFTP server. This step gives you a fallback procedure in case the new software image is corrupt:

```
Phoenix#copy flash TFTP
System flash directory:
File Length  Name/status
 1  7969232 11-2-13.img
[7969296 bytes used, 8807920 available, 16777216 total]
Address or name of remote host [255.255.255.255]? 172.16.24.134
Source file name? 11-2-13.img
Destination file name [11-2-13.img]? <Return>
Verifying checksum for '11-2-13.img' (file # 1)... OK
Copy '11-2-13.img' from Flash to server
 as '11-2-13.img'? [yes/no]y
!!!!!!!!!!!!!!!!!!!!!!!!!!!!!!!!!!!!!!!!!!!!!!!!!!!!!!!!!!!!!!!!!!!!!!!
!!!!!!!!!!!!!!!!!!!!!!!!!!!!!!!!!!!!!!!!!!!!!!!!!!!!!!!!!!!!!!!!!!!!!!!
!!!!!!!!!!!!!!!!!!!!!!!!!!!!!!!!!!!!!!!!!!!!!!!!!!!!!!!!!!!!!!!!!!!!!!!
!!!!!!!!!!!!!!!!!!!!!!!!!!!!!!!!!!!!!!!!!!!!!!!!!!!!!!!!!!!!!!!!!!!!!!!
!!!!!!!!!!!!!!!!!!!!!!!!!!!!!!!!!!!!!!!!!!!!!!!!!!!!!!!!!!!!!!!!!!!!!!!
!!!!!!!!!!!!!!!!!!!!!!!!!!!!!!!!!!!!!!!!!!!!!!!!!!!!!!!!!!!!!!!!!!!!!!!
!!!!!!!!!!!!!!!!!!!!!!!!!!!!!!!!!!!!!!!!!!!!!!!!!!!!!!!!!!!!!!!!!!!!!!!
!!!!!!!!!!!!!!!!!!!!!!!!!!!!!!!!!!!!!!!!!!!!!!!!!!!!!!!!!!!!!!!!!!!!!!!
!!!!!!!!!!!!!!!!!!!!!!!!!!!!!!!!!!!!!!!!!!!!!!!!!!!!!!!!!!!!!!!!!!!!!!!
!!!!!!!!!!!!..!!!!!!!!!!!!!!!!!!!!!!!!!!!!!!!!!!!!!!!!!!!!!!!!!!!!!!!!!
!!!!!!!!!!!!!!!!!!!!!!!!!!!!!!!!!!!!!!!!!!!!!!!!!!!!!!!!!!!!!!!!!!!!!!!
!!!!!!!!!!!!!!!!!!!!!!!!!!!!!
Upload to server done
Flash copy took 00:04:36 [hh:mm:ss]
```

# Upgrade IOS

After the current IOS has been backed up to a TFTP server and the available memory on the router has been checked, you can proceed with the upgrade of the IOS. The new IOS must reside on the TFTP server, as shown below:

```
Phoenix#copy TFTP flash
Proceed? [confirm]<Return>

System flash directory:
File Length  Name/status
 1  7969232 11-2-14.img
[7969296 bytes used, 8807920 available, 16777216 total]
Address or name of remote host [172.16.24.134]?<RETURN>
Source file name? 11-2-14.img
```

```
Destination file name [11-2-14.img]?
Accessing file '11-2-14.img' on 172.16.24.134...
Loading 11-2-14.img from 172.16.24.134 (via Ethernet1): ! [OK]

Erase flash device before writing? [confirm]
Flash contains files. Are you sure you want to erase? [confirm]

System configuration has been modified. Save? [yes/no]:
% Please answer 'yes' or 'no'.

System configuration has been modified. Save? [yes/no]: y
Building configuration...
[OK]

Copy '11-2-14.img' from server
 as '11-2-14.img' into Flash WITH erase? [yes/no]y

%SYS-5-RELOAD: Reload requested
%SYS-4-CONFIG_NEWER: Configurations from version 11.2 may not be
correctly understood.
%FLH: 11-2-14.img from 172.16.24.134 to flash ...

System flash directory:
File Length  Name/status
 1  7969232 11-2-14.img
[7969296 bytes used, 8807920 available, 16777216 total]
Accessing file '11-2-14.img' on 172.16.24.134...
Loading 11-2-14.img from 172.16.24.134 (via Ethernet1): ! [OK]
Erasing                                        device...
eeeeeeeeeeeeeeeeeeeeeeeeeeeeeeeeeeeeeeeeeeeeeeeeeeeeeeeeeeeeee
ee ...erased
Loading 11-2-14.img from 172.16.24.134 (via Ethernet1):
!!!!!!!!!!!!
!!!!!!!!!!!!!!!!!!!!!!!!!!!!!!!!!!!!!!!!!!!!!!!!!!!!!!!!!!!!!!!!!!!
!!!!!!!!!!!!!!!!!!!!!!!!!!!!!!!!!!!!!!!!!!!!!!!!!!!!!!!!!!!!!!!!!!!
!!!!!!!!!!!!!!!!!!!!!!!!!!!!!!!!!!!!!!!!!!!!!!!!!!!!!!!!!!!!!!!!!!!
!!!!!!!!!!!!!!!!!!!!!!!!!!!!!!!!!!!!!!!!!!!!!!!!!!!!!!!!!!!!!!!!!!!
!!!!!!!!!!!!!!!!!!!!!!!!!!!!!!!!!!!!!!!!!!!!!!!!!!!!!!!!!!!!!!!!!!!
!!!!!!!!!!!!!!!!!!!!!!!!!!!!!!!!!!!!!!!!!!!!!!!!!!!!!!!!!!!!!!!!!!!
!!!!!!!!!!!!!!!!!!!!!!!!!!!!!!!!!!!!!!!!!!!!!!!!!!!!!!!!!!!!!!!!!!!
[OK - 7969232/16777216 bytes]
Verifying checksum... OK (0xF865)
Flash copy took 0:07:00 [hh:mm:ss]
```

## Reloading The Router

Depending on what type of router mode you have, when you copy a new version of software to the router, the router will either reload itself or return with the Router# prompt. If the router returns with a prompt, use the **Router# reload** command to restart the router and load the new software. The router **reload** command is as follows:

```
Router# reload
```

# Practice Questions

## Question 1

> Which of the following commands will allow you to review the contents of NVRAM? [Choose the two best answers]
>
> ❑ a.  **show configuration**
>
> ❑ b.  **show protocols**
>
> ❑ c.  **show version**
>
> ❑ d.  **show running-config**
>
> ❑ e.  **show startup-config**

Answers a and e are correct. The **show configuration** and **show startup-config** commands display the router's backup configuration file from NVRAM. The **show protocols, show version,** and **show running-config** commands will allow you to review the contents of RAM, not NVRAM; therefore, answers b, c, and d are incorrect.

## Question 2

> Which of the following router components contains the router's IOS image?
>
> ○ a.  Flash memory
>
> ○ b.  NVRAM
>
> ○ c.  RAM
>
> ○ d.  Interfaces

Answer a is correct. Flash memory contains the IOS images used by the router. If no image resides in Flash memory, the image in ROM will be used. Interfaces provide the network connections for the router; therefore, answer d is incorrect. NVRAM and RAM contain the backup configuration and active configuration files, respectively; therefore, answers b and c are incorrect.

# Question 3

> Which of the following router components contain versions of the router's configuration file? [Choose the two best answers]
>
> ❑ a. Flash memory
>
> ❑ b. NVRAM
>
> ❑ c. RAM
>
> ❑ d. ROM

Answers b and c are correct. NVRAM contains the backup configuration file for the router, while RAM contains the router's active configuration file. Flash memory and ROM do not contain a configuration file. They contain the router's IOS image files; therefore, answers a and d are incorrect.

# Question 4

> Which of the following commands will allow you to review the contents of RAM? [Choose the three best answers]
>
> ❑ a. **show configuration**
>
> ❑ b. **show protocols**
>
> ❑ c. **show version**
>
> ❑ d. **show running-config**
>
> ❑ e. **show startup-config**

Answers b, c, and d are correct. The **show protocols, show version,** and **show running-config** commands allow you to review the contents of RAM. The **show configuration** and **show startup-config** commands allow you to review the router's backup configuration file from NVRAM, not RAM; therefore, answers a and e are incorrect.

## Question 5

> Which command would allow you to add, modify, or delete commands in the startup configuration file?
>
> ○ a. **show startup-config**
> ○ b. **show running-config**
> ○ c. **configure terminal**
> ○ d. **configure memory**

Answer d is correct. The **configure memory** command allows you to enter commands into the startup configuration file stored in NVRAM. Answers a and b are incorrect because they only allow you to view the startup and running configuration files, respectively. Answer c is incorrect because it allows you to add, modify, or delete commands in the running configuration file, but not in the startup configuration file.

## Question 6

> Which command would be used to restore a configuration file to RAM on a Cisco router?
>
> ○ a. **router#copy TFTP running-config**
> ○ b. **router>copy TFTP running-config**
> ○ c. **router#copy TFTP startup-config**
> ○ d. **router>copy TFTP startup-config**

Answer a is correct. To restore a configuration file, the file must be copied from a TFTP server to the Cisco router. This is a trick question, because you must be in EXEC privileged mode to perform this function. Answers b and d are incorrect because the answer implies that the command is initiated from exec mode; you can determine this by the > symbol (versus the # symbol) at the end of the word "router" in answers b and d. Answer c is incorrect because the startup-config file is not in RAM, and the question requires that you copy to the running-config file which is in RAM.

## Question 7

> Which of the following commands will display the running configuration file
> to a console terminal?
>
> ○ a. **router>show running-config**
>
> ○ b. **router#show startup-config**
>
> ○ c. **router#show flash**
>
> ○ d. **router>show version**
>
> ○ e. None of the above

Answer a is correct. The command to display a running configuration file to a
console terminal is **show running-config**. Answer b displays the startup configuration file to the console monitor and is, therefore, incorrect. Answer c is incorrect because it displays any IOS images or configuration files stored in Flash
memory. Answer d displays the software version and hardware on this router and
is, therefore, incorrect.

## Question 8

> If you need to copy the currently executing configuration file into NVRAM,
> which command would accomplish this goal?
>
> ○ a. **router#copy startup-config running-config**
>
> ○ b. **router#copy startup-config TFTP**
>
> ○ c. **router#copy running-config startup-config**
>
> ○ d. **router>copy startup-config running-config**

Answer c is correct. The startup configuration file exists in NVRAM. So, to copy
a configuration file to NVRAM, the current startup configuration file must be
overwritten. Answer a is incorrect because the **startup-config** is not the currently
executing image, and this command is attempting to write the configuration file
to RAM. Answer b is incorrect because the **startup-config** is not the currently
executing configuration file, and TFTP does not exist in NVRAM. Answer d is
incorrect because the **startup-config** is not the currently executing image and
because the command is being executed from exec mode.

## Question 9

Which of the following commands would not set a password on a Cisco router?

○ a. **router(config)#enable secret**

○ b. **router(config-line)#password phoenix**

○ c. **router(config)#service encryption password**

○ d. **router(config)#enable password**

Answer c is correct. The **service encryption password** command is used to encrypt passwords in configuration files. Answer a is incorrect because it is used to set the **enable secret password** command. Answer d is incorrect because it is used to set the **enable password** command. Answer b is incorrect because this command is used to set the Telnet, auxiliary, or console passwords, depending on which line configuration mode the router is in when the command is executed.

## Question 10

In which of the following scenarios would a router boot into the initial configuration dialog after its power has been cycled? [Choose the two best answers]

❏ a. Someone copied the startup configuration file to a TFTP server.

❏ b. The running configuration file was copied to the startup configuration file.

❏ c. It is the first time this router has ever been powered on.

❏ d. The **write erase** command was executed immediately before powering down the router.

Answers c and d are correct. The initial configuration dialog starts anytime a configuration file cannot be found in NVRAM. This occurs when a **write erase** command has been performed on the startup configuration file or when it is the first time the router is being powered on. Copying the running configuration to the startup configuration will not cause the router to boot into the initial configuration dialog; therefore, answer b is incorrect. Answer a is incorrect because copying a startup configuration file to a TFTP server will not cause a router to boot into the initial configuration dialog.

## Question 11

> Which of the following configuration register values would force a router to boot from ROM?
>
> ○ a. 0x2103
>
> ○ b. 0x210F
>
> ○ c. 0x2101
>
> ○ d. 0x2104

Answer c is correct. A configuration register with the value of 0x2101 forces a router to boot from ROM. Only when the boot field has a value of 1 or 0 will the router boot from ROM. Answers a, b, and d are incorrect because all of these values would cause the router to look at the boot commands in the configuration file to determine what IOS to load.

## Question 12

> Where does the running configuration file exist in a Cisco router?
>
> ○ a. NVRAM
>
> ○ b. ROM
>
> ○ c. RAM
>
> ○ d. Flash memory

Answer c is correct. The running configuration file exists in RAM. This file is erased if a router is reloaded or its power is cycled. Answer b cannot be correct because ROM is a read-only device, and configuration files are constantly being updated. Answer a is incorrect because NVRAM is used to maintain the startup configuration file, not the running configuration file. Answer d is incorrect because Flash memory stores a copy of the IOS software, not running configuration files.

# Question 13

> Which is the correct command to back up Cisco IOS software?
>
> ○ a. **router#copy running-config startup-config**
>
> ○ b. **router(config)#copy TFTP flash**
>
> ○ c. **router#copy flash TFTP**
>
> ○ d. **router#copy flash NVRAM**

Answer c is correct. To back up Cisco IOS, you must copy it to a TFTP server or another storage device. Answer a is incorrect because it deals with configuration files, not Cisco IOS software. Answer b is incorrect because this command would be used to restore the Cisco IOS to a router. Answer d is incorrect because **copy flash NVRAM** is not a valid command.

# Question 14

> Which of the following is not a valid Cisco command?
>
> ○ a. **router>show version**
>
> ○ b. **router#show running-config**
>
> ○ c. **router#show startup-config**
>
> ○ d. **router#show RAM**

Answer d is correct. **show RAM** is not a Cisco IOS command. Answers a, b, and c are incorrect because they are Cisco commands.

# Need to Know More?

McNutt, Shawn, Mark Poplar, Jason Waters, and David Stabenaw: *CCNA Routing and Switching Exam Prep.* The Coriolis Group, Scottsdale, AZ, 2000. ISBN 1-57610-440-0. This book is a great complement to the CCNA Cram book. Several chapters have expanded information about router configuration, including instructions on setting up and configuring a test lab.

Chappell, Laura: *Introduction to Cisco Router Configuration.* Cisco Systems Inc., Macmillan Publishing Company, Indianapolis, IN, 1998. ISBN 0-7645-3186-7. A great introduction to Cisco router configuration.

Lammle, Todd, Donald Porter, and James Chellis: *CCNA Cisco Certified Network Associate.* Sybex Network Press, Alameda, CA, 1999. ISBN 0-7821-2381-3. This book is full of helpful information.

Syngress Media, with Richard D. Hornbaker, CCIE: *Cisco Certified Network Associate Study Guide.* Osborne/McGraw-Hill, Berkeley, CA, 1998. ISBN 0-07-882487-7. This book is a great study tool.

The Cisco Web page, **www.cisco.com**, also provides some helpful information. Use the search engine to search for the following topics: password configuration, 2500 software upgrade, and managing configuration files.

# TCP/IP

## Terms you'll need to understand:

✓ Transmission Control Protocol (TCP)

✓ Internet Protocol (IP)

✓ Defense Advanced Research Projects Agency (DARPA)

✓ Advanced Research Project Agency network (ARPAnet)

✓ File Transfer Protocol (FTP)

✓ User Datagram Protocol (UDP)

✓ Telnet

✓ Simple Mail Transfer Protocol (SMTP)

✓ Simple Network Management Protocol (SNMP)

✓ Domain Name System (DNS)

✓ TCP three-way handshake

✓ TCP windowing

✓ Internet Control Message Protocol (ICMP)

✓ Address Resolution Protocol (ARP)

✓ Reverse Address Resolution Protocol (RARP)

## Techniques you'll need to master:

✓ Identifying the functions of the TCP/IP transport layer protocols

✓ Identifying the functions of the TCP/IP network layer protocols

✓ Describing the TCP/IP stack

✓ Explaining the function of the TCP/IP protocols ARP, RARP, and ICMP

This chapter discusses the *Transmission Control Protocol/Internet Protocol* (*TCP/IP*) suite of protocols. The birth and evolution of the Internet was made possible by the creation of the TCP/IP protocol suite. This chapter begins by providing a brief background of TCP/IP; understanding its humble beginnings allows you to truly appreciate the enormity of its use in our world today.

To continue to build on the foundation of internetworking, the TCP/IP protocol suite is mapped to the Open Systems Interconnect (OSI) model. Each of the TCP/IP protocols maps roughly to one of the seven layers of the OSI model. Each of the TCP/IP layers is discussed and broken down to a level of detail to prepare for the CCNA exam. The purpose and function of many of the TCP/IP protocols are discussed in this chapter. IP addressing and subnetting are covered in detail in Chapter 10.

# Background and History of TCP/IP

The importance of TCP/IP in today's society was not expected during its early development. In the early 1970s, Stanford University received funding from DARPA to create a protocol that could exploit the advantages of a packet-switched network and allow communication between dissimilar networks.

DARPA wanted a protocol that could connect different networks and be robust enough to choose among multiple paths to a final destination. DARPA believed that the flexibility inherent to a packet-switched network might be the solution. Stanford University, consequently, produced the IP suite to fulfill these wishes. Meanwhile, DARPA built a hardware infrastructure designed to use the IP as the software and called it *ARPAnet*, which later evolved into the Internet. The IP suite is commonly referred to as TCP/IP in reference to the two best-known protocols.

The IP suite was developed to operate across the networks of a wide variety of institutions. The IP suite allowed networks with different information formats, data rates, error characteristics, and data unit sizes to share a common suite of protocols. It is the adaptability of the IP suite that has made it the most widely used protocol today. Nearly every computer vendor supports at least part of this suite. The TCP/IP suite of protocols has literally evolved from a government-funded research program into packet-switched networks into a ubiquitous media.

# TCP/IP Stack and the OSI Model

TCP/IP is based on a nonproprietary model and allows all vendors to develop applications that are based on the model. The TCP/IP suite has four layers that roughly map to the seven layers of the OSI model; however, it performs all of the

| OSI 7 Layer Model | TCP/IP 4 Layer Model | Services/ Protocols | |
|---|---|---|---|
| Application | Application | Telnet TFTP SMTP | FTP NFS DNS |
| Presentation | | | |
| Session | | | |
| Transport | Transport | TCP | UDP |
| Network | Network | IP | ICMP |
| Data Link | Network Interface | ARP | RARP |
| Physical | | | |

**Figure 9.1**  TCP/IP mapping to the OSI model.

functions of the OSI model. The mapping of the TCP/IP suite to the OSI model is shown in Figure 9.1.

Note that the application layer of the TCP/IP protocol suite maps to the application, presentation, and session layers of the OSI model. The TCP/IP application layer performs the functions described by the OSI model for all three layers. The transport and network layers of the TCP/IP protocol suite perform the functions described by the OSI model for the transport and network layers. Finally, the network interface layer of the TCP/IP protocol performs the same functions as the data link and physical layers of the OSI model.

## Application Layer

The application layer consists of a set of services that provides ubiquitous access to all types of networks. Applications utilize the services to communicate with other devices and remote applications. A large number of TCP/IP services are provided at the application layer. Table 9.1 lists several application layer protocols and their associated port numbers.

 Memorize the port numbers for these protocols. You will find that knowing these protocols by name and number will be beneficial for test-taking and real world engineering.

| Table 9.1 | TCP/IP application layer services. | |
|---|---|---|
| **Service** | **Function** | **Port Number** |
| FTP | File transfer | 21 |
| TFTP | File transfer | 69 |
| Telnet | Terminal emulation | 23 |
| SMTP | Mail transfer | 25 |
| SNMP | Network management | 161, 162 |
| DNS | Domain name resolution | 53 |

## FTP

*FTP* is used to copy a file from one host to another host regardless of the physical hardware or operating system (OS) of each device. FTP identifies a client and server during the file transfer process. In addition, it provides a guaranteed transfer by using the services of TCP. The services that TCP provides are explained in more detail in the next section of this chapter.

## TFTP

*TFTP* was designed to be a lean FTP service. The goal was to develop a protocol that could fit into the limited read-only memory (ROM) space of diskless machines. TFTP is a connectionless protocol that uses the services of the *UDP* for transport. TFTP is used to copy files from one host (server) to another host (client). In many cases, TFTP is used to copy software to a device as it boots up. The function of the TFTP services for Cisco routers is illustrated in Chapter 8. The following is a list of some of the commands that use TFTP:

➤ **copy tftp startup-config**

➤ **copy tftp running-config**

➤ **copy tftp flash**

➤ **copy startup-config tftp**

➤ **copy running-config tftp**

➤ **copy flash tftp**

 The steps for performing these commands were shown in Chapter 8. It is important to understand completely the proper situation in which to use each of these commands. For example, you must know that copying a file to the startup configuration file will write the file to non-volatile random access memory (NVRAM), and copying a file to the running configuration file will write the file to random access memory (RAM).

## Telnet

The Telnet service allows users to act as though their terminal is attached to another device. This process is referred to as *terminal emulation.* Telnet is a very useful protocol in internetworking, because it allows network administrators to view and configure remote devices in the network from one location. Telnet uses the services of TCP to provide a connection-oriented session. An example of using the Telnet service between two devices follows:

```
Router#telnet 204.99.4.36
Trying 204.99.4.36 ... Open
Phoenix>
```

## SMTP

*SMTP* is used to pass mail messages between devices. It uses TCP connections to pass the email we've all grown to love between two mail hosts.

## SNMP

*Simple Network Management Protocol (SNMP)* is used to obtain data on remote devices. Typically, a network management station uses SNMP to poll the devices in a network and to retrieve data regarding the devices' current and past conditions. With SNMP, the network management machine is referred to as the *manager* and all of the remote devices are considered *agents* of the manager. Each of the agents maintains a *management information database* (*MIB*) locally that constantly stores information about that device. The manager systematically polls each of its agents, requesting information from their databases. It then manipulates and organizes the data into a useful format for reporting or displaying on the network management monitor.

## DNS

*DNS* is used to translate hostnames or computer names into IP addresses such as **www.examcram.com** or vice versa. DNS is a hierarchical database of names and their associated IP addresses. DNS is what allows people to enter a word-based address for any device on the Internet. When this occurs, that person's device requests a DNS lookup from a DNS server. The DNS server replies with the IP address associated with that word-based address.

# Transport Layer

The *transport layer* provides an end-to-end connection between two devices during communication by performing sequencing, acknowledgments, checksums, and flow control. The transport layer allows the application layer to ignore the complexities of the network and focus on its primary job. This layer is also responsible for sending data that it receives from the network layer to the appropriate application. An application using the services of the transport layer can use two different protocols: UDP and TCP. Both protocols fulfill the transport layer responsibilities, however, they provide two very different levels of service.

## TCP

TCP provides a connection-oriented, reliable service to the applications that use its services. TCP was designed to add some reliability into the world of IP networking. A description of the main functions of TCP follows:

➤ *Segments application layer data stream*—TCP accepts data from applications and segments it into a desirable size for transmission between itself and the remote device. The segment size is determined while TCP is negotiating the connection between the two devices. Either device can dictate the segment size.

➤ *Provides acknowledgment timers*—TCP maintains timers to identify when packets have taken too long to get to their destination. When an acknowledgment is not received for an IP packet before the expiration of the timer, TCP resends the packet to the destination.

➤ *Enables sequence number checking*—TCP/IP uses sequence numbers to ensure that all packets sent by an application on one device are read in the correct order by an application on another device. The packets might not be received at the transport layer in the correct order, but TCP sequences them in their original order before passing them to the application layer.

➤ *Provides buffer management*—Any time two devices are communicating, the possibility exists that one device can send data faster than the other can accept it. Initially, the receiving device puts the extra packets into a buffer and reads them when it gets a chance. When this data overflow persists, however, the buffer is eventually filled and packets begin to drop. TCP performs some preventive maintenance called *flow control* to avoid this scenario.

➤ *Initiates connection with three-way handshake*—TCP uses the concept of the three-way handshake to initiate a connection between two devices. Figure 9.2 illustrates this procedure. A TCP connection begins with device A by sending a request to synchronize sequence numbers and initiate a connection (a SYN message). Device B receives the message and responds with a SYN message with the sequence number increased by one. Device A responds by sending an acknowledgement message (an ACK) to device B, indicating that the device received the sequence number it expected.

➤ *Performs error and duplication checking*—TCP uses a checksum to identify packets that have changed during transport. If a device receives a packet with a bad checksum, it drops the packet and does not send an acknowledgment

**Figure 9.2**  TCP three-way handshake.

for it. Thus, the sending device resends the packet (hopefully, it will not change during transport this time). In addition, any time TCP receives a duplicate packet, it drops the duplicate.

➤ *Performs acknowledgment windowing to increase efficiency of bandwidth use*— Any time a TCP device sends data to another device, it must wait for the acknowledgment that this data was received. Figure 9.3 illustrates TCP communication between two devices with a window size of 1. To increase the efficiency of bandwidth utilization, TCP can change the window size. If the window size is increased to 2, as shown in Figure 9.4, then the sending device requires only one acknowledgment for every two packets sent. TCP sets the window size dynamically during a connection, allowing either device involved in the communication to slow down the sending data rate based on the other device's capacity. This process is often referred to as *sliding windows* because of TCP's ability to change the window size dynamically.

## TCP Header Format

The TCP header is designed to support all of the functions mentioned previously and many more. The TCP header, illustrated in Figure 9.5, is 20 bytes and encapsulated in an IP packet during transport.

The purpose of each of the fields in the TCP header is as follows:

➤ *Source port*—Identifies the port at which upper-layer source processes receive TCP services.

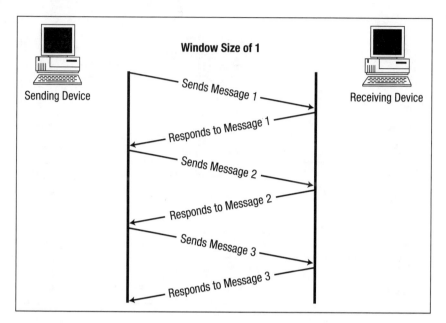

**Figure 9.3** TCP communication with window size of 1.

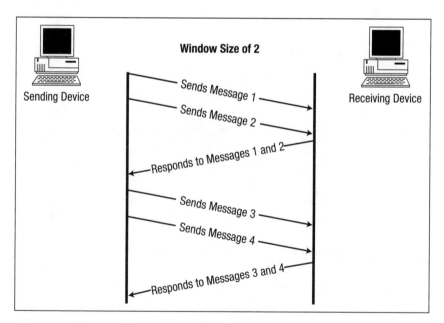

**Figure 9.4** TCP communication with window size of 2.

**Figure 9.5** TCP header format.

➤ *Destination port*—Identifies the port at which upper-layer destination processes receive TCP services.

➤ *Sequence number*—Allows the receiving device to order data correctly before passing it to an application, or to detect missing frames.

➤ *Acknowledgment number*—Identifies which TCP octet is expected next.

➤ *Header length*—Gives the length of the header in 32-bit words. This is necessary because the TCP header can have optional fields in it that can extend the header.

➤ *Reserved*—Reserved for later use. Always set to zero.

➤ *Code bits*—Identifies what type of segment is being sent. For example, the code bit can designate a SYN or ACK segment type.

➤ *Window*—Identifies the number of bits that a device is willing to accept.

➤ *Checksum*—Provides a field that is verified by the receiving device to ensure that data was not manipulated during transport.

➤ *Urgent pointer*—Indicates the end of urgent data.

➤ *Options*—Identifies the maximum TCP segment size. This is the only option that is currently defined.

➤ *Data*—Identifies the payload.

 It is not important to memorize all of the fields in the TCP or IP headers. It is important, however, to understand the overall capabilities of the TCP and IP header.

## UDP

UDP is a transport layer protocol that provides a subset of the functionality of TCP. UDP, however, requires considerably less network resources to perform its job than TCP does. UDP is a connectionless protocol because it does not require acknowledgments or sequence numbers to communicate. UDP simply receives data from the application layer, applies the proper header, and sends the datagram on its merry way. This is why UDP is referred to as a *best-effort protocol*. A comparison to TCP is provided in Table 9.2.

## UDP Header Format

The UDP header requires only eight bytes for all of its information. In comparison with TCP's 20-byte header, the UDP header is very small and requires minimal bandwidth. Figure 9.6 illustrates the UDP header format.

The purpose of each of the fields in the UDP header is as follows:

➤ *Source port*—Identifies the port at which upper-layer source processes receive UDP services.

➤ *Destination port*—Identifies the port at which upper-layer destination processes receive UDP services.

➤ *Header length*—Identifies the length of the UDP in bytes.

➤ *Checksum*—Provides a checksum that covers the UDP header and data.

| UDP Header Format | |
|---|---|
| 16-bit source port number | 16-bit destination port number |
| 16-bit UDP length | 16-bit UDP checksum |
| data | |

**Figure 9.6** UDP header format.

**Table 9.2 Functional comparison of TCP and UDP application layer services.**

| Function | UDP | TCP |
|---|---|---|
| Data segmentation | Every datagram is the same size | Assigns datagram size dynamically for efficiency |
| Reliability | Best effort only | Sequence numbers, acknowledgments, and three-way handshake |
| Flow control | None | Provides buffer management to avoid overflow and lost packets. Uses sliding windows to maximize bandwidth efficiency. |
| Error checking | Checksum | Checksum |

## Ports and Sockets

We have mentioned the purpose of ports and sockets in our explanation for TCP and UDP. This section provides a more detailed look at ports and sockets. A port number identifies a sending or destination application. Every application running on a host uses certain ports or ranges of ports to communicate with applications running on other hosts. It is by these port numbers that TCP or UDP determines which application to pass the data to in the application layer. A total of 65,535 ports exist; however, only a subset of these ports is most commonly used. They are referred to as the *well-known ports*.

The well-known ports have a value between 0 and 1,023. When an application on one device wants to communicate with an application on another device, it must specify the address of the device (IP address) and identify the application (port number). The combination of the sending and destination port numbers and the sending and destination IP addresses defines a *socket*. A socket can be used to define uniquely any UDP or TCP connection. Figure 9.7 illustrates some of the most commonly used ports and their associated applications. Notice that each port number is assigned either to UDP or TCP. All of the well-known port numbers are defined in Request for Comment (RFC) 1700.

# Network Layer

The *network layer* is responsible for path determination and packet switching. The network layer utilizes a logical addressing scheme to make intelligent decisions regarding path determination and packet switching. TCP/IP uses the IP addressing scheme that is explained in detail in Chapter 10. The network layer performs the actual relay of packets from an originating network to a destination network in an efficient manner.

## IP

*IP* is the transport for TCP, UDP, and Internet Control Message Protocol (ICMP) data. TCP and UDP have been explained in detail, and ICMP will be discussed shortly. IP provides an unreliable service. It lets the upper layer protocols such as TCP or application-specific devices worry about reliability. In addition, IP performs as a connectionless service because it handles each datagram as an independent entity. IP performs packet switching and path determination by maintaining tables that indicate where to send a packet based on its IP address. The format of the IP packet header is provided in Figure 9.8.

The purpose of each of the fields in the IP header is as follows:

➤ *Bit version*—Identifies the current version of IP. The current IP version is 4 or IPv4.

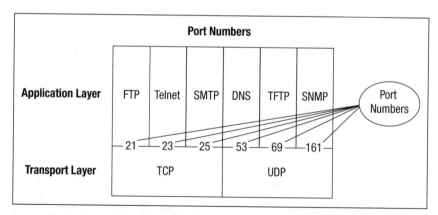

**Figure 9.7**   Commonly used port numbers.

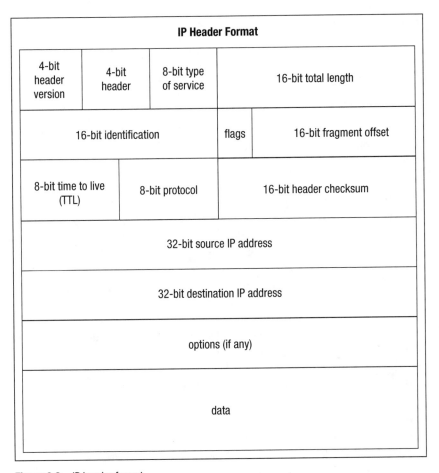

**Figure 9.8** IP header format.

➤ *Header length*—Identifies the number of 32-bit words in the header.

➤ *Type-of-service (TOS)*—Used to provide quality of service for IP data transport. The TOS field is broken into a three-bit precedence bit and four TOS bits.

➤ *Total length*—Provides the total length of the IP datagram in bytes.

➤ *Identification*—Uniquely identifies every packet from the sending device. This field, along with the flags and fragment offset fields, is used for packet fragmentation and reassembly.

➤ *Time-to-live (TTL)*—Sets an upper limit on the number of routers that can switch the packet. It is used to drop packets that are in routing loops.

➤ *Protocol field*—Identifies the protocol to pass the packet to upstream. For example, this protocol could be TCP, UDP, ICMP, or Internet Group Management Protocol (IGMP).

➤ *Checksum*—Provides a cyclical redundancy check of the IP header only.

➤ *Source IP address*—Identifies the IP address of the sending device.

➤ *Destination IP address*—Identifies the IP address of the destination device.

➤ *Options*—Identifies a variable-length list of optional information for the packet.

Chapter 8 provides more detailed information about IP and IP addressing. In addition, you can find a complete account of IP in RFC 791.

## ARP

*ARP* bridges the gap between physical and logical addressing by mapping a known IP address to a physical address. Therefore, if two devices want to communicate, the first device can send a broadcast ARP requesting the physical address for a specified IP address. The receiving device responds with its IP address, and the first device maintains this entry in its ARP cache. If a device does not exist on the same subnet, the sending device addresses the default gateway's physical address and sends the packet to the default gateway.

It is vital to understand the difference between when ARP versus RARP is applicable. One instance where RARP is used is in the case of diskless machines. This is because diskless machines do not have an IP address during the boot sequence.

## RARP

*RARP* provides the exact opposite type of mapping from ARP, i.e., RARP maps a known physical address to a logical address. Diskless machines that do not have a configured IP address when started typically use RARP. These devices send a broadcast requesting an IP address. In these scenarios, a device on the same local area network (LAN) is designed to respond to this broadcast request and supply the IP address for that physical address. Table 9.3 defines both ARP and RARP.

## ICMP

*ICMP* communicates error messages and control messages between devices. Thirteen different types of ICMP messages are defined. The ICMP protocol allows devices to check the status of other devices, query the current time, and perform other functions. The most used function of ICMP is the ping utility (illustrated in Chapter 8). The most common ICMP messages are as follows:

➤ *Destination unreachable*—Indicates that a certain device cannot be contacted.

➤ *Time exceeded*—Indicates that a certain device could not be reached within a specified time limit.

| Table 9.3 | ARP and RARP. | |
|-----------|---------------|---|
| Protocol | Action | Purpose |
| ARP | Maps a known IP address to a physical address | Used to identify the physical address of another workstation |
| RARP | Maps a known physical address to an IP address | Used in diskless environments so machines can determine their IP address from another device on the same LAN |

➤ *Echo*—Requests an echo reply to determine device reachability.

➤ *Echo reply*—Replies to an echo request indicating that a host is reachable.

The **ping** command is extremely useful in troubleshooting network problems. An extended **ping** command is also available in the Cisco Internetwork Operating System (IOS). An extended ping is performed by using the IP **ping** command. After executing this command, you will be given the option to alter many of the variables in the **ping** command. Some example variables include the number of attempts and the size of the packet.

## Network Interface Layer

This layer provides access to the LAN. The physical addressing and network-specific protocols exist at this layer. Token ring, Ethernet, and fiber distributed data interface (FDDI) are some examples of network interface layer protocols.

# Practice Questions

## Question 1

> Which of the following terms does not identify a layer of the TCP/IP model?
>
> ○ a. Application
>
> ○ b. Transport
>
> ○ c. Presentation
>
> ○ d. Network
>
> ○ e. Network interface

Answer c is correct. The presentation layer is only used by the OSI model; therefore, it does not identify a layer of the TCP/IP model. Answers a, b, d, and e all identify separate layers of the TCP/IP model.

## Question 2

> Which of the following services exist at the application layer of the TCP/IP model? [Choose the three best answers]
>
> ❏ a. SMTP
>
> ❏ b. FTP
>
> ❏ c. ICMP
>
> ❏ d. ARP
>
> ❏ e. TFTP

Answers a, b, and e are correct. SMTP, FTP, and TFTP all exist at the application layer of the TCP/IP model. Answer c is incorrect because ICMP exists at the Internet layer of the TCP/IP model. Answer d is incorrect because ARP exists at the network interface layer of the TCP/IP model.

# Question 3

FTP is used to copy files to and from Cisco routers.

○ a. True

○ b. False

Answer b is correct. The protocol used to copy files to and from Cisco routers is TFTP. TFTP is similar in function to FTP, but they are different protocols, and operate differently.

# Question 4

Which of the following services is used to translate word-based addresses into IP addresses?

○ a. SNMP

○ b. SMTP

○ c. IP

○ d. UDP

○ e. DNS

Answer e is correct. DNS is used to translate word-based addresses into IP addresses or vice versa. SNMP and SMTP are TCP/IP application layer services, but do not perform address translation; therefore, answers a, b, and c are incorrect. SNMP is used to monitor remote devices, and SMTP is used to send email between devices. IP is not a service, but a protocol used for addressing. Finally, UDP is a transport layer protocol used for packet sequencing; therefore, answer d is incorrect.

# Question 5

> Which of the following functions is not performed by TCP?
>
> ○ a. Flow control
>
> ○ b. Sequencing
>
> ○ c. Error checking
>
> ○ d. Subnetting

Answer d is correct. Subnetting is not a function performed by TCP; it is a process used to create more networks out of classful IP addresses. Answer a is incorrect because TCP does indeed provide flow control in the form of sliding windows and buffer management. Answer b is incorrect because TCP provides sequencing to ensure that datagrams are read in the correct order on the receiving side. Finally, answer c is incorrect because TCP provides error checking by applying a checksum to the TCP header and encapsulated data.

# Question 6

> Which of the following functions do UDP and TCP both perform? [Choose the two best answers]
>
> ❑ a. Destination and source port numbers
>
> ❑ b. Flow control
>
> ❑ c. Dynamic datagram size allocation
>
> ❑ d. Checksum
>
> ❑ e. Acknowledgments of datagram receipt

Answers a and d are correct. Answer a is correct because the destination and source port numbers are provided in both the UDP and TCP headers. In addition, answer d is correct because both TCP and UDP provide for a checksum in the header to verify accurate delivery. Answer b is incorrect because only TCP performs flow-control type activities in the form of buffer management and sliding windows. Answer c is incorrect because UDP does not set datagram sizes dynamically, but assigns each datagram the same size. Finally, only TCP provides reliability in its data transport; therefore, answer e is incorrect because UDP does not generate acknowledgments for the receipt of datagrams.

# Question 7

> Which of the following are functions of the network layer? [Choose the two best answers]
>
> ❑ a.  Path determination
>
> ❑ b.  Packet switching
>
> ❑ c.  Code formatting
>
> ❑ d.  Reliability
>
> ❑ e.  Physical addressing

Answers a and b are correct. Answer a is correct because the network layer uses the logical address of a packet to determine the best path to take to a destination. In addition, the network layer uses the logical address to make packet-switching decisions; therefore, answer b is correct. Answer c is incorrect because code formatting is performed by the TCP/IP application layer, not the network layer. Answer d is incorrect because the network layer does not provide reliability, but relies on the TCP/IP transport and application layers to provide the reliability. Answer d is incorrect because physical addressing is a function of the TCP/IP interface layer.

# Question 8

> Which of the following are characteristics of the protocol ARP? [Choose the two best answers]
>
> ❑ a.  It resides at the network layer.
>
> ❑ b.  It resides at the network interface layer.
>
> ❑ c.  It maps a known IP address to a MAC address.
>
> ❑ d.  It maps a known MAC address to an IP address.

Answers a and c are correct. Answer a is correct because the protocols ARP, RARP, ICMP, and IP exist at the network layer. Answer c is correct because devices use ARP to determine the physical address (MAC address) for a known IP address. Answer b is incorrect because LAN protocols such as token ring, Ethernet, and FDDI exist at this layer. Answer d is incorrect because the process of mapping a known MAC address to an unknown IP address is accomplished by RARP.

# Question 9

Which transmission layer protocol provides connectionless services?

- ○ a.  UDP
- ○ b.  TCP
- ○ c.  ICMP
- ○ d.  IP
- ○ e.  FTP

Answer a is correct. UDP is a transport layer protocol that provides a best-effort connectionless service. Answer b is incorrect because TCP provides a connection-oriented transport layer service through the use of acknowledgments and sequence numbers. Answer c is incorrect because ICMP is a network layer protocol used for control messaging. Answer d is incorrect because IP is a network layer protocol used for addressing and path determination. Answer e is incorrect because FTP is an application layer protocol used for transferring files between two devices.

# Need to Know More?

 McNutt, Shawn, Mark Poplar, Jason Waters, and David Stabenaw: *CCNA Routing and Switching Exam Prep.* The Coriolis Group, Scottsdale, AZ, 2000. ISBN 1-57610-440-0. This book has a very detailed chapter on TCP/IP.

 Chappell, Laura. *Introduction to Cisco Router Configuration.* Cisco Systems Inc., Macmillan Publishing Company, Indianapolis, IN, 1998. ISBN 0-7645-3186-7. The first three chapters cover some great OSI material.

 Lammle, Todd, Donald Porter, and James Chellis. *CCNA Cisco Certified Network Associate.* Sybex Network Press, Alameda, CA, 1999. ISBN 0-7821-2381-3. Chapter 4 covers IP addressing.

 Stevens, W. Richard. *TCP/IP Illustrated Volume 1.* Addison-Wesley Professional Computing Series, Reading, MA, 1994. ISBN 0-201-63346-9.

 Syngress Media, with Richard D. Hornbaker, CCIE. *Cisco Certified Network Associate Study Guide.* Osborne/McGraw-Hill, Berkeley, CA, 1998. ISBN 0-07-882487-7. Chapter 2 covers IP addressing.

 Tittel, Ed, Kurt Hudson, and J. Michael Stewart. *TCP/IP Exam Cram.* The Coriolis Group, Inc., Scottsdale, AZ, 1998. ISBN 1-57610-195-9.

 **www.cisco.com/univercd/cc/td/doc/cisintwk/ito_doc/ip.htm** on Cisco's Web site provides some excellent information regarding IP.

# IP Addressing
# and Subnetting

. . . . . . . . . . . . . . . . . . . . . . . . . . . . . . . . . . . . . . . . . . . . . . . . . .

## Terms you'll need to understand:

✓ Dotted decimal notation

✓ Classful addressing

✓ Subnetting

✓ Subnet mask

✓ Logical AND

✓ Variable Length Subnet Masking (VLSM)

✓ Classless Interdomain Routing (CIDR)

✓ Ping

✓ Traceroute

## Techniques you'll need to master:

✓ Describing the two parts of IP network addressing

✓ Identifying the different classes of IP addressing

✓ Developing an IP addressing scheme with subnetting

✓ Configuring IP addressing on a Cisco router

✓ Verifying IP addressing on a Cisco router

✓ Monitoring IP addressing on a Cisco router

The proliferation of the Internet into many aspects of our lives has increased the importance of *Internet Protocol (IP)* drastically. The building blocks of the Internet are wires, switches, and routers, but the glue that keeps it together is IP. The secret password into the Internet is a registered IP address. IP has been selected as the protocol of choice for the Internet. This means that vendors, corporations, and consultants work feverishly to develop, utilize, and implement this protocol. It also means that the number of products that utilize the IP are increasing, which ensures the longevity of its importance.

This chapter focuses on explaining the fundamentals of IP addressing. We will explain IP in its binary and decimal forms. The ability to understand IP in both forms is expected of beginning engineers. In addition, this chapter explains classful addressing and identifies the differences among the various classes of IP addresses. After providing a foundation, we'll introduce and explain the concept of subnetting. We will also cover the steps required to configure, verify, and monitor IP on a Cisco router.

# IP Addressing

The purpose of an IP address is to identify uniquely a device to the rest of the digital world. IP addresses have two parts: a *network ID* and a *host ID*. Each plays an important role in uniquely identifying a device. Figure 10.1 illustrates an IP address in binary format divided into its network ID and host ID parts.

The purpose of having two distinct parts of an address is to simplify the process of finding any individual host in a sea of networks. Computers use the network ID to route data to the gateway device of the network quickly. The gateway device of that network then uses the host ID part of the IP address to identify a device on that network. The division of the IP address into two parts allows a quick and accurate method of isolating a host's network, then identifying the host. The concepts of *classful addressing* and *subnetting* increase the complexities of IP addressing a little; nevertheless, they are interesting topics that are staples of networking. Before these topics are tackled, however, it is important to understand the format of an IP address in more detail.

## Dotted Decimal Notation

IP addresses are typically shown in *dotted decimal notation*. This was developed so that people could easily read and write IP addresses. An IP address in its native form is binary. Figure 10.2 illustrates the same binary IP address used in Figure 10.1; however, the address is now displayed in dotted decimal notation. An IP address under IP Version 4 (IPv4) is composed of 32 bits that have been divided into 8-bit groups referred to as *octets* or *bytes*. An IP address in dotted decimal notation specifies the decimal value of each of the four octets separated by dots.

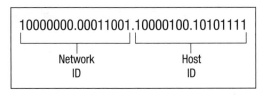

**Figure 10.1**    An IP address that is a two-part network address.

**Figure 10.2**    An IP address in dotted decimal notation.

Each octet can have a decimal value between 0 and 255. Why? The total number of possible values for a binary number with eight bits can be written mathematically as $2^8$. Although $2^8$ has a total value of 256, IP addresses begin with the number 0; therefore, the decimal range starts at 0 and ends with 255 for a total of 256 possible values.

The ability to convert IP addresses to both binary and decimal values is essential to using IP addressing effectively. The difference between the decimal and binary number systems is the number of digits they use. The decimal system uses 10 digits: 0, 1, 2, 3, 4, 5, 6, 7, 8, and 9. The "dec" in the name decimal refers to the 10 digits. The binary number system uses two digits: 0 and 1. The "bi" in the name binary refers to the two digits.

When a decimal number is higher than nine, the proper procedure is to increase the number of digits that are used to represent the number. The first time you increase the number of digits, you indicate this by putting the number 1 to the left of a new character with the value of 0.

The method used to increase a binary number is the same, except it uses only two values. When a binary value is higher than 1, the proper procedure is to increase the number of digits that are used to represent the number by one. The first time you increase the number of digits, you indicate this by putting the number 1 to the left of a new number with the value of 0. Because this binary number equals the same number of increments as the decimal number 2, it is said to have a decimal value of 2.

Adding the decimal value of every bit in the octet derives the total decimal value of an octet. The total decimal value of an octet is displayed in an IP address in dotted decimal notation. Table 10.1 contains a sample of a binary-to-decimal conversion table.

| Table 10.1 | Binary-to-decimal conversion. | |
|---|---|---|
| Binary Value | Bit Conversion | Decimal Value |
| 00000001 | 1 | 1 |
| 00000010 | 2 + 0 | 2 |
| 00000110 | 4 + 2 + 0 | 6 |
| 11110000 | 128 + 64 + 32 + 16 + 0 + 0 + 0 +0 | 240 |
| 11111111 | 128 + 64 + 32 + 16 + 8 + 4 + 2 +1 | 255 |

## Classful Addressing

The number of bits assigned to the network ID and the host ID depends on the number of hosts required on a given network and the number of networks required in an environment. Before the idea of classful addressing was in place, it was the network administrator's responsibility to determine which bits in the 32-bit address to assign to the network ID and which bits to assign to the host ID. If the number of hosts required on a given network was enormous, then a network administrator assigned a large portion of the 32 bits available to host IDs and used a small portion for network IDs. If a large number of networks were required with only a few hosts per network, the network administrator used a small portion of the bits for host IDs and a large number for network IDs.

This method of allocating address space was inefficient, often giving small organizations the right to a large number of IP address spaces. Therefore, IP address space was divided into three classes in the attempt to meet the needs of large and small organizations. (Actually, the IP address was divided into five classes; however, we will focus on the three main classes used by the Internet community.) With the class system, it is possible to assign a corporation address space based on the number of hosts and networks that it requires. This system is referred to as *classful addressing*. Classful addressing divides the $2^{32}$ (4,294,967,296) possible IP addresses into five different classes.

A class A, B, or C IP address can be determined by looking at the first three bits of the address. Figure 10.3 illustrates the relationship between the first three bits of an IP address and its class. Also, note the range in the decimal value for each class. When you understand IP addressing, you will only need to look at the first octet of an IP address in decimal format to determine its class. The class of an IP address governs the number of bits that can be used for network IDs and the number of bits that can be used for host IDs. For example, an organization that is allocated a class B address must use 16 bits to identify its network ID and 16 bits to identify its host ID. It is important to note that this strict rule can be avoided, and most often is, through a process known as *subnetting*.

| Bit Position | 1 | 2–8 | 9–32 |
|---|---|---|---|
| **Class A** | 0 | Network ID | Host ID |

| Bit Position | 1 | 2 | 3–16 | 17–32 |
|---|---|---|---|---|
| **Class B** | 1 | 0 | Network ID | Host ID |

| Bit Position | 1 | 2 | 3 | 4–24 | 25–32 |
|---|---|---|---|---|---|
| **Class C** | 1 | 1 | 0 | Network ID | Host ID |

**Figure 10.3**    Class addressing.

## Class A

Class A addresses are typically assigned to very large organizations, universities, or the military. It is extremely difficult—if not impossible—to get a class A address today. These addresses are identified in binary by the first bit having a value of 0 or in decimal by having a value between 1 and 126. Class A addresses use the first 8 bits to specify the network ID and the last 24 bits to designate the host ID. We will see later that the 24 bits used for the host ID can also be used as network IDs by using the process of subnetting. For now, however, it is only important to understand the division of bits for network and host IDs.

Class A addresses have a maximum of 126 network IDs. This value is arrived at by taking the number of bits used for the network ID to the power of 2. In this case, $2^7$ equals a total of 128. However, the network ID 0.0.0.0 is reserved for the default route, and the network ID 127.0.0.0 is reserved for the loop-back function. Therefore, the range of possible class A network IDs in decimal is 1 to 126.

Each class A network ID can support a total of $2^{24}$-2 (16,777,214) host IDs. The purpose of subtracting two from the possible number of hosts is to remove two special host IDs. Any time every bit in the host ID portion of an IP address has a value of 1, it is considered a *broadcast IP address*, meaning that all hosts should read a message sent to this address. Obviously, no device should have an address that is used for broadcasting information. The second consideration is when every bit in the host ID's binary value is 0. This value is used to distinguish a network number from a host ID. Figure 10.4 illustrates a class A address in decimal and binary formats.

## Class B

Class B addresses are typically assigned to medium and large organizations. These addresses are identified in binary by the first two bits having a value of 10 or in

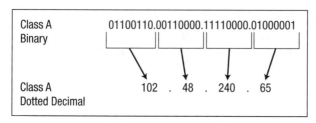

**Figure 10.4** Class A IP address.

decimal by having a value between 128 and 191. Class B addresses use the first 16 bits to specify the network ID and the last 16 bits to designate the host IDs. Because the first two bits of all class B addresses are always 10, however, only 14 bits are available to be used for network IDs. This allows a total of $2^{14}$ (16,384) class B network addresses. Each network ID supports a total of $2^{16}$-2 (65,534) host IDs. Figure 10.5 illustrates a class B address in decimal and binary formats.

## Class C

Class C addresses are typically assigned to small and medium organizations. These addresses are identified in binary by the first three bits having a value of 110 or in decimal by having a value between 192 and 223. Class C addresses use the first 24 bits to specify the network ID and the last 8 bits to designate the host IDs. Because the first 3 bits of a class C address are 110, however, only 21 bits are available to be used for network IDs. This allows a total of $2^{21}$ (2,097,152) class C network addresses. Each network ID supports a total of $2^{8}$–2 (254) host IDs. Figure 10.6 illustrates a class C address in decimal and binary formats.

*Note: It is important to be able to identify the class of an IP address quickly by looking at its decimal or binary value. This skill will serve you well for the exam and your career.*

## Other Classes

Two other classes of addresses are available in the IPv4 address space. These classes are not used as public address space, but have been reserved for specific functions. Class D addresses are identified in binary by the first 4 bits having a

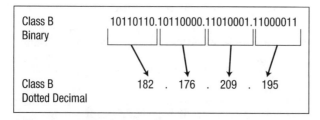

**Figure 10.5** Class B IP address.

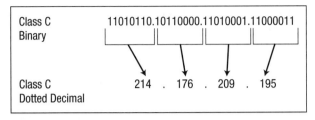

**Figure 10.6**   Class C IP address.

value of 1110 or in decimal by having a value between 224 and 239. Class D addresses have been reserved to support IP *multicasting*, which is the process of using one address to send a message to a group of people. Class E addresses are identified in binary by the first 4 bits having a value of 1111 or in decimal by having a value between 240 and 247. Class E addresses have been reserved for experimental or research use.

## Summary of Classful Addressing

The purpose of assigning classes to the IP address space was to provide a mechanism to assign address space to public and commercial organizations efficiently. This allocation scheme had a fundamental problem, because organizations typically have more than one network. Assigning a company an entire class B address for every separate network in its organization led to a huge waste of address space.

For example, if the XYZ Corporation required enough address space to support two networks that have 5,000 and 1,000 users, respectively, it would be extremely inefficient to assign them two class B addresses. XYZ has a requirement of only 6,000 total addresses for its organization today. One class B provides a total of $2^{16}-2$ (65,534) addresses. If XYZ were given two class B addresses, it would be using only 6,000 out of 131,068 total possible addresses. Furthermore, if XYZ wanted to add another network, this problem would be compounded. This is a grossly inefficient allocation mechanism. Subnetting is the solution to this problem.

## Subnetting

Subnetting creates multiple IP networks from a single allocated class A, B, or C IP network. Subnetting divides a single class A, B, or C network into smaller subnetworks. One of the major goals of allocating IP addresses to organizations based on their size was to have to allocate only one class A, B, or C address to any given organization. Therefore, only one routing entry would have to be maintained per organization. However, organizations had the need for multiple subnetworks within their network. Subnetting allowed for organizations to have multiple networks and the InterNIC to allocate a single class A, B, or C network.

Internet routers need to maintain only one classful network entry per organization because each organization is assigned only one class A, B, or C IP address. (Organizations are typically assigned only one class address; however, this is not always true, thanks to subnetting.) Even though organizations divide their IP address into multiple networks, they still look like one class A, B, or C IP address to the rest of the world. Organizations accomplish this by performing route summarization at the boundary of their network and any other network. Figure 10.7 illustrates this point.

## Default Mask

A *default mask* is a 32-bit number divided into four octets, just like an IP address. A default mask indicates the number of bits that are used to identify the network ID and is implied with all class A, B, and C addresses. Class A addresses imply an 8-bit default mask because the first 8 bits in their addresses designate the network ID. Therefore, the default mask (the number of bits that indicate the network ID) can be represented in decimal format as 255.0.0.0. Table 10.2 illustrates the default masks for class A, B, and C addresses in binary and decimal format. Note that the default mask represents the number of bits used to identify the network ID.

After viewing Table 10.2, it is easy to see that a default mask indicates which bits are used to identify the network ID versus the host ID. Why do we need a default mask if we can already determine this by the class of the IP address? As mentioned previously, organizations often have the need to increase the number of networks in their intranet. However, they are only assigned one IP address and can advertise only one IP address to the Internet. An organization can get around this by using some of the host ID bits as network ID bits. The organization can indicate that it has used some of the host ID bits as network ID bits by providing a subnet mask.

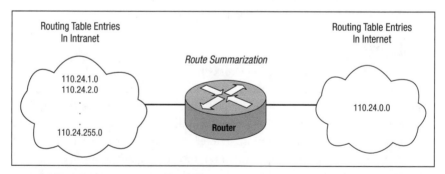

**Figure 10.7**   Class C IP address summarization.

| Table 10.2 | Default masks of class A, B, and C addresses. | |
|---|---|---|
| **Class** | **Binary Notation** | **Dotted Decimal Notation** |
| A | 11111111.00000000.00000000.00000000 | 255.0.0.0 |
| B | 11111111.11111111.00000000.00000000 | 255.255.0.0 |
| C | 11111111.11111111.11111111.00000000 | 255.255.255.0 |

## Subnet Mask

A *subnet mask* is an extension to the default mask. It indicates the number of bits in addition to the default mask that should be used to identify network IDs. What does this do for an organization? It increases the number of networks an organization can create from one class A, B, or C network ID.

For example, if an organization has a registered class C address and needs to create two networks, it must somehow get more network IDs. The organization can accomplish this by using some of the bits designated as host IDs as network IDs. However, the organization must indicate that this class C is no longer using the default 24 bits as a network ID. The organization can indicate this by applying a subnet mask to represent the additional bits that are to be used as network IDs versus host IDs. The subnet mask can be represented in various ways; in this chapter, we will refer to the subnet mask as the default mask plus any additional bits used for network IDs.

## Logical AND

How should the subnet mask be used to determine what the network ID is for an IP address? To determine the network ID and the host ID for an IP address, it is necessary to perform a process known as *logical AND*. This indicates which bits to use as network bits and which bits to use as host bits when deciphering an IP address. When applying the subnet mask to an IP address, each bit starting from the most significant bit to the least significant bit is compared between the IP address and the subnet mask. For example, the first bit of the first octet of the IP address is compared with the first bit of the first octet of the subnet mask. The resulting value from this bit-by-bit comparison is the network ID. The rule set to apply is listed as follows:

➤ If the subnet mask and the IP address both have values of 1, then the resulting network ID bit is 1.

➤ If the subnet mask has a value of 1 and the IP address has a value of 0, then the resulting network ID bit is 0.

➤ If the subnet mask has a value of 0, then the resulting network ID bit is 0.

| Table 10.3 The logical AND process. | |
|---|---|
| **Binary IP Address** | **Dotted Decimal IP Address** |
| 10000001.11111101.11101011.11111010 | 129.253.235.250 |
| **Binary Subnet Mask** | **Dotted Decimal Subnet Mask** |
| 11111111.11111111.11111000.00000000 | 255.255.248.0 |
| **Binary Network ID** | **Dotted Decimal Network ID** |
| 10000001.11111101.11101000.00000000 | 129.253.232.0 |

Table 10.3 illustrates the logical AND process. Note that, in Table 10.3, the only difference between the dotted decimal IP address and the dotted decimal network ID is in the last two octets. The difference between the values in the octet is due to the commingling of network and host bits in the same octet. The logical AND process drops all of the host IDs and retains the network IDs. Therefore, in Table 10.3 we determine that the host 129.253.235.252 is actually part of the network 129.253.232.0.

A computer performs the logical AND process every time it sends a message to another computer. To send a message, a personal computer (PC) must determine whether it should send the message to a device on its local network using its media access control (MAC) address or send it to a default gateway to be forwarded to another network. A PC performs a logical AND on the destination IP address to determine if the message is local or remote. If the result of the logical AND indicates that the destination device is on the same network, the PC looks in its Address Resolution Protocol (ARP) cache for the corresponding MAC address for the destination address. If the MAC address is found, the PC sends the message using the MAC address to the destination. If the MAC address is not found in the ARP cache, the PC performs an ARP search to get the corresponding MAC address.

Table 10.4 illustrates another example of the logical AND process using a class C address. Note that, with a class C address, the only difference in the IP address occurs in the last octet. The reason that the differences are isolated to the last octet is that, in a class C address, only the last octet contains bits assigned to host IDs, so only these bits are available for subnetting.

So far, we have learned that IP addresses are divided into classes to allocate the IP address space to varying sizes of organizations efficiently. Efficient allocation of address space also minimizes the number of entries that need to be maintained in the routing tables of Internet routers. Because organizations required more networks than the InterNIC believed reasonable to assign due to wasted IP address space, a subnet mask was created, giving organizations a tool for increasing the number of networks they had by borrowing bits from the host IDs of their

| Table 10.4   The logical AND process, class C address. | |
|---|---|
| **Binary IP Address** | **Dotted Decimal IP Address** |
| 11000001.11011101.10110001.11101000 | 193.221.177.58 |
| **Binary Subnet Mask** | **Dotted Decimal Subnet Mask** |
| 11111111.11111111.11111111.11100000 | 255.255.255.224 |
| **Binary Network ID** | **Dotted Decimal Network ID** |
| 11000001.11011101.10110001.00100000 | 193.221.177.32 |

assigned IP address space. A subnet mask uses the logical AND process to distinguish between the network ID and the host ID of an IP address.

Next we'll discuss some of the items to consider when determining the number of bits to use for the subnet mask. A bad decision on a subnet mask can place constraints on an organization's future addressing choices.

## Subnetting Consideration

Remember that the purpose of the subnet mask is to give an organization the flexibility to increase the number of networks in its environment. So, you might think that an organization should give itself the maximum number of networks possible with its assigned IP address space. Any time a bit is added to the network ID, however, a bit is removed from the host ID. Therefore, if the number of networks is increased, the number of host IDs available per network is decreased. Table 10.5 illustrates this fact by presenting the number of network and host IDs for class B IP addresses with different subnet masks.

Organizations need to determine the happy medium between sufficient host IDs and network IDs for their specific needs. The cost of changing the subnet mask on thousands of computers because of a scaling issue is not a welcome thought for network administrators. Some of the questions that must be asked before developing a subnet addressing scheme are as follows:

| Table 10.5   Class B networks with various subnet masks. | | | |
|---|---|---|---|
| **Subnet Mask** | **Bits In Subnet Mask** | **Network IDs** | **Host IDs** |
| 255.255.255.0 | 24 | $2^8-2= 254$ | $2^8-2 = 254$ |
| 255.255.255.128 | 25 | $2^9-2= 510$ | $2^7-2 = 126$ |
| 255.255.255.192 | 26 | $2^{10}-2= 1022$ | $2^6-2 = 62$ |
| 255.255.255.224 | 27 | $2^{11}-2= 2046$ | $2^5-2 = 30$ |
| 255.255.255.240 | 28 | $2^{12}-2= 4094$ | $2^4-2 = 14$ |
| 255.255.255.248 | 29 | $2^{13}-2= 8190$ | $2^3-2 = 6$ |

➤ What is the total number of network IDs that my organization needs today?

➤ What is the total number of host IDs that my largest network requires today?

➤ What is the total number of network IDs that my organization will need in the future?

➤ What is the total number of host IDs that my largest network will require in the future?

The answers to these questions will determine how an organization subnets its assigned IP address space. The purpose of asking about current and future requirements is to get an understanding of what is absolutely needed today and what should be planned for the future. To illustrate the process of classful IP addressing, subnetting, the logical AND, and IP addressing considerations, examples using class A and B addresses are provided in the following sections.

## Class A Network Example

This example uses a fictitious company named DGR to illustrate the process of determining the proper subnetting for an organization. DGR has been allocated the class A IP address 114.0.0.0 by the InterNIC. DGR must determine the proper way to use this IP address space to support its current and future needs. To determine these needs, we must answer the four questions suggested previously. These questions are repeated below, along with DGR's responses to them:

➤ What is the total number of network IDs that DGR needs today? Answer: 5,000

➤ What is the total number of network IDs that DGR will need in the future? Answer: 9,000

➤ What is the total number of host IDs that DGR requires on its largest network today? Answer: 1,000

➤ What is the total number of host IDs that DGR requires on its largest network in the future? Answer: 2,000

DGR has been assigned only one network; however, it requires several more to support its current and future requirements. DGR plans to use subnetting to create more network IDs. As mentioned previously, by default, 24 bits are allocated for host IDs with class A IP address space. We know that DGR requires 5,000 networks today and 9,000 in the future. Therefore, to create enough network IDs, bits have to be taken from the host IDs and used for network IDs. How many bits have to be taken from the host ID bits to provide 5,000 network IDs?

DGR requires a total of 13 bits to provide 5,000 network IDs. The number of bits required can be determined by taking $2^{13}$ (8,192 possible networks). A subnet mask of 255.255.248.0 is used to represent the 13 bits of subnetting. However, 13 bits only provide 8,192 total possible networks, which is not enough to support DGR's expected growth. A total of 14 bits is required to ensure that 9,000+ networks can be supported in the future. If DGR uses 14 bits as the subnet mask (a subnet mask of 255.255.252.0), it has a total of $2^{14}$ (16,384) possibilities for network IDs. DGR would prefer to use 14 bits of the host ID to subnet the current 114.0.0.0 class A address; however, taking 13 bits from the host ID would provide a sufficient number of network IDs (subnets) to provide for today's needs. Table 10.6 illustrates the number of bits required to provide 5,000 and 9,000+ network IDs.

DGR must determine if enough bits still remain to provide an adequate number of host IDs. DGR requires 1,000 host IDs today and expects to need 2,000 host IDs in the future. How many bits are required to provide 1,000 host IDs? How many bits are required to provide 2,000 host IDs? How many bits are still available to be used as host IDs?

The number of bits required for 1,000 host IDs is 10, which provides a total combination of 1,022 ($2^{10}-2$). Remember that we subtract 2 to represent the broadcast (all 1s) and the zero (all 0s) value in each network. However, DGR requires 11 bits to provide sufficient host IDs to support its future requirement of 2,000 hosts.

DGR has only 24 bits of host IDs in its class A 114.0.0.0 IP address to use for both hosts and networks. To get enough host IDs for 2,000 users per network and 9,000+ network IDs, however, it would take 14 network ID and 11 host ID bits for a total of 25 bits. DGR is short one bit, so it has to decide whether to limit the number of hosts or networks to have in the future. In this case, DGR would probably opt to use only 13 bits (8,192 networks) for network IDs and 11 bits for host IDs (2,046 host IDs per network). The decision can become more difficult, however, when an organization doesn't have the luxury of owning an entire class A IP address.

## Class C Network Example

In this example, we will define the actual subnets and host IDs. If an organization named CMN has been assigned the IP address space 210.14.12.0, it has been assigned a class C address with a default mask of 255.255.255.0. This organization

| Table 10.6 | The number of bits required for 5,000 and 9,000+ network IDs. | | |
|---|---|---|---|
| **IP Address** | **Subnet Mask** | **Network IDs** | **Host IDs** |
| 114.0.0.0 | 255.255.248.0 | $2^{13} = 8192$ | $2^{11} - 2 = 2046$ |
| 114.0.0.0 | 255.255.252.0 | $2^{14} = 16384$ | $2^{10} - 2 = 1022$ |

requires five networks today and expects to need eight in the future. In addition, CMN expects the largest number of hosts on a given network now and in the future to be 30 users.

CMN requires more networks and must subnet the eight bits allocated to host IDs to provide these networks. To do so, CMN must subnet three bits to provide eight more networks ($2^3$). The subnet mask of this IP address is now 255.255.255.224. The value of the last octet has changed to represent the three bits ($128 + 64 + 32 = 224$) that are now used to identify networks instead of hosts. However, CMN must make sure that it will have enough host IDs left to identify all 30 devices on its largest network. CMN has five bits remaining for host IDs, giving them a total of 30 ($2^5-2$) host IDs per network.

CMN has a total of eight subnets; these are listed on Table 10.7 along with the range of host IDs available for each subnet. A total of 30 host IDs exist for each subnet because the all 0s and all 1s host IDs have not been included. The all 1s host ID is reserved for the broadcast of information. For example, for subnet 210.14.12.64, host ID 210.14.12.95 is the broadcast address because every bit used for determining the host ID is set to 1.

## Summary of Subnetting

We have seen that flexibility has been built into IP addressing via a process known as subnetting, which allows organizations to divide up a classful network ID into a number of other networks. Any device can determine how the IP address was divided by looking at the IP address's subnet mask. This mask indicates which bits have been used for subnetting and which bits are still being used to identify hosts. Of course, each class of IP address has a default mask. Furthermore, we identified some important questions to consider when setting up an addressing scheme. Specifically, we need to know the number of hosts and networks an organization requires in the present and the future.

| Table 10.7 Subnets and host IDs for IP address 210.14.12.0 | | | | |
|---|---|---|---|---|
| **Subnet** | **Lowest Host ID** | **Highest Host ID** | **All 1s Host ID** | **All 0s Host ID** |
| 210.14.12.0 | 210.14.12.1 | 210.14.12.30 | 210.14.12.31 | 210.14.12.0 |
| 210.14.12.32 | 210.14.12.33 | 210.14.12.62 | 210.14.12.63 | 210.14.12.32 |
| 210.14.12.64 | 210.14.12.65 | 210.14.12.94 | 210.14.12.95 | 210.14.12.64 |
| 210.14.12.96 | 210.14.12.97 | 210.14.12.126 | 210.14.12.127 | 210.14.12.96 |
| 210.14.12.128 | 210.14.12.129 | 210.14.12.158 | 210.14.12.159 | 210.14.12.128 |
| 210.14.12.160 | 210.14.12.161 | 210.14.12.190 | 210.14.12.191 | 210.14.12.160 |
| 210.14.12.192 | 210.14.12.193 | 210.14.12.222 | 210.14.12.223 | 210.14.12.192 |
| 210.14.12.224 | 210.14.12.225 | 210.14.12.254 | 210.14.12.255 | 210.14.12.224 |

The ability to decipher subnet masks and classes of IP addresses for the CCNA exam is crucial. The good news is that this ability is also crucial to being proficient at networking in general. So, feel good about spending a significant amount of time practicing the art of subnetting.

## VLSM

One of the main problems IP addressing faces is the number of wasted IP addresses that occur on the networks of organizations. As we demonstrated previously, if an organization requires 30 hosts for its largest network, then all networks end up having to be able to support 30 hosts. Therefore, if a network has only two hosts, it wastes a total of 28 host IDs that could have been used somewhere else. The solution to this problem is *VLSM*.

A network is considered to be using VLSM when more than one subnet mask exists for the entire network. The limiting factor in the past was the ability of routing protocols to decipher IP addresses with different subnet masks. This led to packets being routed down the wrong path or in loops. Many of the newer protocols, however, support VLSM and require that the number of bits used for subnetting be forwarded with route updates, allowing the router to determine if a packet is destined for a particular destination.

## CIDR

*CIDR* is a partial solution to the rapid depletion of IP address space on the Internet. CIDR provides a more efficient method of allocating IP address space by removing the concept of classes such as A, B, and C. CIDR is not constrained by the 8-bit, 16-bit, and 24-bit class boundaries applied in classful addressing. Instead, CIDR associates a value (bit mask) with each IP address that identifies the number of bits used to identify the network portion of the IP address. This method does not waste bits for hosts or networks; additionally, the exact number of bits can be used to identify networks and hosts.

In addition, CIDR reduces the number of routing entries required through *route aggregation*, in which a single routing entry represents IP address space across traditional classful bit boundaries. Internet routers can summarize IP address space to other routers, thus minimizing the number of entries required. In the past, every classful address would require an entry in the routing table.

# Configure and Verify IP Addresses

We have spent a significant amount of time explaining IP addressing. We focused on topics such as classful addressing, subnetting, VLSM, and CIDR. Because of the volume of information presented in these areas, you might think that it is extremely difficult to configure a Cisco router with an IP address. Wrong. The process of configuring a Cisco router with an IP address and subnet mask is very simple. When you have determined your IP addressing scheme, the actual process of configuring the router takes only a few moments. Enter the IP address at the configuration mode of the interface that is being addressed. The actual commands are shown in Listing 10.1.

**Listing 10.1**   Configuring an Ethernet interface with an IP address.

```
Router#configure terminal
Router(config)#interface ethernet 0
Router(config-if)#IP Address 172.16.24.12 255.255.255.0
Router(config-if)#exit
Router(config)#
```

In the previous example, Ethernet interface 0 was configured with the class B address 172.16.24.12. A subnet mask of eight bits was used, as indicated by the mask of 255.255.255.0.

# IP Host Names

With Cisco routers, it is possible to map a literal host name to a numeric IP address. This can often make it easier to navigate around a complex network. For example, if we wanted to map the host name "Coriolis" with the IP address 172.16.30.12, we would perform the following set of commands:

```
Router(config)#ip host coriolis 172.16.30.12
Router(config)#exit
```

Now an administrator can use the literal "Coriolis" in place of the numeric IP address when configuring the router and navigating around the network.

# Verifying IP Addresses

The process of verifying IP addresses is one that you will perform countless times during your career as a network professional. Knowing how to use the many different tools for verifying IP addresses will save you an enormous amount of time in the long run. The three tools that are vital to know for the CCNA exam are ping, Telnet, and traceroute.

## Ping

The ping test is used to test *IP connectivity* between two devices. IP connectivity means that both devices have the ability to send IP packets to each other. Ping tests layer 3 connectivity between two devices. The **ping** command sends Internet Control Message Protocol (ICMP) echo packets to the destination device. The destination device responds with ICMP echo reply packets if it receives the message. If the message does not reach its destination, the last hop sends an ICMP host unreachable packet back to the sending device. An example of a ping between two devices on different networks is shown in Listing 10.2.

**Listing 10.2    Pinging between two devices.**

```
Router>ping 172.16.29.3
Type escape sequence to abort.
Sending 5, 100-byte ICMP echos to 172.16.29.3,
Timeout is 5 seconds
!!!!!
Success rate is 100%, round-trip min/avg/max = 2/4/8 ms
Router>
```

The previous messages indicate that five ICMP echo requests were sent to host 172.16.29.3. If these messages did not reach their destination in five seconds, they would be dropped. An exclamation point is written to the screen each time an ICMP echo reply packet was received by the sending device. Therefore, the sending device received all five ICMP echo requests. A number of variations to the ping test allows the user to extract more detailed information. We encourage you to explore this tool.

## Telnet

The Telnet application can be used to test application layer connectivity between two hosts. The Telnet protocol is explained in more detail in Chapter 7. The Telnet application is used to gain remote access to a host device; therefore, it must travel across all layers of the Open Systems Interconnect (OSI) model to reach its destination. The fact that Telnet passes through all seven layers of both the source and destination devices makes it an effective tool. If we can open a Telnet session, we know that all layers of the OSI model are functioning properly.

## Traceroute

The **traceroute** command is used to determine the actual path a packet takes between its source and destination. The **traceroute** command uses ICMP and the time-to-live (TTL) field in the IP header to map the typical course a packet would take between two destinations. The TTL field's original purpose was to identify transient packets caught in routing loops. This is accomplished by setting the TTL field to some value (usually 255) and subtracting one from the value each time the packet reaches a router. When the TTL field reaches a value of 0, a router drops the packet. The traceroute program capitalizes on the fact that routers drop IP packets with a value of 0. Whenever a router decreases a

TTL packet to a value of 0, it sends an ICMP TTL exceeded message back to the sending device. It is this ICMP message that the traceroute program uses to gather information about each hop between two devices.

For example, if a user sends an ICMP packet to the destination with the TTL field set to 1, the first router in the path to the destination receives the packet and decreases the value of the TTL field. The value of the TTL field is now 0, so the router drops the packet and sends an ICMP host unreachable message back to the sending device. The sending device sends an ICMP packet with the TTL field set to 2. The first router receives the packet and decreases the TTL field, but this time forwards the packet because it still has a TTL of 1. The second router decreases the TTL field to 0 and drops the packet, but still sends an ICMP host unreachable message back to the sending device. The sending device continues this process until the destination device receives the ICMP packet. An example of a traceroute between two devices is shown in Listing 10.3.

**Listing 10.3**  Traceroute between two devices.

```
Router#traceroute 172.16.19.2
Type escape sequence to abort.
Tracing the route to 172.16.19.2

1 172.16.14.254 100 msec 10 msec 4 msec
2 172.16.13.254 100 msec 10 msec 5 msec
3 172.16.63.250 110 msec 12 msec 8 msec
4 172.16.19.2 140 msec *
```

# Monitoring IP

The functioning of IP in a router can be monitored in many ways. Three of the best and most useful commands are the **show ip protocol, show ip interface,** and **show ip route** commands. Although these three commands do not provide a 100-percent comprehensive view of IP, they will provide enough information for the majority of inquiries.

## Show IP Interface

The **show ip interface** command contains a vast amount of information about any interface using the IP protocol. An example of the **show ip interface** command is illustrated in Listing 10.4. The first line of the command output distinguishes whether the interface has data-link connectivity and is administratively active. From an IP perspective, the command output illustrates that the IP interface is using an IP address of 172.16.52.10 with a 24-bit default mask. In addition, the maximum transmission unit (MTU) size of all IP packets has been set to 1,500 bytes. A wealth of information is provided by executing this command.

We encourage you to explore this command and identify key information that can be retrieved with it.

**Listing 10.4    The show ip interface command.**

```
Router#sh ip int e0
Ethernet0 is up, line protocol is up
 Internet address is 172.16.52.10/24
 Broadcast address is 255.255.255.255
 Address determined by non-volatile memory
 MTU is 1500 bytes
 Helper address is not set
 Directed broadcast forwarding is enabled
 Outgoing access list is not set
 Inbound access list is not set
 Proxy ARP is enabled
 Security level is default
 Split horizon is enabled
 ICMP redirects are always sent
 ICMP unreachables are always sent
 ICMP mask replies are never sent
 IP fast switching is enabled
 IP fast switching on the same interface is disabled
 IP multicast fast switching is enabled
 Router Discovery is disabled
 IP output packet accounting is disabled
 IP access violation accounting is disabled
 TCP/IP header compression is disabled
 Probe proxy name replies are disabled
 Gateway Discovery is disabled
 Policy routing is disabled
 Network address translation is disabled
```

# Show IP Protocol

The **show ip protocol** command is used to determine which protocols are performing routing for IP. The command identifies the IP networks that routing is being performed on and displays the protocol name, frequency of protocol updates, and gateways. An example of the **show ip protocol** command is provided in Listing 10.5.

**Listing 10.5    The show ip protocol command.**

```
Router#sh ip prot
Routing Protocol is "eigrp 33"
 Outgoing update filter list for all interfaces is not set
 Incoming update filter list for all interfaces is not set
```

```
Default networks flagged in outgoing updates
Default networks accepted from incoming updates
EIGRP metric weight K1=1, K2=0, K3=1, K4=0, K5=0
EIGRP maximum hop count 100
EIGRP maximum metric variance 1
Redistributing: static, eigrp 33
Automatic network summarization is in effect
Routing for Networks:
 172.16.25.0
Passive Interface(s):
 Serial0
 Serial1
 Serial2
 Serial3
 Serial4
 Serial5
 Serial6
 Serial7
Routing Information Sources:
 Gateway          Distance   Last Update
 Gateway          Distance   Last Update
 148.171.63.2     90         0:00:00
 148.171.63.3     90         0:00:02
 148.171.63.4     90         0:00:02
 148.171.63.11    90         0:00:02
 148.171.63.126   90         0:00:00
Distance: internal 90 external 170
```

## Show IP Route

The **show ip route** command displays the routing table that the router uses to forward packets. The command also displays how it learned of the route, such as static, connected, Interior Gateway Routing Protocol (IGRP), and so forth. This command can be used to understand why a packet follows a certain path when traveling between two devices. An example of the **show ip route** command is provided in Listing 10.6.

### Listing 10.6   The **show ip route** command.

```
Router#sh ip route
Codes: C - connected, S - static, I - IGRP, R - RIP, M - mobile,
   B - BGP
   D - EIGRP, EX - EIGRP external, O - OSPF,
   IA - OSPF inter area
   N1 - OSPF NSSA external type 1, N2 - OSPF NSSA
   external type 2
   E1 - OSPF external type 1, E2 - OSPF external type 2,
```

```
E - EGP
i - IS-IS, L1 - IS-IS level-1, L2 - IS-IS level-2,
* - candidate default
U - per-user static route, o - ODR
```

Gateway of last resort is 172.16.50.1 to network 0.0.0.0

```
C    172.16.50.0 is directly connected, Ethernet0
C    172.16.51.0 is directly connected, Ethernet1
S    140.71.0.0/16 [1/0] via 172.16.50.3
S*   0.0.0.0/0 [1/0] via 172.16.50.1
E    172.16.29.0/16 via 172.16.50.1
```

# Practice Questions

## Question 1

An IP address is listed below in dotted decimal format. Please indicate the corresponding binary value of this IP address.

112.14.12.8

○ a.  01100000.00110000.01101111.10110111

○ b.  0.11.0.11

○ c.  01110000.00001110.00001100.00001000

○ d.  01110000.00001110.11000000.00110011

Answer c is correct. The conversion of these binary bits yields a decimal value of 112.14.12.8. Answer a can be identified quickly as incorrect by noting that the fourth octet begins with a 1, but its value is not greater than 128. Answer b can be eliminated immediately, because it is not in the format of a binary IP address. Answer d can be judged to be incorrect by determining the decimal value of either the third or fourth octet. It is important to note that it was not necessary to convert each one of the answers above into decimal format. It is much quicker to eliminate the obviously wrong answers (like b) and then isolate reasons to remove other answers before converting any values.

## Question 2

How many of the following addresses are class B addresses? [Choose the two best answers]

❑ a.  130.15.130.254

❑ b.  10100000.11000000.11111111.11110000

❑ c.  11010001.11001100.10101010.00001111

❑ d.  127.0.0.0

Answers a and b are correct. The first octet of answer a has a decimal value of 130. The first octet of all class B addresses must be in the range of 128 through 191; therefore, this is a correct answer. Answer b's first two bits are 10, which is also a characteristic of a binary class B address. Answer c is incorrect because the value of its first two bits is 11. This is not a characteristic of a class B address. Finally, answer d has the decimal value of a loop-back address, not a class B address.

# Question 3

> How many of the following characteristics describe this IP address and subnet mask? [Choose the two best answers]
>
> 194.122.14.5 255.255.255.0
>
> ❏ a. It has a host ID of 14.5.
> ❏ b. It has a class C address.
> ❏ c. It has a network ID of 194.122.14.
> ❏ d. It is a class B address.
> ❏ e. It has a network ID of 194.122.

Answers b and c are correct. The IP address 194.122.14.5 is a class C address, so answer b is correct and answer d is incorrect. This can be determined by noting that the decimal value of the first octet is in the range of 192 and 223. Also, if this IP address were converted to binary, the three bits would have a value of 110. Class C addresses, by default, use the first three octets to represent the network ID and the last octet to represent the host ID; therefore, the network prefix is 194.122.14, and the host ID is 5. Answer a is incorrect because the default mask of a class C IP address is 24 bits, so the bits in the third octet are used for the network ID, not the host ID. Likewise, answer e is incorrect because it should include the third octet as part of the network ID.

# Question 4

> How many of the following characteristics describe this IP address? [Choose the two best answers]
>
> 10001000.00011000.00011000.00001111
>
> ❏ a. It is a class A address.
> ❏ b. It is a class B address.
> ❏ c. It has a host ID of 24.15.
> ❏ d. It has a host ID of 24.24.15.
> ❏ e. It has a host ID of 24.16.

Answers b and c are correct. The first step in solving this problem is to convert the IP address into decimal format. If you fail in this conversion, you are probably going to answer incorrectly. Therefore, make sure that you are proficient at the binary-to-decimal conversion. You could also determine that this was a class B address by looking at the two leading bits, 10. This tells you that only the last 16 bits need to be converted to determine the host ID. These types of techniques will save you valuable time on the exam. Answer a is incorrect because the address is not a class A address. Answer d is incorrect because the second octet would not be used to identify a host ID. Finally, answer e is incorrect because the dotted decimal value of the fourth octet is 15, not 16.

## Question 5

> Which of the following is not true when deciphering a subnet ID from an IP address and subnet mask?
>
> O a. If the subnet mask and the IP address both have values of 1, the resulting network ID bit is 1.
>
> O b. If the subnet mask has a value of 1 and the IP address has a value of 1, the resulting network ID bit is 0.
>
> O c. If the subnet mask has a value of 1 and the IP address has a value of 0, the resulting network ID bit is 0.
>
> O d. If the subnet mask has a value of 0, the resulting network ID bit is 0.

Answer b is correct. It specifies that a network ID bit of 0 is the result when comparing a subnet mask bit with a value of 1 and an IP address with a value of 1. This is not one of the rules used to decipher network IDs, so b is the correct answer. Answers a, c, and d are the three rules presented in the chapter for deciphering network IDs from an IP address with a subnet mask, so these answers are incorrect.

## Question 6

> A subnet mask can have a value of 0.255.255.0.
>
> O a. True
>
> O b. False

Answer b is correct. A subnet mask must use contiguous bits when masking an IP address, and the ones must be first. Therefore, the subnet mask of 0.255.255.0 (or 00000000 11111111 11111111 00000000) is invalid. If the beginning 0 were changed to a 255, the subnet mask would be valid.

# Question 7

Which of the following tools can be utilized to test IP connectivity between two devices? [Choose the three best answers]

☐ a. Ping

☐ b. Telnet

☐ c. Traceroute

☐ d. **show ip interface**

☐ e. **show ip protocol**

Answers a, b, and c are correct. These answers are all different tools mentioned in this chapter for testing IP connectivity between two devices. Answers d and e are used to monitor IP addresses and the functioning of IP within a local router.

# Question 8

Which of the following tools will identify the address of intermediate hops between two destinations?

○ a. Traceroute

○ b. Telnet

○ c. Ping

○ d. Rlogin

○ e. TCP

Answer a is correct. The **traceroute** command can be used to identify the address of every intermediate hop between two locations. Answer b is incorrect because the **telnet** command is used to obtain remote control of a destination device. Answer c is incorrect because the **ping** command only tells users if they have IP connectivity. Answer d is a command used for remote access on Unix machines. Finally, answer e is incorrect because TCP is a layer 4 protocol that is not used for testing IP connectivity.

## Question 9

Which of the following commands will show the MTU size used by the interface?

○ a. **show ip route**

○ b. **show ip interface**

○ c. **show ip protocol**

Answer b is correct. The **show ip interface** command displays a wealth of information regarding the interface specified, including the MTU size. Answers a and c are incorrect because neither of these commands displays information regarding the MTU size of an interface.

## Question 10

The default mask of a class A IP address is which of the following?

○ a. 255.0.0.255

○ b. 255.255.0.0

○ c. 255.0.0.0

○ d. 255.255.255.0

Answer c is correct. Class A addresses have a default mask of eight bits or 255.0.0.0. Answer a is incorrect because all default masks are contiguous bits. Answer b is the default mask of a class B IP address, not a class A IP address. Answer d is incorrect because it is the default mask of a class C IP address, not a class A IP address.

# Need to Know More?

McNutt, Shawn, Mark Poplar, Jason Waters, and David Stabenaw: *CCNA Routing and Switching Exam Prep.* The Coriolis Group, Scottsdale, AZ, 2000. ISBN 1-57610-440-0. This book is a great complement to the CCNA Cram book. Chapter 7 covers IP addressing and subnetting.

Chappell, Laura. *Introduction to Cisco Router Configuration.* Macmillan Publishing Company, Indianapolis, IN, 1998. ISBN 0-7645-3186-7. Cover to cover, this book is packed with great information.

Lammle, Todd, Donald Porter, and James Chellis. *CCNA Cisco Certified Network Associate.* Sybex Network Press, Alameda, CA, 1999. ISBN 0-7821-2381-3. Chapter 4 covers IP addressing.

Stevens, W. Richard. *TCP/IP Illustrated, Volume 1.* Addison-Wesley Professional Computing Series, Reading, MA, 1996. ISBN 0-201-63346-9. A great resource for TCP/IP information.

Syngress Media, with Richard D. Hornbaker, CCIE. *Cisco Certified Network Associate Study Guide.* Osborne/McGraw-Hill, Berkeley, CA, 1998. ISBN 0-07-882487-7. Chapter 2 covers IP addressing.

Tittel, Ed, Kurt Hudson, and J. Michael Stewart. *TCP/IP Exam Cram.* The Coriolis Group, Inc., Scottsdale, AZ, 1997. ISBN 1-57610-195-9. This book is packed with great information on TCP/IP.

**http://www.cisco.com/univercd/cc/td/doc/cisintwk/ito_doc/ip.htm** on Cisco's Web site provides some excellent information regarding IP.

# Routing Protocols

**Terms you'll need to understand:**

✓ Route table
✓ Metric
✓ Routing protocol
✓ Convergence
✓ Routing loop
✓ Distance vector

✓ Link state
✓ Hop count
✓ Counting to infinity
✓ Split horizon
✓ Route poisoning
✓ Hold-down timers

**Techniques you'll need to master:**

✓ Understanding the path determination function of a router

✓ Understanding the switching function of a router

✓ Explaining the goals of routing protocols

✓ Listing the types of routing protocols

✓ Understanding the problems distance vector and link state routing protocols encounter when dealing with network topology changes

✓ Describing techniques to increase the stability of distance vector and link state routing protocols

✓ Configuring a router with the Routing Information Protocol (RIP)

✓ Configuring a router with the Interior Gateway Routing Protocol (IGRP)

✓ Explaining the services of separate and integrated multiprotocol routing

This chapter presents information about routing protocols. Because the path determination and switching functions of a router rely on routing protocols, we'll discuss the goals and types of routing algorithms and protocols. We'll review the strengths and weaknesses of two popular routing algorithms and highlight techniques to mitigate the weaknesses. In addition, we'll list router configuration commands to enable routing protocols.

# Routing Activities

Routing occurs within the network layer (layer 3) of the Open Systems Interconnect (OSI) model. By sending packets from source network to destination network, the network layer gives its best effort in the delivery of end-to-end services. Getting packets to their next hop requires a router to perform two basic activities: path determination and packet switching.

*Path determination* involves reviewing all available paths to a destination network and choosing the optimal route on which to send a packet. Network topology information used to determine optimal routes is collected and stored in *route tables*, which contain information such as the destination network, the next hop, and an associated *metric* (or the cost of sending packets to that next hop).

*Packet switching* involves changing a packet's physical destination address to that of the next hop; however, the packet's destination logical address remains constant during the packet switching process. Review Chapter 4 for more specific examples of path determination and packet switching.

# Routing Algorithms and Protocols

Routers choose the optimal or best route based on the available route information. A *routing algorithm* aids in the collection of route information and the determination of the best path. These algorithms may vary in several aspects. They may differ based on the goals they were designed to achieve with an internetwork. In addition, several types of routing algorithms exist to suit specific internetwork requirements. The metrics used by different routing algorithms also vary.

A *routing protocol* is a standard method of implementing a particular routing algorithm. For the purpose of our discussions, routing protocols mean the routing algorithm or the protocol that implements it.

## Goals of Routing Protocols

As the needs of internetworks changed, new routing protocols were created to meet those needs and goals. For example, a routing protocol that functioned well in a small internetwork five years ago may experience problems in the large internetworks in use today.

Routing protocols have been designed to meet one or more of the following design goals:

➤ Flexibility

➤ Optimality

➤ Rapid convergence

➤ Robustness

➤ Simplicity

## Flexibility

A routing protocol should be flexible. It should be able to adapt quickly to its ever-changing network environment. If a network segment goes down, a flexible routing protocol is able to detect that event and determine the next best path to use while the segment is down. When the network segment becomes available, the routing protocol should also update its route table to reflect that event. Flexible routing protocols can also adapt to changes in network variables, such as network bandwidth and delay.

## Optimality

The optimality of a routing protocol gauges its ability to choose the best route correctly. The metrics used by the protocol affect its optimality. For example, one protocol may heavily weight number of hops as its metric, whereas another may use a combination of number of hops and network delay.

## Rapid Convergence

*Convergence* occurs when all routers within an internetwork agree on the optimal routes through the internetwork. Network events like routes going down or becoming available cause routers to recalculate optimal paths and distribute update messages about network routes. These messages permeate the entire network until all routes converge and agree on optimal routes. Slow convergence of the routing protocol can cause problems such as a routing loop.

A *routing loop* occurs when two or more routers have not yet converged and are broadcasting their inaccurate route tables. In addition, they are most likely still switching packets based on their inaccurate route tables. Figure 11.1 illustrates this case. An event has just occurred within the network—router A lost its path to network 5. While router A is updating its route table, it receives an update from router B that says network 5 is one hop away.

Router A increases the counter by one and adds this new information to its route tables. In turn, router A broadcasts its updated route table to router C, which updates its table and broadcasts the erroneous information to router D. Router D

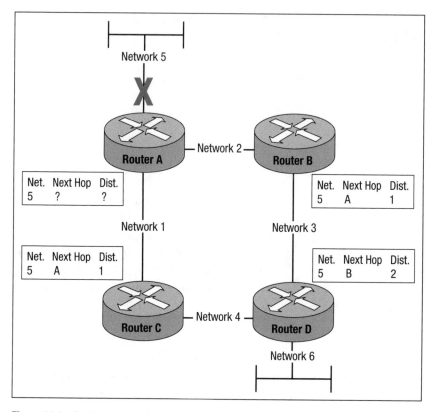

**Figure 11.1** Routing loop.

updates its table and propagates the misinformation to router B. Figure 11.2 illustrates this situation.

This cycle will continue ad infinitum. If packets traversing the network are destined for network 5, they will loop between router A and router B until the packet becomes too old and is discarded.

## Robustness

Robust and stable routing protocols perform correctly during unusual and unpredictable network events. High utilization, hardware failures, or incorrect configurations can create significant problems within a network. A robust routing protocol is stable during a variety of network situations.

## Simplicity

The simplicity of a routing protocol refers to its ability to operate efficiently. Because routing protocols collect and store route information, the protocol is competing for the router's limited physical resources. A routing protocol must perform its functions with minimal administrative overhead.

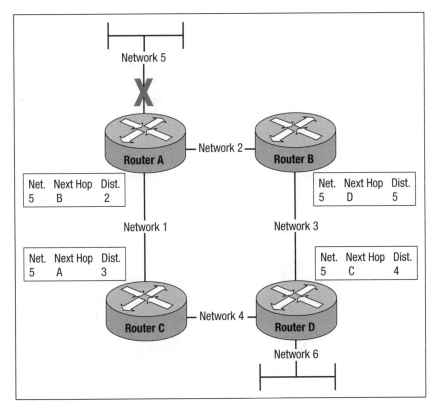

**Figure 11.2**    Routing loop updated.

# Types of Routing Protocols

Routing protocols can also be categorized by type. The type of routing protocol deployed within an internetwork should be based on the organizational requirements.

Types of routing protocols include:

➤ Static or dynamic

➤ Single-path or multipath

➤ Flat or hierarchical

➤ Interior or exterior

➤ Distance vector or link state

## Static or Dynamic

A network administrator configures static routes manually. When defining a *static route*, the administrator configures the destination network, next hop, and appropriate metrics. The route does not change until the network administrator changes it. Static routes function well in environments where the network is simple and network traffic is predictable.

*Dynamic routes* adjust to changes within the internetwork environment automatically. When network changes occur, routers begin to converge by recalculating routes and distributing route updates. The route update messages permeate the network, which causes more routers to recalculate their routes. This route update process continues until all routers have converged.

Occasionally, static routes augment dynamic routes. In a dynamically routed environment, a router discards a packet if the destination network does not appear in the route table. However, a static route can be configured to handle this situation. A *default route* (that points to a router) can be established to receive and attempt to process all packets for which no route appears in the routing table.

## Single-Path or Multipath

When calculating the optimal path for a particular network, some routing protocols simply choose the best *single-path* to a destination network. Others allow more than one optimal path if the paths have equal metric values. A *multipath protocol* enables traffic multiplexing using the multiple paths and offers additional advantages over single-path protocols, such as reliability.

## Flat or Hierarchical

A routing environment is considered *flat* if all routers are peers to each other. Routers that use a flat routing protocol may communicate with any other router in the network as directly as possible. Like static routing, a flat routing protocol functions well in simple and predictable network environments.

Alternatively, a *hierarchical* routing environment contains several routers that compose a backbone. Most traffic from non-backbone routers usually traverses the backbone routers (or at least travels to the backbone) in order to reach another non-backbone router. Within a hierarchical routing environment, autonomous systems (sometimes referred to as *domains* or *areas*) can be established. Being part of the same autonomous system enables a group of routers to share network topology information with each other, but that same information is not shared outside the group. Although several layers or tiers may exist within the hierarchy, the routers at the highest level comprise the backbone. Typically, the network backbone comprises its own autonomous system or domain.

## Interior or Exterior

An *interior routing* protocol operates within a single autonomous system or domain. These protocols are typically implemented within an organization's private network. Routers that are running interior routing protocols are considered *intradomain routers*; they only need to know about other routers within their domain. Conversely, an *exterior routing* protocol conveys routing information between domains. Exterior routing protocols are in use within the Internet. *Interdomain routers* need to know how to route traffic between autonomous systems and can protect against errors or problems with one domain from affecting another.

### Distance Vector or Link State

*Distance vector* protocols require each router to send all or a large part of its route table to its neighboring routers. *Link state* protocols require each router to send the state of its own interfaces to every router in the internetwork. Distance vector protocols are simple and straightforward, but they converge slowly, which can cause routing loops. Link state protocols converge quickly, but they require more of the router's central processing unit (CPU) and memory resources. Distance vector and link state routing protocols are widely used. They will be explored in more detail later in the chapter.

Each routed protocol can be implemented in one or more routing protocols. The routing protocols (or standard set of rules) actually enable the router to determine the best path. Common routing protocols include:

➤ RIP

➤ IGRP

➤ Open Shortest Path First (OSPF)

➤ Enhanced Interior Gateway Routing Protocol (EIGRP)

➤ Border Gateway Protocol (BGP)

➤ Exterior Gateway Protocol (EGP)

BGP and EGP are both exterior routing protocols and differ significantly from their interior counterparts. Table 11.1 lists the common interior routing protocols and their characteristics.

*Note: IGRP and EIGRP are Cisco proprietary routing protocols. They are only supported on Cisco routers.*

## Routing Metrics

Routing protocols use many different metrics to determine the optimal route. These variables can be used individually or in combination with one another to create the metric defined within a given routing protocol.

| Table 11.1 | Interior routing protocols. | | | | |
|---|---|---|---|---|---|
| Routing Protocol | Static or Dynamic | Single-Path or Multipath | Flat or Hierarchical | Interior or Exterior | Distance Vector or Link State |
| RIP | Dynamic | Single-path | Flat | Interior | Distance vector |
| IGRP | Dynamic | Multipath | Flat | Interior | Distance vector |
| OSPF | Dynamic | Multipath | Hierarchical | Interior | Link state |
| EIGRP | Dynamic | Multipath | Flat | Interior | Advanced distance vector |

Metrics used in routing protocols include:

➤ Bandwidth

➤ Delay

➤ Load

➤ Path length

➤ Reliability

## Bandwidth

The available capacity of a network link is known as its *bandwidth*. Typically, a 10Mbps Ethernet link is preferable to a 56Kb Frame Relay link. However, if other metrics such as delay are considered, the Ethernet link may not be the optimal path.

## Delay

*Network delay* refers to the amount of time necessary to move a packet through the internetwork from source to destination. Delay is a conglomeration of several other variables, including physical distance between source and destination, bandwidth and congestion of intermediate links, and port queues of intermediate routers.

## Load

*Load* is an indication of how busy a network resource is. CPU utilization and packets processed per second are two valuable factors when calculating the load.

## Path Length

In some routing protocols, *path length* refers to the sum of the costs of each link traversed up to the destination network. Other routing protocols refer to path length as the *hop count*, which is the number of passes through a router that a packet makes on its way to the destination network.

### Reliability

This metric allows the network administrator to assign a numeric value arbitrarily to indicate a reliability factor for the link. Some network links go down more than others do; some are easily repaired and become available relatively quickly. The reliability metric is simply a method used to capture an administrator's experience with a given network link.

A routed protocol such as the Internet Protocol (IP) or IPX is concerned with the movement of user traffic. A routing protocol such as RIP or OSPF is concerned with maintaining route tables.

# Distance Vector vs. Link State

This section highlights the similarities and differences between two types of widely used routing protocols: distance vector and link state.

## Distance Vector Overview

A distance vector routing protocol sends all or part of its route table across the network, but only to its neighbors. The route table contains the distance and direction to any network within its domain. Figure 11.3 provides an overview of the distance vector process.

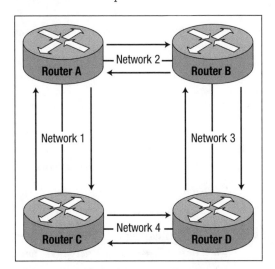

**Figure 11.3**   Distance vector process overview.

Periodically, router A broadcasts its entire route table to its neighbors, router B and router C. Router B updates the route information it received by increasing the metric value, which is usually the hop count, by one. Router B then compares the route information it just received and updated with the existing route information from its route table. Router B replaces existing route information with an updated entry only if the updated route information has a lower calculated metric. Router B then broadcasts its route table to its direct neighbors, router D and router A. This process occurs regularly and in all directions for all directly connected neighbors. Although this process enables routers to accumulate network distance information, the routers do not know the network's exact topology.

*Note: The default value for RIP updates to occur is every 30 seconds.*

## Link State Overview

A *link state* routing protocol (sometimes referred to as *shortest path first*) sends only the state of its own network links across the network, but it sends this information to every router within its domain. This process enables routers to learn and maintain full knowledge of the network's exact topology and how it is interconnected. Figure 11.4 provides an overview of the link state process.

Link state routing protocols rely on several components to acquire and maintain knowledge of the network:

➤ Router C broadcasts and receives link state packets to and from other routers via the network. Link state packets contain the status of a router's links or network interfaces.

➤ Router C builds a topology database of the network.

➤ Router C runs a Shortest Path First (SPF) algorithm against the database and generates an SPF tree of the network with router C as the root of the tree.

➤ Router C populates its route table with optimal paths and ports to transmit data through to reach each network.

## Network Discovery

When a router starts up, it must undergo a *network discovery* process. This process enables the router to begin communicating with other routers on the network.

Figure 11.5 illustrates the network discovery process for distance vector protocols. Router A has just started up and is configured to run a distance vector.

Router A begins the discovery process by identifying its neighbor, router B. Router A begins populating its route table with its directly connected networks, networks 1 and 2, which receive a metric of 0. It passes its route table to router B and

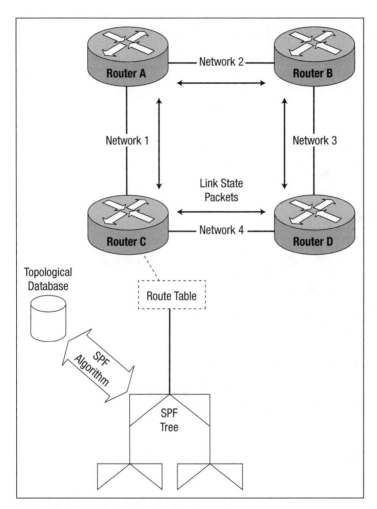

**Figure 11.4**  Link state process overview.

receives router B's entire route table. Router A increases the distances of each entry by one hop. After the distances have been updated, router A will already have better routes to networks 1 and 2, but not network 3. Router A increases the distance to network 3 by one hop and stores it in its route table.

The network discovery process for link state protocols is similar to that of distance vector protocols. Instead of route tables, routers exchange link state packets and use that information to build their topology databases, SPF trees, and route tables. Refer to Figure 11.4 for an example of the link state discovery process.

Regardless of whether a router uses a distance vector or link state routing protocol, the router dynamically discovers its network environment. It can then use its route table to perform the packet-switching function.

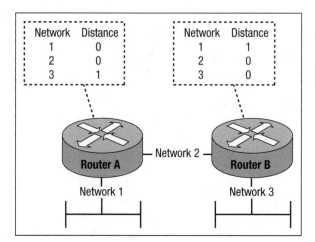

Network 1

Network 3

**Figure 11.5** Distance vector network discovery.

# Topology Changes

After the router has discovered the network, it must also keep up with network topology changes. Depending on the protocol used, a router transmits route information periodically or when a network event occurs. Routers detect changes in the network topology via these updates.

Most distance vector protocols handle topology changes through regularly scheduled updates. After a specified interval, a router broadcasts its route table to its neighbor. Route recalculation occurs if necessary and updates in the network topology are broadcast. The route distribution timers are not synchronized across routers.

Link state protocols rely on network events to address topology changes. If a router detects a network event (such as one of its neighbors is no longer reachable or a new neighbor appears), it triggers an update. The router broadcasts the state of its links to all other routers within the domain. Upon receiving the update, other routers update their topology database and broadcast the state of their links also. When all updates have been received, each router updates its SPF tree and route tables accordingly. At this point, the network has converged. Event-triggered updates have a ripple effect within a network.

# Distance Vector Problems

The fact that route updates with a distance vector protocol occur after a specified interval can become problematic. With RIP, route updates are broadcast every 30 seconds by default. As a result, distance vector protocols converge slowly. Routing loops and the problems they create were discussed previously in this chapter. Routing loops create a condition know as *counting to infinity*, where the distance metric is continually increased because the network has not fully converged. Refer to Figures 11.1 and 11.2 for examples of a routing loop and counting to infinity.

## Distance Vector Remedies

One technique to remedy a count-to-infinity situation involves a maximum hop count. Although this count will not prevent a routing loop, it does reduce the time that the routing loop exists. A maximum hop count (represented in Figure 11.6), when reached, forces a router to mark a network unreachable, rather than increase the distance metric.

Routing loops also occur when information that contradicts information sent previously is broadcast back to a router. Router A sends information about network 5 to router B. *Split horizon* prevents a router from sending information it received about a network back to the neighbor that originally sent the information. For example, split horizon prohibits router B and router C from sending any information about network 5 back to router A. Refer to Figure 11.7 as an example.

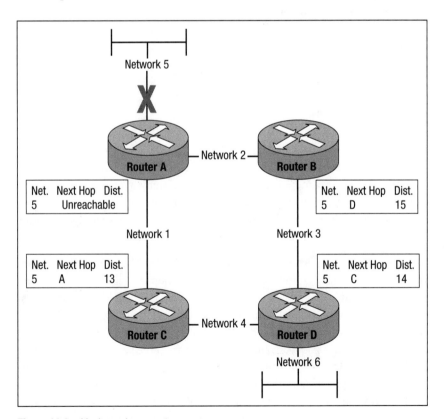

**Figure 11.6**   Maximum hop count.

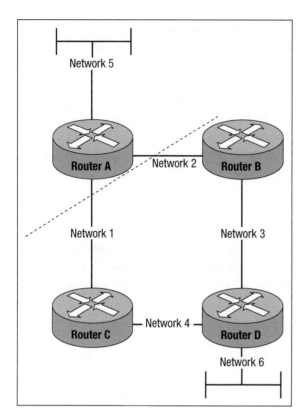

**Figure 11.7** Split horizon.

*Route poisoning* occurs when a router detects that a network is down and immediately marks it as unreachable. This route update is broadcast throughout the network. While the other routers slowly converge, the router maintains this poisoned route in its route table and ignores updates from other routers about better routes to the network. The poisoned route is removed after several update cycles. Route poisoning works well with another technique called *hold-down timers*.

A *hold-down timer* indicates that no updates to a particular route should be accepted until the timer expires. A hold-down condition is triggered when a router receives an update from its neighbor indicating that a reachable network has just gone down. The router marks the network as unreachable and starts its hold-down timer. While the timer is active, updates from any other router are ignored. Updates about the unreachable network are only accepted from the neighboring router that initially indicated the unreachable network while the timer is active. If the neighboring router indicates that the network is reachable again, the router stops the hold-down timer and updates its route table. When the hold-down timer expires, the router marks the network reachable and receives updates from any router.

The following techniques help to stabilize distance vector protocols:

➤ Maximum hop count

➤ Split horizon

➤ Route poisoning

➤ Hold-down timers

# Link State Problems

Because link state routing protocols have knowledge of the entire network and converge quickly, they do not suffer from the same problems as distance vector protocols. One problem that affects link state protocols is the significant memory and processor resources required from the router itself when acquiring and maintaining full knowledge of large networks. As updates move through the network, each router must receive the update, recalculate its information, and send its own link information. Of course, this type of overhead affects the ability of the router to move user data packets through the network.

A second shortcoming of link state protocols is the amount of network bandwidth that can be consumed while the network converges. Routers flood updates about the state of their links to every other router in the network, so the amount of bandwidth consumed is significant. As routers collect link information from each other, the amount of bandwidth available for end-user communications is reduced. This high level of bandwidth utilization typically occurs on initialization of the network or when several routers start up simultaneously.

Additional problems can occur during the link state update process itself. It is imperative that each router receives all of the packets in a timely manner and that the updates are synchronized. For example, if one part of the network receives route information before another part, convergence may take longer, or SPF trees and route tables may store inaccurate information. Additionally, as routers attempt to move link state packets through the network, they may be doing so without fully constructed SPF trees or route tables.

The following problems may occur within networks using link state protocols:

➤ Router resource usage

➤ Network bandwidth consumption

➤ Update synchronization

# Link State Remedies

One remedy for link state problems involves minimizing the resources required to build and maintain route tables. The time between periodic updates can be lengthened to reduce the processing resources required. Also, routers can be identified to serve as border routers. The border routers can then exchange route summaries with other border routers and each core router to reduce the bandwidth consumed during the update process and to isolate update processes to hierarchical areas. The border router then passes updates to the routers within its area.

Another technique involves coordinating link state updates. Time stamps and sequence numbers can be attached to the link state packet. Routers then realize when they receive inaccurate or old link state packets.

 The following techniques help to stabilize link state protocols:

➤ Minimize router resource usage by lengthening update frequency or exchanging route summaries.

➤ Coordinate updates with time stamps or sequence numbers.

Both distance vector and link state routing protocols have demonstrated their worth over time. Each has advantages that may suit a particular network design perfectly. Several factors must be considered when choosing a routing protocol, including business policies and operational issues. Table 11.2 provides a quick comparison of distance vector and link state routing protocols.

# Routing Protocol Configuration and Review

This section highlights the basic router commands necessary to add the RIP and IGRP to a router configuration.

## RIP

Table 11.3 lists the router configuration commands necessary to enable RIP on a router.

| Table 11.2 Distance vector versus link state routing protocols. | |
| --- | --- |
| **Distance Vector** | **Link State** |
| Sees the network from its neighbor's perspective | Sees the entire network from its own perspective |
| Distance metrics accumulate from router to router | Calculates shortest path to other routers |
| Route updates occur periodically | Route updates are event-triggered |
| Convergence is slow | Convergence is fast |
| Broadcasts entire route table to neighbors | Broadcasts link status information to all other routers |

**Table 11.3  RIP configuration commands.**

| Task | Router Prompt | Command Syntax |
|---|---|---|
| Enter global configuration mode | RouterA# | **configure terminal** |
| Enter RIP configuration mode | RouterA (config)# | **router rip** |
| Configure network 172.16.0.0 to be advertised | RouterA (config-router)# | **network 172.16.0.0** |
| Exit configuration mode | RouterA (config-router)# | <CTRL>Z |

The **show IP protocol** command displays detailed information about each IP routing protocol that has been configured on the router.

The following output displays the results of the **show IP protocol** command after RIP has been configured.

**Listing 11.1  RIP configuration display.**

```
RouterA#
RouterA#show ip protocol <Return>
Routing Protocol is "rip"
  Sending updates every 30 seconds, next due in 2 seconds
  Invalid after 180 seconds, hold down 180, flushed after 240
  Outgoing update filter list for all interfaces is not set
  Incoming update filter list for all interfaces is not set
  Redistributing: rip
  Default version control: send version 1, receive any version
    Interface       Send  Recv   Key-chain
    Ethernet0       1     1      2
    Loopback0       1     1      2
    Serial0         1     1      2
  Routing for Networks:
    172.16.0.0
  Routing Information Sources:
    Gateway         Distance     Last Update
    172.16.24.252       120      00:00:12
  Distance: (default is 120)

RouterA#
```

*Note: By default, RIP sends updates every 30 seconds. Also, the RIP hold-down timer is set to 180 seconds, and a neighbor router has an IP address of 172.16.24.252.*

| Table 11.4 IGRP configuration commands. | | |
|---|---|---|
| **Task** | **Router Prompt** | **Command Syntax** |
| Enter global configuration mode | RouterA # | **configure terminal** |
| Enter IGRP routing protocol configuration mode for autonomous system 1 | RouterA (config)# | **router igrp 1** |
| Configure network 172.16.0.0 to be advertised | RouterA (config-router)# | **network 172.16.0.0** |
| Exit configuration mode | RouterA (config-router)# | <CTRL>Z |

# IGRP

Table 11.4 lists the router configuration commands necessary to enable IGRP on a router.

The following output displays the results of the **show IP protocol** command after IGRP has been configured.

### Listing 11.2 IGRP configuration display.

```
RouterA#
RouterA#show ip protocol <Return>
Routing Protocol is "igrp 1"
  Sending updates every 90 seconds, next due in 7 seconds
  Invalid after 270 seconds, hold down 280, flushed after 630
  Outgoing update filter list for all interfaces is not set
  Incoming update filter list for all interfaces is not set
  Default networks flagged in outgoing updates
  Default networks accepted from incoming updates
  IGRP metric weight K1=1, K2=0, K3=1, K4=0, K5=0
  IGRP maximum hopcount 100
  IGRP maximum metric variance 1
  Redistributing: igrp 1
  Routing for Networks:
    172.16.0.0
  Routing Information Sources:
    Gateway          Distance      Last Update
    172.16.24.252        100       00:00:15
  Distance: (default is 100)
RouterA#
```

*Note: By default, IGRP sends updates every 90 seconds. Also, the IGRP maximum hop count is set to 100, and a neighbor router has an IP address of 172.16.24.252.*

# Advanced Distance Vector Protocol

Both distance vector and link state routing protocols have performed well under a variety of network conditions. Based on the specific needs of an organization, one may be more preferable than the other; however, each type has shortcomings. An *advanced distance vector protocol* combines the strengths of distance vector and link state protocols. EIGRP is Cisco's proprietary advanced distance vector protocol.

Like distance vector protocols, advanced distance vector protocols use distance metrics, but the metrics are more accurate than simple hop counts for determining the best path. In the event that distance metrics are equal for multiple best paths, routers supporting an advanced distance vector protocol add both or all routes to its route table and load balance traffic across those routes. But unlike distance vector protocols, an advanced distance vector protocol does not periodically send route updates across the network. It relies on topology changes to trigger when route updates are to be sent.

Like link state protocols, an advanced distance vector protocol converges quickly. It is also much more efficient in its use of a router's resources and network bandwidth when sending route updates than link state protocols.

In addition to resolving some of the shortcomings of distance vector and link state protocols, advanced distance vector protocols support integrated routing.

## Integrated Multiprotocol Routing

Although a router can support multiple routing and routed protocols, it keeps those protocols isolated. The protocols have no knowledge of or impact on each other. This concept is referred to as *ships-in-the-night routing*. *Integrated multiprotocol routing* permits these different protocols to have knowledge of each other and allows different protocols to share resources. Rather than using several routing protocols to support multiple routed protocols, integrated routing enables a network administrator to use a single routing protocol to support multiple routed protocols.

Benefits of integrated routing include:

➤ Carrying route updates that can be used by multiple routing protocols

➤ Minimizing the use of network and router resources

➤ Maintaining separate route tables for each routing protocol

➤ Simplifying network administration

➤ Supporting path selection and packet switching for multiple routed protocols

| Table 11.5 EIGRP configuration commands. | | |
|---|---|---|
| **Task** | **Router Prompt** | **Command Syntax** |
| Enter global configuration mode | RouterA# | **configure terminal** |
| Enter EIGRP routing protocol configuration mode for autonomous system 1 | RouterA (config)# | **router eigrp 1** |
| Configure network 172.16.0.0 to be advertised | RouterA (config-router)# | **172.16.0.0** |
| Exit configuration mode | RouterA (config-router)# | <CTRL>Z |

EIGRP also supports integrated routing, and IP, Novell IPX, and AppleTalk protocols. Table 11.5 lists the router configuration commands necessary to enable EIGRP on a router.

The following output displays the results of the **show IP protocol** command after EIGRP has been configured.

**Listing 11.3** EIGRP configuration display.

```
RouterA#
RouterA#show ip protocol <Return>
Routing Protocol is "eigrp 1"
  Outgoing update filter list for all interfaces is not set
  Incoming update filter list for all interfaces is not set
  Default networks flagged in outgoing updates
  Default networks accepted from incoming updates
  EIGRP metric weight K1=1, K2=0, K3=1, K4=0, K5=0
  EIGRP maximum hopcount 100
  EIGRP maximum metric variance 1
  Redistributing: igrp 1, eigrp 1
  Automatic network summarization is in effect
  Routing for Networks:
    172.16.0.0
  Routing Information Sources:
    Gateway         Distance      Last Update
    172.16.24.252        90       0:00:06
  Distance: internal 90 external 170
RouterA#
```

*Note: EIGRP does not periodically send updates. Also, the EIGRP maximum hop count is set to 100 by default, and a neighbor router has an IP address of 172.16.24.252.*

# Practice Questions

## Question 1

> Which of the following are basic functions of a router? [Choose the two best answers]
>
> ❑ a. Packet switching
>
> ❑ b. Packet filtering
>
> ❑ c. Path determination
>
> ❑ d. Rapid convergence

Answers a and c are correct. Routers packet switch when they have determined the best path. Path determination is the process of choosing the best network path from all available network paths. Packet filtering is a technique used to control inbound and/or outbound packets to or from a router; therefore, answer b is incorrect. Rapid convergence is a design goal of some routing protocols; therefore, answer d is incorrect.

## Question 2

> Network routing information distributed among routers is stored in which of the following?
>
> ○ a. Flash memory
>
> ○ b. Route table
>
> ○ c. Metric table
>
> ○ d. NVRAM

Answer b is correct. Route tables contain information about destination networks and the next hop along the optimal path to get there. Flash memory contains the operating system images used by the router; therefore, answer a is incorrect. Metric information is contained within a router's route table; therefore, answer c is incorrect. NVRAM contains the router's active configuration files; therefore, answer d is incorrect.

# Question 3

Which of the following is not an interior routing protocol?

○ a. RIP

○ b. IGRP

○ c. OSPF

○ d. BGP

Answer d is correct. BGP is designed to communicate route information between autonomous systems; therefore, it is an exterior routing protocol. RIP, IGRP, and OSPF are routing protocols used to communicate route information within an autonomous system; therefore, answers a, b, and c are incorrect.

# Question 4

Which of the following routing protocols communicates route information by sending the state of its links to all routers in its domain?

○ a. BGP

○ b. RIP

○ c. IGRP

○ d. OSPF

Answer d is correct. OSPF is a link state routing protocol that passes the state of its links to all routers within its domain. BGP is an exterior routing protocol that communicates reachability information between domains; therefore, answer a is incorrect. RIP and IGRP are distance vector protocols that send all or part of their route tables to their neighbors; therefore, answers b and c are incorrect.

## Question 5

Which of the following conditions is a problem experienced by distance vector routing protocols?

○ a. Split horizon

○ b. Route poisoning

○ c. Counting to infinity

○ d. Maximum hop count

○ e. Hold-down timers

Answer c is correct. Counting to infinity can result from the slow convergence inherent with distance vector protocols. Split horizon, route poison, maximum hop count, and hold-down timers are techniques used to reduce the occurrence and impact of the counting-to-infinity situation; therefore, answers a, b, d, and e are incorrect.

## Question 6

What router command will display the routing protocol settings (such as timers and neighbors) configured on a router?

○ a. **show protocol**

○ b. **show routing protocol**

○ c. **show ip protocol**

○ d. **show running-config**

Answer c is correct. The **show ip protocol** command displays all routing protocols that are active on the router. In addition, it displays other values such as timers, neighbors, and when the next update will be sent. The **show protocol** command displays information about routed protocols such as IP and IPX; therefore, answer a is incorrect. The **show routing protocol** command is invalid; therefore, answer b is incorrect. The **show running-config** command displays some routing protocol information, such as the networks that are being advertised to other routers; therefore, answer d is incorrect.

# Question 7

> Which techniques help to mitigate the shortcomings of link state protocols?
> [Choose the two best answers]
>
> ❑ a.  Maximum hop count
>
> ❑ b.  Minimize router resource usage
>
> ❑ c.  Coordinate updates
>
> ❑ d.  Route poisoning

Answers b and c are correct. Lengthening the update frequency or exchanging router summaries at specific border routers helps to minimize router resource usage; therefore, answer b is correct. Also, attaching time stamps or sequence numbers on link state packets helps to coordinate update information between routers; therefore, answer c is correct. A maximum hop count and route poisoning address problems with distance vector protocols; therefore, answers a and d are incorrect.

# Question 8

> Which router commands, if executed from the global configuration prompt, enable RIP routing for network 172.16.0.0?
>
> ○ a.  **router rip 1** and **network 172.16.0.0**
>
> ○ b.  **router rip all**
>
> ○ c.  **router rip** and **network 172.16.0.0**
>
> ○ d.  **network 172.16.0.0**

Answer c is correct. The **router rip** command enables RIP routing and the **network 172.16.0.0** command enables the router to advertise that network to other routers. Answers a and b are incorrect because the **router rip** command requires no additional parameters. Answer d is incorrect because you must first enter routing protocol configuration mode before configuring a network to be advertised.

# Question 9

Which router commands, if executed from the global configuration prompt, enable IGRP routing for autonomous system 1 and network 172.16.0.0?

○ a.  **router igrp 1** and **network 172.16.0.0**

○ b.  **router igrp 172.16.0.0**

○ c.  **router igrp** and **network 172.16.0.0**

○ d.  **network 172.16.0.0**

Answer a is correct. The **router igrp 1** command enables IGRP routing for autonomous system 1, and the **network 172.16.0.0** command enables the router to advertise that network to other routers. The **router igrp** command requires an autonomous system to be specified, so answers b and c are incorrect. Answer d is incorrect because you must first enter routing protocol configuration mode before configuring a network to be advertised.

# Question 10

Which of the following statements is a benefit of integrated routing?

○ a.  Supporting path selection and packet switching for multiple routed protocols

○ b.  Carrying route updates that can be used by multiple routing protocols

○ c.  Minimizing the use of network and router resources

○ d.  Maintaining separate route tables for each routing protocol

○ e.  All of the above

Answer e is correct. All of the answers are benefits of integrated routing. Simplifying network administration and replacing the native routing algorithm are also benefits of integrated routing.

## Question 11

Which of the following conditions are problems experienced by link state routing protocols? [Choose the three best answers]

❑ a. Split horizon

❑ b. High router resource usage

❑ c. High network bandwidth consumption

❑ d. Unsynchronized updates

❑ e. Hold-down timers

Answers b, c, and d are correct. Problems with high router resource usage and high network bandwidth can occur during convergence as link state packets flood the network. If link state packet updates are not synchronized, inaccurate SPF trees and route tables may result, and convergence may take longer. Split horizon and hold-down timers are techniques used to reduce problems in distance vector routing protocols; therefore, answers a and e are incorrect.

# Need to Know More?

 McNut, Shawn, Mark Poplar, Jason Waters, and David Stabenaw: *CCNA Routing and Switching Exam Prep*. The Coriolis Group, Scottsdale, AZ, 2000. ISBN 1-57610-440-0. This book is a great complement to the CCNA Cram book.

 Moy, John T. *OSPF: Anatomy of an Internet Routing Protocol*. Addison-Wesley Publishing Company, Reading, MA, 1998. ISBN 0-20163-472-4. This book gives detailed information about various Internet routing protocols, then focuses specifically on OSPF.

 Parkhurst, William R. *Cisco Router OSPF: Design and Implementation Guide*. McGraw-Hill, New York, NY, 1998. ISBN 0-07048-626-3. This book reviews routing protocol configuration commands and also discusses advanced topics such as route redistribution between routing protocols.

 **www.cisco.com/public.technotes/tech_protocol.shtml**, the official Cisco documentation Web site, discusses the routing protocol Web pages for IGRP/EIGRP and OSPF. You can also review more information about exterior routing protocols such as BGP and EGP.

 **www.cis.ohio-state.edu/hypertext/information/rfc.html**, the computer and information science Web site at Ohio State University, provides information about Internet Request for Comments (RFC) documents. For detailed information about a distance vector routing protocol, look up RFC 1058, which describes RIP. RFCs 1388 and 1723 provide updated information about RIP. For detailed information about a link state routing protocol, review RFC 1131, which lists the OSPF specification. RFC 1247 provides updated information about OSPF.

# Internet Package Exchange (IPX)

## Terms you'll need to understand:

- ✓ NetWare
- ✓ Internet Packet Exchange (IPX)
- ✓ Network Operating System (NOS)
- ✓ Network Basic Input/Output System (NetBIOS)
- ✓ NetWare shell
- ✓ NetWare Core Protocol (NCP)
- ✓ Sequence Packet Exchange (SPX)
- ✓ Routing Information Protocol (RIP)
- ✓ Network interface card (NIC)
- ✓ Encapsulation
- ✓ Ticks
- ✓ Hop count
- ✓ NetWare Link State Protocol (NLSP)
- ✓ Service Advertisement Protocol (SAP)

## Techniques you'll need to master:

- ✓ Describing the Novell IPX protocol stack
- ✓ Listing key features and characteristics of Novell IPX
- ✓ Understanding IPX addressing
- ✓ Describing IPX encapsulation types
- ✓ Explaining IPX SAPs
- ✓ Configuring the IPX protocol on a router
- ✓ Monitoring IPX status and activity on a router
- ✓ Troubleshooting IPX activity on a router

This chapter introduces NetWare and the IPX protocol. Like Internet Protocol (IP), IPX resides at the network layer of the Open Systems Interconnect (OSI) model. This chapter describes how the NetWare protocol suite maps to the OSI model and covers IPX addressing, encapsulation, and SAPs. IPX commands for configuring, monitoring, and troubleshooting IPX are also listed.

In the early 1980s, Novell, Inc. created a proprietary suite of protocols for local area networks (LANs) entitled *NetWare*. Derived from Xerox Network Systems, NetWare defined protocols for the upper five layers of the OSI model. It is considered a NOS and provides support for file sharing, printing, database access, and various applications. Like other NOSs, NetWare is based on a client-server architecture where clients (such as personal computers, PCs) request services from different servers (such as printers).

# NetWare Protocol Suite

Figure 12.1 shows the relationship between the OSI model and the NetWare protocol suite.

## Upper Layer

NetWare supports many applications, such as email and other industry-standard protocols. For example, NetWare includes emulation software that supports *NetBIOS* application interfaces. NetBIOS is a common session-layer interface

**Figure 12.1** NetWare protocol suite.

specification from IBM and Microsoft. Also, NetWare provides an additional service, a *NetWare shell*, that determines whether application calls require network services. The NetWare shell interrogates the calls and sends them to lower-layer protocols for additional network services, if necessary. The *NetWare Core Protocol* (*NCP*) is a collection of server routines that satisfies requests from other applications, like a NetWare shell.

## Transport Layer

*SPX* is the transport protocol used within NetWare. Similar to other transport protocols, SPX provides reliable, connection-oriented services that supplement NetWare's network layer protocol.

## Network Layer

NetWare uses IPX as its network layer protocol. Like other network protocols, IPX supports the routing of information from a source network, through any intermediate networks, to the destination network. Also, IPX is connectionless. That is, it does not require acknowledgment of each packet it transmits; SPX provides that capability. IPX relies on RIP to exchange network routing information.

## Data Link and Physical Layers

NetWare supports several different media access protocols and physical media types. NetWare can run over an Ethernet or token ring LAN. It can also operate in several wide area network (WAN) environments, including Integrated Services Digital Network (ISDN), Point-to-Point Protocol (PPP), and Frame Relay (Chapters 14 through 16 discuss WAN protocols in detail).

# IPX Addressing

Similar to addressing within an IP network, an IPX logical address contains a network number and a node number. Although an IPX logical address can contain up to 80 bits, a network administrator defines the IPX network number, which can contain a maximum of 32 bits. The node number is provided by the media access control (MAC) address of the *NIC* and can be up to a maximum of 48 bits. Because MAC addresses are virtually unique, it is nearly impossible for two devices within the same network to possess the same node number. Also, using the MAC address as the node's logical address eliminates the need for the Address Resolution Protocol (ARP) to determine the physical address. Figure 12.2 depicts a router connected to four IPX networks.

*Note: Serial interfaces do not have physical MAC addresses. In that event, IPX uses the MAC address of another interface.*

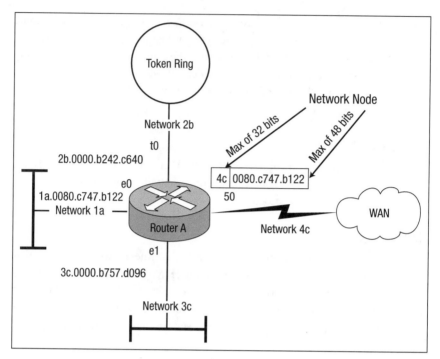

**Figure 12.2** IPX network and node addressing.

 An IPX address consists of a network number and a node number that is the node's MAC address. For example, if a node's MAC address is 0080.c729.b112 and it resides on IPX network 1a, the IPX address for that node would be 1a.0080.c729.b112.

# IPX Encapsulation

Novell's IPX supports various encapsulation types; several of those can be configured on a single router interface. As IPX packets are passed to the data link layer, the packets are encapsulated into one of several framing types supported by NetWare. However, you need to assign each encapsulation type to a unique network number on the router's interface. (The encapsulation type you select depends on the router's interface.) Table 12.1 lists the four Ethernet encapsulation types and the corresponding Cisco Internetwork Operating System (IOS) names that you will need to use when configuring the router.

Even though a single interface can support multiple encapsulation types, clients and servers that use different encapsulation types cannot communicate directly, but do so instead via the router.

| IPX Name | Cisco IOS name | Usage |
|---|---|---|
| Ethernet II | arpa | With TCP/IP and DECnet |
| Ethernet 802.2 | sap | With NetWare version 4.x and OSI routing |
| Ethernet SNAP | snap | With TCP/IP and AppleTalk |
| Ethernet 802.3 | novell-ether | With NetWare versions 2.x and 3.x |

The default encapsulation types for Cisco routers are:

➤ Ethernet: novell-ether

➤ Token Ring: sap

➤ Fiber distributed data interface (FDDI): snap

# IPX Routing

RIP, the routing protocol used by IPX, is a distance vector routing protocol and (in version 2 of RIP) relies on ticks and hop count as its metrics. A *tick* is a measure of delay time, about 1/18th of a second. In RIP version 2, ticks serve as the primary value used in determining the best path. If two or more network paths have the same tick value, RIP then uses *hop count* (the number of routers the packet must traverse) to break the tie. If multiple network paths have equal tick values and hop counts, RIP either uses a user-defined tiebreaker or loads balance across the paths.

*Note: Although IPX uses RIP as its default, two other routing protocol choices exist: Novell's NLSP and Cisco's Enhanced Interior Gateway Protocol (EIGRP).*

# IPX Service Advertisement

In an IPX network, servers *advertise* (that is, broadcast the services they offer and their addresses) across the network. These advertisements are defined within the SAP and are supported by all versions of NetWare. Clients learn of services that are being provided by issuing SAP broadcast queries and receiving SAP responses. SAP broadcasts traverse the network on a regular basis, every 60 seconds by default. Routers also receive SAP broadcasts, learn of services offered, and store the information in SAP tables. However, routers do not forward SAP broadcasts; they share SAP table information with other routers. Like SAP broadcasts, SAP table information is forwarded every 60 seconds by default. Figure 12.3 illustrates SAP broadcasts within an IPX network.

**Figure 12.3** SAP broadcasts.

A unique hexadecimal number identifies the services within a SAP broadcast. Table 12.2 lists some common SAP services.

One example of a SAP broadcast involves a *Get Nearest Server* (*GNS*) request. Figure 12.4 presents the GNS process. A client workstation typically issues this type of request when it needs to log in to the network. The client broadcasts the GNS request across the network, and both the NetWare file server and the router receive the request. If a file server resides on the network, it replies with a GNS SAP. If no file server responds and the router knows of another file server, the router responds with information from its SAP table.

| Table 12.2   Common SAP services. | |
|---|---|
| **Hex Number** | **SAP Description** |
| 0004 | NetWare file server |
| 0007 | Print server |
| 0024 | Router |
| 039B | Lotus Notes server |

**Figure 12.4** GNS process.

Key features of IPX include:

➤ The logical address is 80 bits (network.node).

➤ The interface MAC address is the node address.

➤ A router interface can support multiple encapsulation protocols.

➤ RIP is the default routing protocol.

➤ Servers advertise their services in SAP packets.

# Configuring IPX

Configuring Novell IPX on a router requires that both global and interface parameters be set. Global configuration includes starting the IPX routing process and enabling load balancing. Interface configuration includes assigning unique network numbers and defining encapsulation settings.

Table 12.3 lists the global configuration commands necessary to enable IPX routing. These commands must be executed from the global configuration prompt.

| Table 12.3 IPX global configuration commands. | |
|---|---|
| **Command** | **Description** |
| **ipx routing** [node] | Enables Novell IPX routing |
| **ipx maximum-paths** [paths] | Enables round-robin load balancing across multiple equal metric paths |

The following output lists the interface configuration command required for IPX routing on an interface. You must configure this command for each interface connected to an IPX network

```
ipx network number [encapsulation encapsulation-type] [secondary]
```

where "*number*" indicates a unique IPX network number; "encapsulation *encapsulation-type*" is optional and indicates the framing that will be used (sap, snap, and so forth); "secondary" is optional and indicates whether an additional encapsulation type exists on the current interface.

To further illustrate, the IPX network configuration depicted in Figure 12.2 would require the following commands to be executed:

```
RouterA (config)#
RouterA (config)# ipx routing
RouterA (config)# ipx maximum-paths 2
RouterA (config)# interface ethernet 0
RouterA (config-if)# ipx network 1a encapsulation sap
RouterA (config-if)# exit
RouterA (config)# interface tokenring 0
RouterA (config-if)# ipx network 2b encapsulation snap
RouterA (config-if)# exit
RouterA (config)# interface ethernet 1
RouterA (config-if)# ipx network 3c encapsulation sap
RouterA (config-if)# exit
RouterA (config)# interface serial 0
RouterA (config-if)# ipx network 4d encapsulation snap
RouterA (config-if)# exit
RouterA (config)#
```

# Monitoring IPX

After configuring IPX on the router, the commands listed in this section enable you to monitor IPX activity.

The **show ipx interface** command displays IPX status and parameters configured on each interface. Sample output from this command is shown in Listing 12.1.

## Listing 12.1   The **show ipx interface** command.

```
Ethernet0 is up, line protocol is up
  IPX address is 1A.00e0.b055.28e1,SAP [up] line-up,
     RIPPQ:0,SAPPQ:0
 Delay of this IPX network,
     in ticks is 1 throughput 0 link delay 0
 IPXWAN processing not enabled on this interface.
 IPX SAP update interval is 1 minute(s)
 IPX type 20 propagation packet forwarding is disabled
 Outgoing access list is not set
 IPX Helper access list is not set
 SAP GNS processing enabled,delay 0 ms,output filter list not set
 SAP Input filter list is not set
 SAP Output filter list is not set
 SAP Router filter list is not set
 Input filter list is not set
 Output filter list is not set
 Router filter list is not set
 Netbios Input host access list is not set
 Netbios Input bytes access list is not set
 Netbios Output host access list is not set
 Netbios Output bytes access list is not set
 Updates each 60 seconds, aging multiples RIP: 3 SAP: 3
 SAP interpacket delay is 5 ms, maximum size is 480 bytes
 RIP interpacket delay is 5 ms, maximum size is 432 bytes
 IPX accounting is disabled
 IPX fast switching is configured (enabled)
 RIP packets received 25913, RIP packets sent 4
 SAP packets received 122226, SAP packets sent 3
```

This interface has been configured for IPX network 1a with encapsulation type sap. It sends sap broadcasts every 60 seconds.

Listing 12.2 shows the **show ipx route** command output. This command displays the contents of the IPX route table.

## Listing 12.2   The **show ipx route** command.

```
Codes:C-Connected primary network,c-Connected secondary network
     S-Static,F-Floating static,L-Local (internal),W-IPXWAN
     R-RIP,E-EIGRP,N-NLSP,X-External,s-seconds,u-uses

4 Total IPX routes. Up to 2 parallel paths and 16 hops allowed.

No default route known.
```

```
C    1A (SAP),              Et0
R        1002 [02/01] via 1A.00aa.0047.5aa6,   45s, Et0
R    361FB7A0 [02/01] via 1A.0080.5f65.abbd,   51s, Et0
R    5F78776E [21/01] via 1A.0080.5f78.776e,    1s, Et0
```

This router can reach four IPX networks. It is directly connected to network 1a and has learned (via RIP) of three other IPX networks that it can reach via its Ethernet 0 interface.

The **show ipx servers** command displays the IPX server list stored in the SAP table. Sample output from the command is shown in Listing 12.3.

### Listing 12.3   The **show ipx server** command.

```
Codes: S - Static, P - Periodic, E - EIGRP, N - NLSP,
       H - Holddown, + = detail
22 Total IPX Servers
Table ordering is based on routing and server info
  Type Name                Net        Address           Port Route Hops
  Itf
P    4 HOUSTON_FS_01       361FB7A0.0000.0000.0001:0451 2/01 1   Et0
P    7 HOUSTON_PS_01       10008022.0080.c780.d9c7:0451 2/01 1   Et0
P   2C BKUPEXECv7_01       361FB7A0.0000.0000.0001:400D 2/01 1   Et0
P  107 HOUSTON_FS_01       361FB7A0.0000.0000.0001:8104 2/01 1   Et0
P  23F HOUSTON_FS_01       361FB7A0.0000.0000.0001:907B 2/01 1   Et0
P  26B HOUSTON_____     361FB7A0.0000.0000.0001:0005 2/01 1   Et0
P  278 HOUSTON_____     361FB7A0.0000.0000.0001:4006 2/01 1   Et0
P  30C 0060B00294C400CG    10008022.0060.b002.94c4:400C 1/00 1   Et0
P  30C 0060B096AB7910C4    10008022.0060.b096.ab79:400C 1/00 1   Et0
P  30C 0060B096AB7920C4    10008022.0060.b096.ab79:401C 1/00 1   Et0
P  30C 0060B096AB79B0C4    10008022.0060.b096.ab79:402C 1/00 1   Et0
P  30C 0060B0CC836B10C4    10008022.0060.b0cc.836b:400C 1/00 1   Et0
P  30C 0060B0CC836BA0C4    10008022.0060.b0cc.836b:401C 1/00 1   Et0
P  30C 0060B0CC836BB0C4    10008022.0060.b0cc.836b:402C 1/00 1   Et0
P  30C 0800098A09E400CE    10008022.0800.098a.09e4:400C 1/00 1   Et0
P  355 00202055777_APPS    10008022.00a0.c959.91d2:6000 1/00 1   Et0
P  39B 002020HOUSTONNOT    10008022.0080.5f78.776e:6000 1/00 1   Et0
P  535 PS_CLR_03           10008022.0800.1104.175a:5005 1/00 1   Et0
P  640 IWEARPOLLY          10008022.0080.c780.e9c1:E885 1/00 1   Et0
P  640 HOUSTON_APPS_01     10008022.00a0.c959.91d2:E885 1/00 1   Et0
P  64E HOUSTON_APPS_01A    10008022.00a0.c959.91d2:4068 1/00 1   Et0
P  82B HOUSTON_FS_01       361FB7A0.0000.0000.0001:400D 2/01 1   Et0
```

This router has received SAPs from several different types of servers.

Listing 12.4 gives the **show ipx traffic** command output. This command displays the number and type of IPX packets transmitted and received by the router.

## Listing 12.4   The **show ipx traffic** command.

```
System Traffic for 0.0000.0000.0001 System-Name: RouterA
Rcvd:   165726 total, 37463 format errors,
        0 checksum errors, 0 bad hop count,
        15539 packets pitched, 155441 local destination,
        0 multicast
Bcast:  155405 received, 6 sent
Sent:   7 generated, 0 forwarded
        0 encapsulation failed, 0 no route
SAP:    17409 SAP requests, 0 SAP replies, 22 servers
        104725 SAP advertisements received, 0 sent
        0 SAP flash updates sent, 112 SAP format errors,
        last seen from 0.0000.0
        000.0000
RIP:    8284 RIP requests, 1 RIP replies, 4 routes
        17633 RIP advertisements received, 0 sent
        0 RIP flash updates sent, 0 RIP format errors
Echo:   Rcvd 0 requests, 0 replies
        Sent 0 requests, 0 replies
        2024 unknown: 0 no socket, 0 filtered, 2024 no helper
        0 SAPs throttled, freed NDB len 0
Watchdog:
        0 packets received, 0 replies spoofed
Queue lengths:
        IPX input: 0, SAP 0, RIP 0, GNS 0
        SAP throttling length: 0/(no limit),
        0 nets pending lost route reply
        Delayed process creation: 0
EIGRP:  Total received 0, sent 0
        Updates received 0, sent 0
        Queries received 0, sent 0
        Replies received 0, sent 0
        SAPs received 0, sent 0
NLSP:   Level-1 Hellos received 0, sent 0
        PTP Hello received 0, sent 0
        Level-1 LSPs received 0, sent 0
        LSP Retransmissions: 0
        LSP checksum errors received: 0
        LSP HT=0 checksum errors received: 0
        Level-1 CSNPs received 0, sent 0
        Level-1 PSNPs received 0, sent 0
        Level-1 DR Elections: 0
        Level-1 SPF Calculations: 0
        Level-1 Partial Route Calculations: 0
```

This router has received more than 100,000 SAP advertisements from various servers.

*Note: Given the high number of SAP advertisements that are broadcast through an IPX network, IPX is considered chatty.*

# Troubleshooting IPX

The commands listed in this section provide information to assist you in diagnosing problems with IPX.

You must be connected to the router's console or configure log messages to be displayed to your terminal session before you will be able to view any debug messages.

The **debug ipx routing activity** command displays IPX routing update information:

```
IPX routing debugging is on

IPXRIP: posting full update to 1A.ffff.ffff.ffff
        via Ethernet0 (broadcast)
IPXRIP: suppressing null update to 1A.ffff.ffff.ffff
```

The **debug ipx sap activity** command displays IPX SAP packet information:

```
IPX service debugging is on

IPXSAP: posting update to 1A.ffff.ffff.ffff
        via Ethernet0 (broadcast) (full)
IPXSAP: posting update to 1A.ffff.ffff.ffff
        via Ethernet0 (broadcast) (full)
IPXSAP: posting update to 1A.ffff.ffff.ffff
        via Ethernet0 (broadcast) (full)
```

The **no debug all** command quickly turns off any debug commands that are active.

You can use the following commands to monitor and troubleshoot IPX activity:

➤ **show ipx interface**

➤ **show ipx route**

➤ **show ipx server**

➤ **show ipx traffic**

➤ **debug ipx routing activity**

➤ **debug ipx sap activity**

# Practice Questions

## Question 1

> Which of the following protocols is used within the transport layer of the NetWare protocol suite?
>
> ○ a. Ethernet
>
> ○ b. UDP
>
> ○ c. SPX
>
> ○ d. ARP

Answer c is correct. SPX is the transport layer protocol used within NetWare's protocol suite. Answer a is incorrect because Ethernet is a data link layer protocol that supports NetWare. UDP is a transport layer protocol, but it is used within the TCP/IP suite, so answer b is incorrect. Answer d is incorrect because ARP resides at the network layer within the TCP/IP suite.

## Question 2

> Which of the following is a valid and complete IPX address?
>
> ○ a. 0080.c747.b122
>
> ○ b. 1a.0080.c747.b122
>
> ○ c. 1a.172.16.101.123
>
> ○ d. 1a

Answer b is correct. It is a complete IPX logical address for network 1a and node 0080.c747.b122. Answer a is incorrect because it is a node address (MAC address) and is incomplete. Answer c contains an IPX network number (1a), but also includes an IP address, so it is incorrect. Answer d is only the IPX network number; therefore, it is incorrect.

## Question 3

Which of the following is the default routing protocol within an IPX network?

○ a. RIP

○ b. NLSP

○ c. EIGRP

○ d. IGRP

Answer a is correct. RIP is the default routing protocol within an IPX network. Although NLSP and EIGRP can be used as the routing protocol for IPX, they are not the default; therefore, answers b and c are incorrect. IGRP is not supported within IPX; therefore, answer d is incorrect.

## Question 4

IPX RIP version 2 uses which of the following metrics to determine the best path? [Choose the two best answers]

❏ a. Bandwidth

❏ b. Hop count

❏ c. Load

❏ d. Ticks

Answers b and d are correct. Hop count and ticks (delay) are the two metrics used within IPX RIP version 2. Bandwidth and load are not used in RIP, but in more sophisticated routing protocols such as EIGRP and OSPF; therefore answers a and c are incorrect.

## Question 5

Which of the following are Cisco names for standard IPX encapsulation types? [Choose the five best answers]

❑ a. arpa

❑ b. sap

❑ c. ethernet

❑ d. token

❑ e. snap

❑ f. novell-ether

❑ g. novell

Answers a, b, d, e, and f are correct. Cisco's encapsulation name for Ethernet II is arpa; for Ethernet_802.2, it's sap; for Ethernet_SNAP and Token Ring_SNAP, it's snap; for Ethernet_802.3, it's novell-ether; and for Token-Ring, it's token. Answers c and g are incorrect because ethernet and novell are not IPX encapsulation types.

## Question 6

Which configuration command must be executed for each interface supporting IPX?

○ a. **ipx routing**

○ b. **ipx protocol**

○ c. **ipx interface**

○ d. **ipx network**

Answer d is correct. The **ipx network** command assigns a network number to a router interface. This command must be repeated for each IPX network that the router must support. The **ipx routing** command enables IPX routing within the router; therefore, answer a is incorrect. Answers b and c are also incorrect because **ipx protocol** and **ipx interface** are not valid commands.

# Question 7

> Which of the following statements represent a feature of an IPX environment? [Choose the answers that best apply]
>
> ❑ a.  A logical address is 80 bits (network.node).
>
> ❑ b.  The interface MAC address is the node address.
>
> ❑ c.  A router interface can support multiple encapsulation protocols.
>
> ❑ d.  RIP is the default routing protocol.
>
> ❑ e.  Servers advertise their services in SAP packets.

Answers a, b, c, d, and e are correct. They are all features of an IPX environment.

# Question 8

> Which router command displays the contents of the router's SAP table?
>
> ○ a.  **show ipx traffic**
>
> ○ b.  **show ipx route**
>
> ○ c.  **show ipx server**
>
> ○ d.  **show ipx interface**

Answer c is correct. The **show ipx server** command displays the information learned through SAP advertisements. Answer a is incorrect because the **show ipx traffic** command displays the number and type of IPX packets transmitted and received by the router. The **show ipx route** command displays the contents of the IPX routing table, so answer b is incorrect. The **show ipx interface** command displays IPX status and parameters configured on each interface; therefore, answer d is incorrect.

## Question 9

---

snap is the default IPX encapsulation type for which type of LAN interface?
[Choose the two best answers]

❑ a. Ethernet

❑ b. Token ring

❑ c. FDDI

❑ d. Serial

---

Answers b and c are correct—snap is the default encapsulation type for both token ring and FDDI. The default encapsulation type for Ethernet is novell-ether; therefore, answer a is incorrect. Because a serial interface is a WAN interface, it does not have a default encapsulation type; therefore, answer d is incorrect.

## Question 10

---

Which of the following reside within the upper layers of the NetWare protocol suite? [Choose the three best answers]

❑ a. NCP

❑ b. NetBIOS emulation

❑ c. NOS

❑ d. NetWare shell

---

Answers a, b, and d are correct. NCP is a collection of server routines that interfaces with other applications. NetBIOS is a common session layer interface specification from IBM and Microsoft. A NetWare shell determines whether application calls require network services. Answer c is incorrect because NetWare itself is considered a NOS and cannot be a protocol within NetWare.

# Need to Know More?

McNutt, Shawn, Mark Poplar, Jason Waters, and David Stabenaw: *CCNA Routing and Switching Exam Prep*. The Coriolis Group, Scottsdale, AZ, 2000. ISBN 1-57610-440-0. This book is a great complement to the CCNA Cram book. Chapter 8 covers IPX.

Chappell, Laura. *Novell's Guide to LAN/WAN Analysis: IPX/SPX*. IDG Books Worldwide, Foster City, CA, 1998. ISBN 0-76454-508-6. This book provides additional information about IPX, SPX, RIP, and NCP. It also introduces techniques for performing network analysis, troubleshooting, and optimization within a NetWare environment. The book includes a CD-ROM that contains a demonstration version of LAN analyzer software.

Cisco Systems, *Cisco IOS Solutions for Network Protocols, IPX, APP Vol 2*. ISBN 1-57870-050-7. This book provides exhaustive information about implementing and troubleshooting IPX within a network utilizing Cisco IOS.

Using Cisco's documentation CD, you can immediately access Cisco's entire library of end-user documentation, selected product news, bug databases, and related information. The documentation CD-ROM is produced monthly.

**www.cisco.com**, the official Cisco Web site, contains several Cisco white papers on topics such as connecting Novell LANs to the Internet and NLSP route aggregation when you search for "Novell IPX."

# IP and IPX Access Lists

. . . . . . . . . . . . . . . . . . . . . . . . . . . . . . . . . . . . . . . .

### Terms you'll need to understand:

✓ IP standard access list

✓ IP extended access list

✓ Service Advertisement Protocol (SAP)

✓ IPX standard access list

✓ IPX extended access list

✓ IPX SAP filter

### Techniques you'll need to master:

✓ Configuring standard access lists for IP

✓ Configuring extended access lists for IP

✓ Configuring standard access lists for IPX

✓ Configuring extended access lists for IPX

✓ Configuring IPX SAP filters

✓ Monitoring access list operations on the router

✓ Verifying access list operations on the router

This chapter covers access lists for IP and IPX traffic. *Access lists* allow network administrators to restrict access to certain networks, devices, and services. They provide an effective means of applying security within an organization; they also permit or deny specific types of traffic to pass through an interface. The types of IP traffic they filter can be based on source or destination address or address range, protocol, precedence, type of service, icmp-type, icmp-code, icmp-message, igmp-type, port, or state of the TCP connection. These filtered types can also be based on the source or destination address, sockets, protocol number, and SAP type. In addition, other IPX access lists restrict other types of traffic; however, these additional categories are not covered, because they are beyond the scope of the CCNA exam. A full list of access lists is provided in Table 13.1.

Access lists provide a powerful set of tools that can deny and permit users to access specific applications or hosts. The trade-off for using access lists, however, is that they require processing power to compare packets entering or exiting an interface with the entries in the list. Figure 13.1 illustrates how routers filter packets to restrict network access.

A wide variety of access lists can be applied to a router interface. This chapter focuses only on the IP standard and extended access lists, IPX SAP access lists, and IPX standard and extended access lists.

# IP Access Lists

IP access lists are used to deny or permit specific traffic into or out of an interface on a router. They filter IP source and destination addresses and protocol- or service-specific traffic. IP access lists are of two types: *standard* and *extended*. The difference between the two is the precision by which each can filter IP traffic.

| Table 13.1 Types of access lists. | |
| --- | --- |
| **Numeric Range** | **Description** |
| 1 through 99 | IP standard access list |
| 100 through 199 | IP extended access list |
| 200 through 299 | Protocol type-code access list |
| 300 through 399 | DECnet access list |
| 600 through 699 | AppleTalk access list |
| 700 through 799 | 48-bit media access control (MAC) address access list |
| 800 through 899 | IPX standard access list |
| 900 through 999 | IPX extended access list |
| 1,000 through 1,099 | SAP access list |

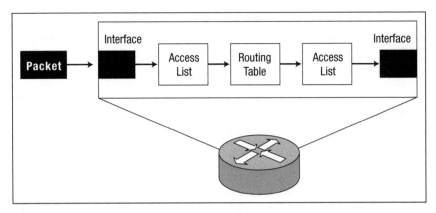

**Figure 13.1**    Access list architecture.

# IP Standard Access Lists

IP standard access lists filter traffic based on the source IP address or address range. Therefore, administrators can use this tool to restrict access to specific users and allow access to others. The lists are applied to the interface of a router where traffic is to be filtered, and they restrict access into or out of the interface. The direction in which traffic is restricted is determined by the Cisco command used to apply the access list to the interface.

## IP Standard Access List Commands

Creating and applying an access list to an interface consists of two steps, both of which are performed in configuration mode. First, the access list must be created. A single access list can consist of many access list *statements*. An access list *number* identifies an individual access group that can consist of many access list *entries*. In addition, the order in which access list entries are created plays an important role in the behavior of the access list. When traffic passes through the interface, it is compared with each access list entry in the order in which the entry was created. If the traffic matches an access list entry, the indicated function (permit or deny) of the access list entry is performed on the traffic. When a packet is permitted entry, the router caches the entry, and any subsequent packets in this session are granted access without being applied against the access list. All access lists have an implicit **deny all** statement at the end of the list. Thus, if the traffic does not match any entry, it is denied access into or out of the interface. The command to create an access list is as follows:

```
Access-list access-list-number {deny|permit} source [source-wildcard]
```

The format of this previous command listing is typical of Cisco commands. The listing can be interpreted as follows. The nonitalicized words should be written exactly as shown. In this case, the pipe symbol (|) indicates that either **deny** or

**permit** should be written, but not both. The italicized words indicate that a character string must be written in this field. In this case, the character string would be a number. The square brackets indicate that a field is optional. A brief description of each field is provided in Table 13.2.

The **source-wildcard** field, referred to as a *wildcard mask*, is used to identify bits in an IP address that have meaning and bits that can be ignored. In this case, the wildcard mask is referred to as a *source-wildcard*, indicating that it is a wildcard mask of the source IP address. A source-wildcard mask is applied to a source IP address to determine a range of addresses to permit or deny.

At first, the best way to learn wildcard masks is to convert the mask from decimal to binary format. The wildcard mask is applied by comparing the IP address bits with the corresponding IP wildcard bits. A 1 bit in the wildcard mask indicates that the corresponding bit in the IP address can be ignored. Thus, the IP address bit can be either a 1 or 0. A 0 in the wildcard mask indicates that the corresponding bit in the IP address must be strictly followed. Thus, the value must be exactly the same as specified in the IP address. Tables 13.3 and 13.4 illustrate how to apply a source-wildcard mask to a source address to determine a range of addresses.

Tables 13.3 and 13.4 illustrate that the first three octets must be strictly followed; therefore, the values of these octets must be 172.16.16 to be a match. The 1 bits in the fourth octet, however, indicate that any value between 0 and 255 will result in a match. Therefore, any host with the IP address of 172.16.16.0 through 172.16.16.255 is a match for this source IP address and source-wildcard mask.

The next step is to apply the access list to an interface. The syntax for doing so is as follows:

```
ip access-group access-list-number {in|out}
```

The **access-list-number** is the number used to identify the access list. This number must be the same as specified in the **access-list** command used to create the previously shown entries. The **in|out** option indicates whether this list is to filter

| Table 13.2   IP standard access list command field descriptions. | |
|---|---|
| Identifier | Description |
| access-list-number | A dotted decimal number between 1 and 99 |
| deny | Denies access if condition is matched |
| permit | Permits access if condition is matched |
| source | Number of the network or host from which the packet is being sent |
| source-wildcard | Wildcard bits to be applied to the source |

**Table 13.3    Applying a source-wildcard mask to a source IP address in binary format.**

| Source Address in Bits | Binary |
|---|---|
| Source address | 10101100.00010000.00010000.00000000 |
| Source-wildcard | 00000000.00000000.00000000.11111111 |
| Result | 10101100.00010000.00010000.any |

**Table 13.4    Applying a source-wildcard mask to a source IP address in decimal format.**

| Source Address in Bits | Binary |
|---|---|
| Source address | 172.16.16.0 |
| Source-wildcard | 0.0.0.255 |
| Result | 172.16.16.any |

on inbound or outbound traffic through the interface. It is important to remember that the access list is being applied to a specific interface on a router, rather than to all of the interfaces on the router.

## Creating and Applying an IP Standard Access List

The network in Figure 13.2 is used to illustrate IP standard access lists further.

In this example, suppose you want to permit the following devices to have access to the network 172.16.4.0:

➤ Any device on network 172.16.14.0

➤ Any device on network 172.16.3.0 except 172.16.3.5

➤ Only the device with the IP address of 172.16.12.4 on network 172.16.12.0

Applying an IP standard access list to a router interface involves two steps. The first step is to create the access list to indicate all of the source addresses that are permitted or denied access. The second step is applying the access list to the interface on which you are restricting either outbound or inbound traffic. By applying the **access-group** command to interface Ethernet 0, you can restrict access to network 172.16.4.0. The commands to create this access list are as follows:

```
Router#configure terminal
Router(config)#access-list 5 permit 172.16.14.0 0.0.0.255
Router(config)#access-list 5 deny 172.16.3.5 0.0.0.0
Router(config)#access-list 5 permit 172.16.3.0 0.0.0.255
Router(config)#access-list 5 permit 172.16.12.4 0.0.0.0
Router(config)#access-list 5 deny 0.0.0.0 255.255.255.255
```

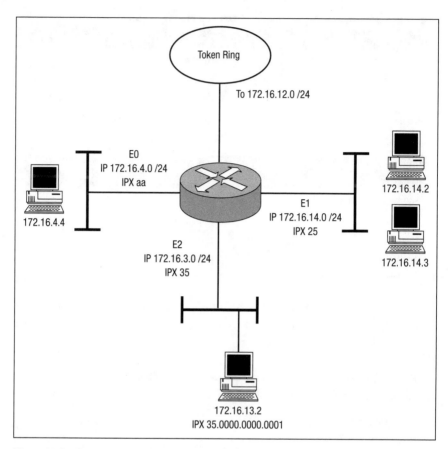

**Figure 13.2**  Basic network used to explain access lists.

These commands restrict and permit the traffic detailed in the requirements. The first **access-list** entry permits access to all users from network 172.16.14.0 to pass through the access list on Ethernet 0. Note that the source-wildcard of 0.0.0.255 indicates that every host ID in the last octet can be ignored, thus allowing all IP addresses between 172.16.14.0 and 172.16.14.255 access. The second **access-list** command denies host ID 172.16.3.5 to pass through the access list. Note that the source-wildcard of 0.0.0.0 indicates that only the source address specified (172.16.3.5) is denied access. The third **access-list** command permits all users on network 172.16.3.0 to pass through the access list. Note that host ID 172.16.3.5 will still not be allowed to pass through the access list, because any traffic from this host was dropped by the previous **deny** command. The order in which a **permit** or **deny** command is placed in an access list is extremely important.

When adding new entries to existing access lists, it is sometimes necessary to reorder the access list so that it will filter traffic correctly. Often, the best way to reorder the entries is to copy all of the entries into a text file, add or remove the required entries, and reorder them in that text file. After you have them ordered correctly, add them all to the router configuration.

The fourth **access-list** entry permits only user 172.16.12.4 to pass through the access list. Finally, the last **access-list** command in italics is implicit whenever an access list is created; therefore, any packet not generated by the router with the access list that does not match one of the permit entries is dropped. You do not have to configure this **deny** entry.

Before these access list entries can filter traffic, they must be applied to the interface as an access group. The access lists are going to be applied to outbound packets on Ethernet 0. Therefore, any packet attempting to travel out interface Ethernet 0 must match one of the entries in access group 5. The steps to configure an outbound access list on Ethernet 0 are as follows:

```
Router#config t
Enter configuration commands, one per line. End with CNTL/Z.
Router(config)#interface ethernet 0
Router(config-if)#ip access-group 5 out
```

The **access-group 5** has been applied to the outbound Ethernet 0 interface. Now, every packet that is sent out the Ethernet 0 interface will be checked to see if it matches. More complicated scenarios for restricting access through an interface exist. Sometimes a network administrator wants to permit only a range of IP addresses through an access list. However, it is more complicated to permit access to a range of IP addresses that do not fall exactly on octet bit boundaries. A second example follows to illustrate this scenario.

Continue to use the network provided in Figure 13.2; however, in this case, you want to allow the following devices to have access only to the network 172.16.4.0. Therefore, you want to permit access to any device with the IP address between 172.16.3.32 through 172.16.3.39.

For this scenario, you must determine the proper source-wildcard mask to apply to allow access to devices in the IP address range 172.16.3.32 through 172.16.3.39. Start with the IP address 172.16.3.32 to create this access list. Next, apply a network mask that allows eight incremental bits in the fourth octet. Table 13.5

illustrates the proper source IP address and source-wildcard mask in binary and decimal format for this example.

Table 13.5 illustrates that, by applying the source-wildcard mask of 0.0.0.7, a range of IP addresses that do not fall on an octet boundary has been allowed. Each permitted address is determined by taking the bits indicated as ignored bits by the source-wildcard mask and listing the possible permutations. A few good rules to know are as follows:

➤ When grouping IP addresses, the group size is always a power of 2 (2, 4, 8, 16, and so forth).

➤ Anytime IP addresses are grouped together, the first IP address in the group is divisible by the size of the group. For example, a group of eight IP addresses can start only on multiples of eight (8, 16, 24, and so forth).

➤ The wildcard mask is always one less than the group size. For example, a group of eight has a wildcard mask of seven. A group of 64 has a wildcard mask of 63.

Although IP standard access lists provide a powerful set of tools for restricting access, they can only restrict access based on the source IP address. IP extended access lists increase the variables that can be used to restrict access through an interface.

## IP Extended Access Lists

IP standard access lists filter traffic based on the source IP address only; therefore, administrators can use this tool to restrict access to specific users only. Because administrators wanted more control of the traffic that could travel through interfaces,

| Table 13.5 | Applying a source-wildcard mask to a source IP address in binary format. | |
| --- | --- | --- |
| **Source Address in Bits** | **Binary** | **Decimal** |
| Source address | 10101100.00010000.00000011.00100000 | 172.16.3.32 |
| Source-wildcard | 00000000.00000000.00000000.00000111 | 0.0.0.7 |
| Permitted address 1 | 10101100.00010000.00010000.00100000 | 172.16.3.32 |
| Permitted address 2 | 10101100.00010000.00010000.00100001 | 172.16.3.33 |
| Permitted address 3 | 10101100.00010000.00010000.00100010 | 172.16.3.34 |
| Permitted address 4 | 10101100.00010000.00010000.00100011 | 172.16.3.35 |
| Permitted address 5 | 10101100.00010000.00010000.00100100 | 172.16.3.36 |
| Permitted address 6 | 10101100.00010000.00010000.00100101 | 172.16.3.37 |
| Permitted address 7 | 10101100.00010000.00010000.00100110 | 172.16.3.38 |
| Permitted address 8 | 10101100.00010000.00010000.00100111 | 172.16.3.39 |

Cisco responded with IP extended access lists, which perform the same basic function as standard access lists (permitting and denying IP packets through an interface), but extend the types of IP traffic that can be filtered. Consequently, IP extended access lists allow for more precise filtering of IP traffic. Whereas IP standard access lists allow only source IP address filtering, IP extended access lists provide source and destination IP address filtering. In addition, IP extended access lists filter on layer 4 protocol such as Transmission Control Protocol (TCP) and User Datagram Protocol (UDP), look into the TCP or UDP header, and allow filtering on TCP/UDP port numbers. Table 13.6 provides a list of some of the most common layer 4 protocols and TCP port numbers that are filtered using IP extended access lists.

Memorizing these TCP and UDP port numbers is a good move for the CCNA exam. While there are many other port numbers, these are the port numbers that are most important for the exam.

In addition, IP extended access lists allow filtering based on the IP precedence field, TOS field, icmp-type, icmp-code, icmp-message, igmp-type, and TCP-established connections. This book only covers source and destination address, IP protocol, and TCP/UDP port numbers.

## IP Extended Access List Commands

The steps taken to create and apply an IP extended access list are the same as those used for an IP standard access list. First, create the access list entries. Second, apply the access list group to the interface where you want to filter traffic.

It is important to enter IP extended access list entries in the correct order. Also, an implicit **deny all** traffic entry is at the end of every IP extended access list.

| Table 13.6 | Common port numbers filtered using IP extended access lists. | |
|---|---|---|
| **Protocol** | **Port Number** | **Protocol Name** |
| TCP | 21 | File Transfer Protocol (FTP) |
| TCP | 23 | Telnet |
| TCP | 25 | Simple Mail Transfer Protocol (SMTP) |
| UDP | 53 | Domain Name System (DNS) |
| UDP | 69 | Trivial File Transfer Protocol (TFTP) |
| UDP | 80 | Hypertext Transfer Protocol (HTTP) |
| UDP | 161, 162 | Simple Network Management Protocol (SNMP) |

The command to create an IP extended access list is very similar to the command used to create an IP standard access list. However, the additional filtering capabilities require some additional fields in the command. The command to create an access list is as follows:

```
access-list access-list-number {deny|permit} protocol source
source-wildcard [operator port [port]]  destination [destination-
wildcard] [operator port [port]]
```

Because how to read the command list was covered in the IP standard access list section, only the additional fields are discussed here. The first noticeable difference is the addition of the **protocol** field. This field is typically filled with TCP or UDP (other possibilities exist, but these are beyond the scope of this book and the CCNA exam). The **operator port [port]** field is used to indicate the TCP/UDP port or range of ports for the **source** and **source-wildcard** fields. In addition, the **destination** and **destination-wildcard** fields are added with their corresponding **operator port [port]** field. Basically, the fields necessary to filter traffic on source and destination address, IP protocol (TCP or UDP), and port numbers have been added. In addition, the **access-list-number** field must now be a number between 100 and 199, as indicated in Table 13.1. A complete list of all of the fields in the IP extended access list command is provided in Table 13.7.

To apply an IP extended access list, use the same IP access group command that is used for standard access lists. Simply apply the access list to the interface where you want to filter traffic.

## Creating and Applying an IP Extended Access List

To illustrate the use of the IP extended access list functionality, continue to use the network in Figure 13.2. In this example, you want to extend the types of traffic being filtered. Suppose you want to permit the following traffic to pass through your access list:

➤ Any device on network 172.16.14.0 is permitted to communicate with any device on network 172.16.4.0 using the IP, TCP, and port number 23 (Telnet).

➤ Device 172.16.14.2 is permitted to communicate with device 172.16.4.4 using the IP, UDP, and UDP port number 69 (TFTP).

➤ Device 172.16.14.3 is permitted to communicate with any device on any network using IP and TCP for any port number.

The following commands create this access list:

```
Router#configure terminal
Router(config)#access-list 105 permit tcp 172.16.14.0 0.0.0.255
172.16.4.0 0.0.0.255 eq 23
```

```
Router(config)#access-list 105 permit udp host 172.16.14.2
host 172.16.4.4 eq 69
Router(config)#access-list 105 permit tcp host 172.16.14.3 any any
Router(config)#access-list 105 deny any any
```

Let's discuss these access list entries. The first entry performs the extended functionality by indicating that only TCP traffic from any device on network 172.16.14.0 (indicated by the source-wildcard mask of 0.0.0.255) is permitted to communicate with 172.16.4.0 (indicated by the destination-wildcard of 0.0.0.255) using the TCP port number (indicated by the operator **eq** and the port number 23). The operator **eq** stands for equal to. A subset of the different possible operators is supplied in Table 13.8.

The second entry introduces the word "host" into the command; this is a short way of indicating the wildcard mask 0.0.0.0. However, the "host" word precedes the IP address, versus the traditional trailing wildcard mask. So, in this entry, only the device with the IP address of 172.16.14.2 has been allowed to communicate only with the device 172.16.4.4 using the UDP for the port number 69 (TFTP).

| Table 13.7 | Access list command field descriptions. |
|---|---|
| **Access List Command** | **Description** |
| **access list-number** | Identifies the access list for which it belongs |
| **deny** | Denies access if condition is matched |
| **permit** | Permits access if condition is matched |
| **protocol** | Name or number of the IP protocol |
| **source** | Number of the network or host from which the packet is being sent |
| **source-wildcard** | Wildcard bits to be applied to the source |
| **destination** | Number of the network or host from which the packet originated |
| **destination-wildcard** | Wildcard bits to be applied to the destination |
| **precedence** | Filter packets by precedence level |
| **tos** | Filter packets by type of service |
| **icmp-type** | Filter packets by icmp-type |
| **icmp-code** | Filter packets by icmp-code |
| **icmp-message** | Filter packets by icmp-message |
| **igmp-type** | Filter packets by igmp-type |
| **operator** | Compares source or destination ports |
| **port** | Decimal value or name of a TCP or UDP port |
| **established** | Indicates an established connection |
| **log** | Causes an information logging entry |

| Table 13.8 | Extended access list command field descriptions. |
|---|---|
| Operator | Meaning |
| eq | Match only packets on a given port number |
| lt | Match only packets with a lower port number |
| gt | Match only packets with a greater port number |
| range | Match only packets in the range of port numbers |

The third entry introduces the word "any" into the command. Similar to the word "host" in the preceding condition, the "any" word is a short way of indicating any source or destination address with the wildcard mask of 255.255.255.255. This mask indicates that all IP addresses are being described, and therefore, it does not matter what source or destination IP address is specified. In this case, all destination addresses have been described. So in this entry, the device with the IP address of 172.16.14.3 has been allowed to communicate with any device using the TCP for any port number.

The last entry in italics is the implicit **deny all** statement. It is not necessary to add this entry, because it is always there.

The second step is applying the access list to the interface that you are restricting. Specify whether you are filtering outbound or inbound traffic by adding the key word "out" or "in" to the end of the command. In this example, apply the access list to Ethernet 1 to illustrate the ability of IP extended access lists to filter traffic based on destination address as well as source address. The command to apply the access group to the interface is as follows:

```
Router#config t
Enter configuration commands, one per line. End with CNTL/Z.
Router(config)#interface ethernet 1
Router(config-if)#ip access-group 105 in
```

In summary, extended access lists are used to increase the preciseness of your filtering. The steps performed to create and apply access lists do not change.

# IPX Access Lists

The basic concepts that applied to IP standard and extended access lists apply also to IPX access lists. The main difference is that these lists filter IPX addresses or other IPX-related items. The four types of IPX access lists are listed in Table 13.9.

This book does not cover IPX NetBIOS access lists, because they are beyond the scope of the CCNA exam. Before proceeding, refer to Table 13.1 to memorize the access list number ranges for these IPX access lists.

| Table 13.9   Types of IPX access lists. | |
|---|---|
| **Name** | **Function** |
| IPX Standard access list | Restricts access based on IPX source and destination address |
| IPX Extended access list | Restricts access based on IPX source and destination address, IPX protocol, and source and destination sockets |
| SAP access list | Restricts access based on IPX SAP |
| IPX NetBIOS access list | Restricts IPX Network Basic Input/Output System (NetBIOS) traffic based on NetBIOS names |

It is vital to know the numbers associated with each type of access list. This will save you time on the CCNA exam, because you will be able to rule out incorrect answers quickly.

# IPX Standard Access Lists

The IPX standard access lists follow the same rules as IP access lists. The general rules to remember are:

> ➤ The order in which access list entries are configured determines the order in which traffic is checked.

> ➤ The implicit **deny all** statement exists at the bottom of every IPX access list.

The **access-list** command is used to create a standard IPX access list. Because this is the same command used to create the IP standard access list, the router uses the access list number to differentiate between IP and IPX standard access lists. The command format is as follows:

```
access-list access-list-number {deny|permit} source-
network[.source-node [source-node-mask]] [destination-
network[.destination-node [destination-node-mask]]]
```

To illustrate IPX access lists, use the network shown in Figure 13.2.

## Creating and Applying an IPX Standard Access List

In this example, you are going to deny IPX network 25 access to IPX network aa, but allow IPX network 35 to access IPX network aa. The first step is to create the access lists:

```
Router#configure terminal
Router(config)#access-list 805 deny 25 aa
Router(config)#access-list 805 permit 35 aa
```

In the previous example, the **deny** statement is not actually required because of the implicit **deny all** at the end of all access lists; it is provided here to illustrate the example. Although it was not shown in this example, source- and destination-wildcard masks could have been used to specify ranges of addresses. Refer to the IP standard and extended access lists shown previously for the steps to apply wildcard masks.

The next step is to apply the access list to an interface. This step is the same for IP standard and extended access lists; simply pick the appropriate interface where you want to filter the traffic and assign the access list to that interface. The command to perform this step is as follows:

```
Router#config t
Enter configuration commands, one per line. End with CNTL/Z.
Router(config)#interface ethernet 0
Router(config-if)#ipx access-group 805 out
```

Note that the command changed from **ip access-group** to **ipx access-group**; otherwise, it is exactly the same command.

Spend most of your time understanding IP access lists thoroughly. After you have mastered this skill, understanding IPX access lists is trivial, because the only real difference is the type of logical address being used.

The concept of using the word "any" to represent all addresses was introduced during the discussion of IP standard and extended access lists. IPX standard and extended access lists use the number -1 to perform the same function. For example, suppose you want to allow any network address except IPX network 25 to access IPX network aa. The access list entries would be created as follows:

```
Router#configure terminal
Router(config)#access-list 805 deny 25 aa
Router(config)#access-list 805 permit -1 -1
```

In this example, IPX network 25 was denied access to IPX network aa first. This command must be performed first, because all traffic is compared with the access list in the order in which the entries are configured. Therefore, any traffic from IPX network 25 is denied based on the first entry, and all other IPX network traffic is allowed to pass through, because it matches the second entry.

## IPX Extended Access Lists

IPX extended access lists increase the preciseness with which IPX traffic can be filtered. IPX extended access lists allow filtering on source and destination addresses, IPX protocol, and source and destination sockets. The command format for an IPX extended access list is as follows:

```
access-list access-list-number {deny|permit} protocol source
[source-wildcard] source-socket destination [destination-wildcard]
destination-socket
```

The previous command extended the IPX standard access list functionality by adding the **protocol** and the **source** and **destination socket** fields. The **protocol** field is used to describe IPX protocols, such as Sequence Packet Exchange (SPX) or SAP. The **socket** field is similar to the **port** field used with IP extended access lists. It uses a number to identify a specific service.

Continue to use the example network in Figure 13.2 to illustrate IPX extended access lists. Suppose you want to allow all IPX networks except 35 to use all IPX protocols and sockets to use the services of IPX network 15. The commands to configure this scenario would be as follows:

```
Router#configure terminal
Router(config)#access-list 905 deny -1 35 0 15 0 0
Router(config)#access-list 905 permit -1 -1 0 0 15 0 0
```

Note that all IPX protocols (indicated by the -1) and all IPX sockets (indicated by the 0) are indicated in both entries; however, it was explicitly identified in the first entry that IPX network 35 cannot access IPX network 15. In the second entry, all networks were identified as being allowed to use all services on the destination network 15. The IPX access list can be applied to interface Ethernet 0 as follows:

```
Router#config t
Enter configuration commands, one per line. End with CNTL/Z.
Router(config)#interface ethernet 0
Router(config-if)#ipx access-group 905 out
```

## IPX SAP Filters

As explained in Chapter 9, SAP messages are a common source of traffic on IPX networks. Typically, Novell servers generate SAP advertisements to communicate the different services that they offer. Administrators often want to filter what advertisements are delivered to specific networks, so they create IPX SAP filters and apply them to the appropriate interfaces. The command to create an IPX SAP filter is as follows:

```
access-list access-list-number {deny|permit} source [source-
wildcard] [service-type [server-name]]
```

To illustrate an IPX SAP filter, suppose you want to filter all SAP type 4 (file server) messages from IPX server 35.0000.0000.0001 from reaching IPX network aa. First, create the access list entry using the following commands:

```
Router#configure terminal
Router(config)#access-list 1005 deny 35.0000.0000.0001 4
Router(config)#access-list 1005 permit -1
```

In the previous example, the specific server 35.0000.0000.0001 was denied from sending SAP type 4 messages and permitted every other address to send any SAP type. Remember that an implicit **deny all** is on every access list.

Second, apply the access list to an interface using the commands as follows:

```
ipx output-sap-filter access-list number
ipx input-sap-filter access-list number
ipx router-sap-filter access-list-number
```

IPX designates the direction of traffic to filter by using the keyword "output," "input," or "router" in the command. This is different from an IP access list that designates the direction in which to filter traffic by adding the word "out" or "in" to the end of the command. Therefore, to apply the example to an interface, simply perform the following command:

```
Router#config t
Enter configuration commands, one per line. End with CNTL/Z.
Router(config)#interface ethernet 0
Router(config-if)#ipx output-sap-filter 1005
```

# Monitor and Verify Access Lists

After you have configured all your access lists, it is important to be able to review your entries and to determine that you are filtering traffic in the manner intended. Many different methods exist to monitor and verify access lists. For the scope of this book and the CCNA exam, we will illustrate only two of the more basic methods. Please refer to the *Cisco Command Reference* to identify some of the other methods used to monitor access lists. To determine which access lists you have applied to specific interfaces, use the **show ip interface** command as follows:

```
Router# show ip interface
Ethernet 0 is up, line protocol is up
      Internet address is 172.16.4.4, subnet mask is
255.255.255.0
      Broadcast address is 255.255.255.255
```

```
        Address determined by non-volatile memory
        No helper address
        No secondary address
        Outgoing access list 5 is set
        Inbound access list is not set
        Proxy ARP is enabled
        Security level is default
        Split horizon is enabled
        ICMP redirects are always sent
        ICMP unreachables are always sent
        ICMP mask replies are never sent
        IP fast switching is enabled
        Gateway Discovery is disabled
        IP accounting is disabled
        TCP/IP header compression is disabled
Router#
```

The entry identifying the outbound access list is highlighted. To get a more detailed look at the type of access lists that you have applied, use the **show access-lists** command as follows:

```
Router>show access-lists
Standard IP access list 5
permit 172.16.14.0, wildcard bits 0.0.0.255
deny 172.16.3.5, wildcard bits 0.0.0.0
permit 172.16.4.0, wildcard bits 0.0.0.255
permit 172.16.12.4, wildcard bits 0.0.0.0
Extended IP access list 105
permit tcp 172.16.14.0 0.0.0.255 172.16.4.0 eq 23
permit udp host 172.16.14.2 host 172.16.4.4 eq 69
permit tcp host 172.16.14.3 any any
deny 0.0.0.0 255.255.255.255
Router>
```

# Practice Questions

## Question 1

Which of the following commands will apply an IP standard access list to an interface?

- ○ a. **ip access-group 204 in**
- ○ b. **ip access group 110**
- ○ c **ip access-group 45 out**
- ○ d **ip access-group 105 out**
- ○ e **ipx access-group 805 in**

Answer c is correct. The command in answer c identifies an IP standard access list by the access list number 45, which is the proper numeric range for identifying an IP standard access list. Answer a is incorrect because it uses the access list number 204, which is reserved for protocol type access lists not IP standard access lists. Answer b is incorrect because the command is not in the correct format. In addition, it should specify whether the access group is being applied against inbound or outbound packets with the "in" or "out" identifiers. The command format should be **ip access-group**, not **ip access group**. Answer d is incorrect because it identifies an IP extended access list (access list number 105), not an IP standard access list. Answer e is incorrect because it identifies an IPX standard access list, not an IP extended access list.

## Question 2

Which of the following can be used to permit or deny traffic with IP standard access lists? [Choose the two best answers]

- ❏ a. Source IP address
- ❏ b. A range of source IP addresses
- ❏ c. Destination IP address
- ❏ d. A range of destination IP addresses

Answers a and b are correct. IP standard access lists allow IP traffic to be filtered based on source IP addresses; they also allow both individual as well as a range of IP addresses to be specified. Answers c and d are incorrect because IP standard access lists do not filter traffic based on individual or a range of destination IP addresses.

# Question 3

> For an IP standard access list, which source IP address and source-wildcard mask would indicate all IP addresses from IP network 172.16.23.0 /24?
>
> ○ a.  172.16.23.4 0.0.0.0
>
> ○ b.  172.16.23.0 0
>
> ○ c.  172.16.23.0 0.0.0.255
>
> ○ d.  172.16.23.0 0.0.255.0

Answer c is correct, because it uses a wildcard mask of 0.0.0.255 to identify any bit combination in the fourth octet; therefore, any source IP address with the value of 172.16.23.0 through 172.16.23.255 is identified. Answer a is incorrect because it identifies only the IP address 172.16.23.4. All the bits in every octet must be strictly followed as indicated by the source-wildcard mask of 0.0.0.0. Answer b is incorrect because it identifies only the source IP address of 172.16.23.0. Answer d is incorrect because the source-wildcard mask of 0.0.255.0 indicates that any combination of bits in the third octet is identified; however, the fourth octet must be strictly followed. This source IP address and source-wildcard mask combination indicates that the third octet can be any value, but the fourth must be 0.

# Question 4

> Which of the following commands will apply an IP extended access list to an interface?
>
> ○ a.  **ip access-group 204 in**
>
> ○ b.  **ip access group 110**
>
> ○ c.  **ip access-group 115 out**
>
> ○ d.  **ip access-group 95 out**
>
> ○ e  **ipx access-group 805 in**

Answer c is correct. The command in answer c identifies an IP extended access list by the correct numeric range of 100 through 199 for IP extended access lists. Answer a is incorrect because it uses the access list number 204, which is reserved for protocol type access lists. Answer b is incorrect because the command is not in the correct format; it should be **ip access-group**, not **ip access group**. In addition, the command should specify whether the access group is being applied to inbound or outbound packets with the "in" or "out" identifiers. Answer d is incorrect because it identifies an IP standard access list (access list number 95), not an IP extended access list. Answer e is incorrect because it identifies an IPX standard access list, not an IP extended access list.

## Question 5

Which of the following can be used to permit or deny traffic with IP extended access lists? [Choose the three best answers]

❑ a. Source IP addresses

❑ b. Destination IP addresses

❑ c. IP sequence number

❑ d. TCP or UDP port numbers

Answers a, b, and d are correct. Answers a and b are correct because IP extended access lists allow traffic to be filtered based on both source and destination IP addresses. Answer d is correct because IP extended access lists allow traffic to be filtered based on TCP or UDP port numbers. Please refer to Table 13.6 to see a list of the different items the IP extended access lists can use to filter traffic. Answer c is incorrect because IP extended access lists do not filter traffic based on IP sequence number.

## Question 6

What is the valid range for an IP extended access list?

○ a. 1 through 99

○ b. 100 through 199

○ c. 800 through 899

○ d. 900 through 999

Answer b is correct. IP extended access lists are identified by the numeric range of 100 through 199. Answer a is incorrect because the numeric range of 0 through 99 identifies IP standard access lists. Answer c is incorrect because the numeric range of 800 through 899 identifies IPX standard access lists. Answer d is incorrect because the numeric range of 900 through 999 identifies IPX extended access lists.

## Question 7

> Which of the following commands identifies an IPX extended access list?
>
> ○ a.  **ipx access-group 899 in**
>
> ○ b.  **ipx access-group 905 in**
>
> ○ c.  **ipx access-list 910 out**
>
> ○ d.  **ipx access-group 105 out**

Answer b is correct. The numeric range for an IPX extended access list is from 900 through 999. Answer a is incorrect because an access group number of 899 refers to an IPX standard access list, not an IPX extended access list. Answer c is incorrect because the command format of **ip access-list 910 out** is incorrect; the correct format is **ipx access-group**, not **access-list**. Answer d is incorrect because the number 105 is not in the correct range for an IPX extended access list. The number 105 identifies an extended access list.

## Question 8

> Which of the following IP standard access lists would deny the host 172.16.23.2? [Choose the two best answers]
>
> ❑ a.  **access-list** 5 deny 172.16.23.0 0.0.0.255
>
> ❑ b.  **access-list** 105 deny host 172.16.23.2
>
> ❑ c.  **access-list** 25 deny host 172.16.23.2
>
> ❑ d.  **access-list** 5 deny 172.16.24.2 0.0.0.255

Answers a and c are correct. Answer a denies traffic with the source address between 172.16.23.0 and 172.16.23.255. The source-wildcard mask of 0.0.0.255 for answer a indicates that all bit combinations in the fourth octet are identified. Answer c denies only traffic with the source IP address of 172.16.23.2. Answer b is incorrect because the access list number is 105, which identifies an IP extended access list, not an IP standard access list, although this command would function correctly. Answer d is incorrect because it indicates that source IP addresses 172.16.24.0 through 172.16.24.255 are denied access, which does not include source IP address 172.16.23.2.

# Question 9

> Which of the following IP extended access list entries would permit Telnet (TCP port 23) from IP source addresses 172.16.29.0 through 172.16.29.255 to access any destination address?
>
> ○ a. **access-list** 105 permit tcp 172.16.29.0 0.0.0.255 any eq 23
>
> ○ b. **access-list** 105 permit tcp 172.16.29.0 0.0.0.255 172.16.0.0 0.0.255.255 eq 23
>
> ○ c. **access-list** 105 permit tcp host 172.16.29.10 any eq 23
>
> ○ d. **access-list** 105 permit udp 172.16.29.0 0.0.0.255 any eq 23

Answer a is correct. Answer a specifies that TCP traffic with the IP port number of 23 should be permitted from IP source addresses 172.16.29.0 through 172.16.29.255 to any destination IP address. Answer b is incorrect because this access list permits TCP traffic with the IP port number of 23 from source IP addresses 172.16.29.0 through 172.16.29.255 only to the destination IP addresses 172.16.0.0 through 172.16.255.255. Answer c is incorrect because it only permits the host 172.16.29.10. Answer d is incorrect because it permits UDP traffic, not TCP traffic.

# Question 10

> Which of the following commands can be used to show access lists? [Choose the three best answers]
>
> ❑ a. **show ip interfaces**
>
> ❑ b. **show ipx interfaces**
>
> ❑ c. **show access-lists**
>
> ❑ d. **show access lists**

Answers a, b, and c are correct, because they will all show configured access lists. Answer d is incorrect because the command format is wrong; it should be **show access-lists**, not **show access lists**.

# Need to Know More?

 McNutt, Shawn, Mark Poplar, Jason Waters, and David Stabenaw: *CCNA Routing and Switching Exam Prep*. The Coriolis Group, Scottsdale, AZ, 2000. ISBN 1-57610-440-0. This book is a great complement to the CCNA Cram book.

 Chappell, Laura. *Introduction to Cisco Router Configuration*. Cisco Systems Inc., Macmillan Publishing Company, Indianapolis, IN, 1998. ISBN 0-7645-3186-7. This book is a great reference for introductory material about Cisco router configuration.

 Lammle, Todd, Donald Porter, and James Chellis. *CCNA Cisco Certified Network Associate*. Sybex Network Press, Alameda, CA, 1999. ISBN 0-7821-2381-3. Chapter 4 covers IP addressing.

 Syngress Media with Richard D. Hornbaker, CCIE. *Cisco Certified Network Associate Study Guide*. Osborne/McGraw-Hill, Berkeley, CA, 1998. ISBN 0-07-882487-7. Chapter 2 covers IP addressing.

 www.cisco.com/univercd/home/home.htm, Cisco's documentation home page, contains samples and syntax for all access list related commands.

# Wide Area Networking: Point-to-Point

**Terms you'll need to understand:**

✓ Point-to-Point Protocol (PPP)

✓ High-level Data Link Control (HDLC)

✓ Password Authentication Protocol (PAP)

✓ Challenge Handshake Authentication Protocol (CHAP)

✓ Link Control Protocol (LCP)

**Techniques you'll need to master:**

✓ Identifying PPP operations to encapsulate wide area network (WAN) data on Cisco routers

✓ Differentiating between the following WAN services: Frame Relay, integrated services digital network (ISDN), HDLC, and PPP

This chapter provides an overview of WAN protocols and services. It introduces four common protocols then delves into PPP communication. PPP components and operations are discussed, and the configuration and monitoring commands are presented.

# WAN Services

Because WANs cover long distances,organizations typically subscribe to an outside provider for WAN services. These services (usually telephone and data) are routed from an interface at one, end of the customer's network through the provider's network to the other end of the customer's network. Figure 14.1 illustrates a WAN service provider's network cloud.

Table 14.1 defines the commonly used terms presented in Figure 14.1.

It is the provider's responsibility to provide the customer with the parameters necessary to connect to their network. The WAN provider's network appears as a cloud to the customer, who simply makes a point-to-point connection to the remote site.

The main interface between the customer and provider networks occurs between the *data terminal equipment* (*DTE*) and the *data communication equipment* (*DCE*). The customer's router usually serves as the DTE device and performs the packet switching function. Sometimes, DTE devices are bridges or terminals. The DCE attaches to the DTE and provides clocking, converts the data into a suitable format, and switches the data across the provider's network. DCE devices include modems, *channel service unit/data service unit* (*CSU/DSU*), and *terminal adapter/network termination 1* (*TA/NT1*). Figure 14.2 depicts DTE devices (routers) and DCE devices within a WAN.

The DTE/DCE interface serves as the boundary where responsibility for the network traffic shifts between the customer's network and the WAN provider's

| Table 14.1 Common WAN service provider terms. | |
|---|---|
| **Term** | **Description** |
| Customer premise equipment (CPE) | Devices that are physically located on the subscriber's premises. These devices are either owned by the customer or leased from the WAN service provider. |
| Demarcation (Demarc) | The point where the CPE ends and the local loop begins, usually in the customer's main data closet. |
| Local loop (last mile) | Cabling that extends from the Demarc into the service provider's Central Office. |
| Central office (CO) | The WAN service provider's switching facility that provides the nearest point of presence (POP) for the service. The CO is also referred to as the service provider's POP. |

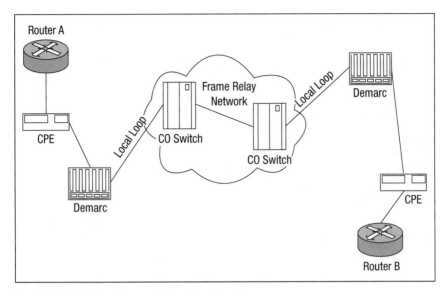

**Figure 14.1** WAN service provider's network cloud.

**Figure 14.2** DTE/DCE interface.

network. It can support several common types of WAN service connections when the DTE is a Cisco router. The first type involves switched services. Switches within the provider's network transmit data from one customer DTE to that customer's other DTEs. *Frame Relay* and *ISDN* are examples of packet-switched and circuit-switched services, respectively.

The second type involves connecting remote devices to a central mainframe. *Synchronous data link control* (*SDLC*) is the protocol used in these types of point-to-point or point-to-multipoint connections. SDLC is a bit-synchronous data link protocol that supports legacy IBM networks.

A third type involves connecting peer devices. HDLC and PPP can be used to encapsulate the data for transmission to peer DTE devices. Table 14.2 lists the types of connectivity of common WAN services, and Figure 14.3 highlights common types of connections and services supported by Cisco routers.

In the remainder of this chapter, we'll be discussing how to employ the HDLC and PPP protocols on a leased line.

# HDLC Overview

HDLC is the default encapsulation used by Cisco routers over synchronous serial links. HDLC is an ISO standard data link protocol. It specifies a method to encapsulate data over synchronous serial links using frame characters and checksums.

Cisco routers use a proprietary version of HDLC. Typically, HDLC is used on leased lines between two Cisco devices. If you need to establish a link between a Cisco router and a non-Cisco device, you must use PPP encapsulation instead of HDLC.

 The ISO standard HDLC does not support multiple protocols on a single link. However, Cisco's proprietary HDLC adds a field that allows it to support multiprotocol environments.

The command to enable HDLC on an interface is relatively simple—**encapsulation hdlc** from interface configuration mode. Because HDLC is the default encapsulation type used by Cisco routers, the only time you may need to use this command is when an interface has been configured with another encapsulation type, and you need to change it back to HDLC.

# PPP Overview

PPP encapsulates network layer information for transmission over point-to-point links. It was designed by developers on the Internet and is described by a series of

| Table 14.2 Connectivity of common WAN services. | |
|---|---|
| **Type** | **Connects To** |
| Frame Relay, ISDN | A device in a WAN service provider's network |
| SDLC | An IBM enterprise data center computer (mainframe hosts) |
| HDLC, PPP | A peer device on the WAN |

**Figure 14.3**  Common WAN services supported by Cisco routers.

documents called *Request for Comments (RFC)*, namely, 1661, 1331, and 2153. Figure 14.4 shows how PPP's layered architecture relates to the Open Systems Interconnect (OSI) model.

PPP consists of two main components:

➤ *Link Control Protocol (LCP)*—Establishes, configures, and tests the connection

➤ *Network Control Program (NCP)*—Configures many different network layer protocols

## PPP Physical Layer

PPP can operate on a variety of DTE/DCE physical interfaces, including:

➤ Asynchronous serial

➤ Synchronous serial

➤ High-speed serial interface (HSSI)

➤ ISDN

Other than what is required by a particular physical interface, PPP makes no special transmission rate requirements.

**Figure 14.4** The OSI reference model and PPP.

# PPP Connections

It is the responsibility of the LCP within PPP to establish, configure, test, maintain, and terminate the point-to-point connection. Four phases occur during the LCP process:

➤ Link establishment

➤ Link quality determination

➤ Network-layer protocol negotiation

➤ Link termination

During link establishment, LCP opens the connection and negotiates configuration parameters. Acknowledgment frames must be sent and received before this phase can be considered completed successfully.

The link quality determination phase involves testing the connection to determine whether the line quality is sufficient to support the network-layer protocols. Although this phase seems very important, it is optional.

In the third phase, the appropriate network-layer protocols are configured. *Network control programs (NCPs)* configure PPP to support different networklayer protocols, including Internet Protocol (IP), Internet Packet Exchange (IPX), and AppleTalk. The PPP devices transmit NCP packets to select and configure one or more network-layer protocols. After each selected network-layer protocol has been configured, data can begin to be transmitted across the link. If the LCP terminates a link, it notifies the NCP, which takes appropriate action.

The link termination phase can be initiated by the LCP at any time. Link termination can occur from events such as a user request, a loss of carrier, or the expiration of a time-out parameter.

# PPP Authentication

PPP authentication occurs during the link quality determination phase; therefore, authentication is optional. The caller (or calling side of the link) must transmit information to ensure that the caller is authorized to establish the connection. This is accomplished by a series of authentication messages being sent between the routers. PPP supports two types of authentication: PAP and CHAP.

## PAP

PAP uses a two-way handshake to allow remote hosts to identify themselves. After the link has been established and the link establishment phase is complete, PAP performs the following steps:

1. The remote host initiates the call, sends a username and password to the local host, and continues to send the information until it is accepted or rejected.

2. The local host receives the call and accepts or rejects the username and password information. If the local host rejects the information, the connection is terminated.

## CHAP

CHAP uses a three-way handshake to force remote hosts to identify themselves after the link establishment phase. CHAP performs the following steps after the link establishment phase is complete:

1. The local router that received the call sends a challenge packet to the remote host that initiated the call. The challenge packet consists of an ID, a random number, and either the name of the local host performing the authentication or a username on the remote host.

2. The remote host must respond with its encrypted unique ID, a one-way encrypted password, the remote hostname or a username, and a random number.

3. The local router performs its own calculation on the response values. It accepts or rejects the authentication request based on whether the value it received from the remote host matches the value it calculated.

Like PAP, CHAP terminates the connection immediately if the local host rejects the authentication request.

During the PAP process, the username and password information is sent from the remote host in clear text, so PAP is not a strong protocol. It offers no protection from a network analyzer capturing the information and using it. Because CHAP uses secret, encrypted passwords and unique IDs, it is a much stronger protocol than PAP. You can choose only one type of authentication, so CHAP is definitely recommended; however, PAP is better than no authentication at all.

## LCP Configuration Options

Cisco routers support several configuration options for LCP:

➤ Authentication options include PAP and CHAP.

➤ By reducing the amount of data that must be transmitted, data compressions increase the throughput on a network link. The data is compressed as it is sent and decompressed as it is received. LCP compression options include Stacker or Predictor.

➤ The error-detection options within LCP activate processes to detect errors. The Quality and Magic Number protocols help to ensure reliable connections.

➤ The multilink PPP configuration option supports load balancing over PPP links. This option is supported in Cisco Internetwork Operating System (IOS) 11.1 and later.

Table 14.3 summarizes the different configuration options within LCP.

*Note: RFC 1548 describes the different PPP LCP configuration options in detail.*

| Table 14.3 | LCP configuration options. | | |
| --- | --- | --- | --- |
| **Option** | **Function** | **Protocol** | **Command** |
| Authentication | Requires a password | PAP | **ppp authentication pap** |
| | Performs a challenge handshake | CHAP | **ppp authentication chap** |
| Compression | Compresses data at the source | Stacker | **ppp compress stacker** |
| | Reproduces data at the destination | Predictor | **ppp compress predictor** |
| Error detection | Monitors the data dropped on the link, avoids frame looping | Quality, Magic Number | **ppp quality** **<number 1 - 100>** |
| Multilink | Performs load balancing across multiple links | MP | **ppp multilink** |

# Configuring PPP

Configuring PPP on a Cisco router requires that both global and interface configuration commands be executed on both the local and remote routers. Figure 14.5 presents an example of two routers that need to establish a PPP link.

A username and password must be set, so the following global configuration command must be executed:

```
Username name password secret-password
```

In this command, *name* and *secret-password* indicate the name of the remote host and the password to use for authentication. The password must be the same on both the local and remote routers. Table 14.4 lists the interface commands that must be executed to configure PPP. Figure 14.6 presents the global and interface configuration commands for router A and router B.

**Figure 14.5**    PPP.

**Figure 14.6**    PPP configuration.

**Table 14.4    PPP interface commands.**

| Command | Description |
| --- | --- |
| encapsulation ppp | Encapsulates data on this interface as PPP |
| ppp authentication pap | Enables password checking for incoming calls |
| ppp authentication chap | Forces incoming calls to answer password challenges |

# Monitoring PPP

You can monitor PPP activity with the **show interface** and **debug ppp chap** commands. The **show interface** command enables you to view PPP LCP and NCP information. Listing 14.1 shows an example of PPP activity on an interface.

**Listing 14.1    PPP activity with the show interface command.**

```
RouterA#sh int s0
Serial0 is up, line protocol is up
  Hardware is HD64570
  Internet address is 172.16.1.1/16
  MTU 1500 bytes, BW 1544 Kbit, DLY 20000 usec,
    rely 255/255, load 1/255
  Encapsulation PPP, loopback not set, keepalive set (10 sec)
  LCP Open
  Open: IPCP, CDPCP
  Last input 00:00:06, output 00:00:06, output hang never
  Last clearing of "show interface" counters never
  Input queue: 0/75/0 (size/max/drops); Total output drops: 0
  Queueing strategy: weighted fair
  Output queue: 0/1000/64/0 (size/max total/threshold/drops)
    Conversations  0/2/256 (active/max active/max total)
    Reserved Conversations 0/0 (allocated/max allocated)
  5 minute input rate 0 bits/sec, 0 packets/sec
  5 minute output rate 0 bits/sec, 0 packets/sec
    34 packets input, 1303 bytes, 0 no buffer
    Received 34 broadcasts, 0 runts, 0 giants, 0 throttles
    0 input errors, 0 CRC, 0 frame, 0 overrun, 0 ignored, 0 abort
    72 packets output, 2819 bytes, 0 underruns
    0 output errors, 0 collisions, 14 interface resets
    0 output buffer failures, 0 output buffers swapped out
    41 carrier transitions
    DCD=up  DSR=up  DTR=up  RTS=up  CTS=up
RouterA#
```

The **debug ppp chap** command displays the CHAP packet exchanges and PAP exchanges. Listing 14.2 displays an example authentication handshake sequence.

**Listing 14.2**   PPP authentication sequence with the **debug ppp chap** command.

```
RouterA# debug ppp chap
Serial0: Unable to authenticate. No name received from peer
Serial0: Unable to validate CHAP response.
        USERNAME pioneer not found.
Serial0: Unable to validate CHAP response.
        No password defined for USERNAME pioneer
Serial0: Failed CHAP authentication with remote.
Remote message is Unknown name
Serial0: remote passed CHAP authentication.
Serial0: Passed CHAP authentication with remote.
Serial0: CHAP input code = 4 id = 3 len = 48
```

*Note:* The **debug ppp chap** command displays the reason why the CHAP request failed.

Once you have finished examining the debug output, use the **no debug all** command to turn off the debugging feature.

# Practice Questions

## Question 1

> Which of the following commands allows you to monitor a PPP authentication sequence on interface serial 0?
>
> ○ a. **sh ppp**
>
> ○ b. **sh ppp s0**
>
> ○ c. **debug ppp authentication s0**
>
> ○ d. **debug ppp authentication**

Answer d is correct. **debug ppp authentication** displays the authentication handshake sequence as it is occurring. Answers a, b, and c are incorrect because they are all invalid commands.

## Question 2

> Which protocol is responsible for establishing, configuring, testing, maintaining, and terminating PPP connections?
>
> ○ a. BRI
>
> ○ b. PRI
>
> ○ c. LCP
>
> ○ d. NCP

Answer c is correct. LCP has the primary responsibility for a PPP connection. Answer d is incorrect, because NCP is responsible for the configuration supporting network-layer protocols. Answers a and b are incorrect because BRI and PRI are not components within PPP.

## Question 3

> Which of the following is an authentication type that would be appropriate
> for an environment that requires strong encrypted passwords?
>
> ○ a. PAP
>
> ○ b. CHAP
>
> ○ c. LCP
>
> ○ d. NCP

Answer b is correct. CHAP uses encrypted passwords, making it a much stronger protocol than PAP. Answer a is incorrect because PAP uses clear text to send passwords. Answers c and d are incorrect because neither is an authentication type.

## Question 4

> Which of the following physical interfaces will PPP operate on?
>
> ○ a. asynchronous serial
>
> ○ b. synchronous serial
>
> ○ c. HSSI
>
> ○ d. ISDN
>
> ○ e. all of the above

Trick! question

Answer e is correct. PPP can operate on a variety of DTE/DCE physical interfaces, including asynchronous serial, synchronous serial, HSSI, and ISDN.

## Question 5

Which PPP authentication protocol uses a three-way handshake?

○ a. PAP

○ b. CHAP

○ c. LCP

○ d. NCP1

Answer b is correct. The CHAP three-way handshake includes the local host requesting authentication, the remote host sending an encrypted response, and the local host comparing the received information then accepting or rejecting the connection. PAP only uses a two-way handshake, so answer a is incorrect. LCP and NCP1 are not authentication protocols, so answers c and d are incorrect.

# Need to Know More?

McNutt, Shawn, Mark Poplar, Jason Waters, and David Stabenaw: *CCNA Routing and Switching Exam Prep.* The Coriolis Group, Scottsdale, AZ, 2000. ISBN 1-57610-440-0. This book is a great complement to the CCNA Cram book. Chapters 12 and 13 contain information on PPP.

Downes, Kevin, Merilee Ford, H. Kim Lew, Steve Spanier, and Tim Stevenson. *Internetworking Technologies Handbook, 2nd Edition,* MacMillan Publishing Company, Indianapolis, IN, 1998. ISBN 1-57870-102-3. Chapters 12 and 13 present more information about PPP.

Reed, Kenneth. *Data Network Handbook.* Van Nostrand Reinhold Publishing, New York, NY, 1996. ISBN 0-442-02299-9. Chapter 11 provides more information about voice and data telecommunications.

Syngress Media, with Richard D. Hornbaker, CCIE. *Cisco Certified Network Associate Study Guide.* Osborne/McGraw-Hill, Berkeley, CA, 1998. ISBN 0-07-882487-7. Chapter 10 addresses wide area networking.

Using Cisco's documentation CD, you can immediately access Cisco's entire library of end-user documentation, selected product news, bug databases, and related information. The documentation CD-ROM is produced monthly.

**www.cisco.com,** the official Cisco Web site, contains several Cisco white papers on topics such as PPP configuration and troubleshooting.

**www.cis.ohio-state.edu/hypertext/information/rfc.html,** the Computer and Information Science Web site at Ohio State University, provides information about Internet RFC documents. You can review detailed information on PPP in RFCs 1661, 1331, and 2153.

# Wide Area Networking: Integrated Services Digital Network (ISDN)

**Terms you'll need to understand:**

✓ ISDN

✓ Basic rate interface (BRI)

✓ Primary rate interface (PRI)

✓ Functions

✓ Reference points

✓ Dial-on-demand routing (DDR)

**Techniques you'll need to master:**

✓ Stating a relevant use and context for ISDN networking

✓ Identifying ISDN protocols, function groups, reference points, and channels

✓ Describing Cisco's implementation of ISDN BRI

This chapter continues the overview of wide area network (WAN) protocols and services. It discusses the use and context for ISDN networking and addresses ISDN components, and configuration and monitoring commands.

# ISDN Overview

*ISDN* refers to the call processing system that enables voice, data, graphics, music, and video to be transmitted over our existing telephone system. ISDN offers several advantages over existing analog modem lines. For example, ISDN connection speeds begin at 64Kbps, whereas typical modem speeds hover between 28.8Kbps and 56Kbps. The call setup time for an ISDN call is also much quicker. ISDN can transmit data packets, voice, or video. ISDN is a viable solution for remote connectivity (telecommuting) and access to the Internet. ISDN also supports any of the network-layer protocols supported by the Cisco Internetwork Operating System (IOS) and encapsulates other WAN services, such as Point-to-Point Protocol (PPP).

ISDN can be used to:

➤ Add bandwidth for telecommuting

➤ Improve Internet response times

➤ Carry multiple network-layer protocols

➤ Encapsulate other WAN services

## Basic Rate Interface and Primary Rate Interface

ISDN can be ordered as either *BRI* or *PRI*. An ISDN BRI service contains two bearer channels (or B channels) of 64Kbps and one data channel (or D channel) of 16Kbps. The B channel carries user data, and the D channel carries signaling and control information. The maximum throughput for BRI is 128Kbps (two B channels at 64Kbps). In North America and Japan, an ISDN PRI service uses a T1 line that contains 23 B channels and one D channel that enables a maximum throughput of 1.544Mbps. In Europe, PRI service uses an E1 line that contains 30 B channels, enabling a throughput of 2.048Mbps.

## ISDN Protocols

The International Telecommunication Union Telecommunication (ITU-T) standardization sector is an international body that develops worldwide standards for telecommunications technologies. In 1984, ITU-T published a comprehensive list of standard ISDN protocols, organized into groups that address certain topics. Table 15.1 presents some of the ISDN protocols.

| Table 15.1   ITU-T standard ISDN protocols. | | |
|---|---|---|
| **Topic** | **Protocol** | **Example** |
| Telephone network and ISDN | E-series | E.164, international ISDN addressing |
| ISDN concepts, aspects, and interfaces | I-series | I.100, concepts, structures, and terminology |
| Switching and signaling | Q-series | Q.931, ISDN network layer between terminal and switch |

## Functions and Reference Points

ISDN functions and reference points are the items that describe ISDN service provider standards. Functions and reference points enable you to articulate your needs clearly as you work with service providers to engineer, implement, and maintain ISDN services. *Functions* represent devices or hardware functions within ISDN. Table 15.2 presents basic ISDN devices and their functions.

*Reference points* describe the logical interfaces between ISDN functions like TAs or NT1s. Table 15.3 lists common ISDN reference points.

Normally, you can connect up to eight ISDN-capable devices on a single ISDN line, enabling them to share the ISDN bandwidth. These devices may be things such as ISDN-capable phones, faxes, routers, and/or terminal adapters. Figure 15.1 shows an example of two routers connected to ISDN services.

| Table 15.2   ISDN devices and functions. | | |
|---|---|---|
| **Device Name** | **Abbreviation** | **Function** |
| Terminal adapter | TA | Converts RS-232, V.35, and so forth into BRI signals |
| Terminal end-point 1 | TE1 | Indicates a router or other device that has a native ISDN interface |
| Terminal end-point 2 | TE2 | Indicates a router or other device that requires a TA for its BRI signals |
| Network termination 1 | NT1 | Converts BRI signals for use by the ISDN line |
| Network termination 2 | NT2 | Indicates a device that supports on-premises ISDN concentration, such as a PBX; a more complex NT1 that also performs layer 2 and 3 functions |
| Local termination | LT | The part of the local exchange that terminates the local loop |
| Exchange termination | ET | The part of the exchange that communicates with other ISDN components |

| Table 15.3 | ISDN reference points. |
| --- | --- |
| Abbreviation | Logical Interface Between |
| R | TE2 and TA |
| S | TE1 and NT2 |
| T | NT1 and NT2 |
| U | NT1 and LT |

In Figure 15.1, router A is a TE1 device that already has a built-in BRI connection. Conversely, router B does not have a built-in BRI connection; it has a serial connection and is considered a TE2 device. It requires a TA to convert the serial signals into BRI signals. Both router A and router B (with a TA device) can connect to the NT1 device.

If your router has a BRI interface, you only need to attach an NT1 device to connect to ISDN services. If your router does not have a BRI interface, you need to attach a TA and an NT1 to connect to ISDN services. In North America, ISDN BRIs can be provisioned without an NT1. In this case, the customer is responsible for providing the NT1 and power for the NT1. Unlike analog telephone lines, if you want a BRI to stay up during a power outage, you must supply uninterrupted power to the NT1. In Europe, ISDN BRIs are provisioned with the NT1 included.

**Figure 15.1**   SDN Example.

*Note: An ISDN BRI usually interfaces with an NT1 device, and an ISDN PRI usually interfaces with a channel service unit/data service unit (CSU/DSU).*

## DDR

*DDR* works with ISDN to establish and terminate network connections, as traffic dictates. DDR configuration commands define host and ISDN connection information. An access list and DDR dialer group define what type of traffic should initiate an ISDN call. You can configure multiple access lists to look for different types of *interesting* traffic. Interesting traffic is simply network traffic that (when it arrives at the router) triggers the router to initiate the ISDN connection. Figure 15.2 illustrates the DDR process when router A calls router B.

When the router notices interesting traffic, it refers to its ISDN information and initiates setup of the ISDN call through its BRI or PRI and NT1 device. When the connection is established, normal routing occurs between the two end devices. After interesting traffic stops being transmitted over the ISDN connection, the connection idle timer begins. When the idle timer expires, the connection is terminated.

# Configuring ISDN

You must perform both global and interface configuration tasks when configuring a router for ISDN. Global configuration tasks include specifying the type of ISDN switch your router connects to at the provider's central office (CO) and defining what type of traffic is interesting. Table 15.4 lists the ISDN global configuration commands.

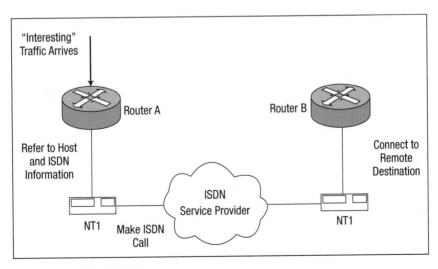

**Figure 15.2**   DDR with ISDN.

**Table 15.4   ISDN global configuration commands.**

| Command | Description |
|---|---|
| **ISDN switch-type** switch-type | Defines an ISDN switch type |
| **dialer-list dialer-group protocol** | Defines or restricts (permits or denies) |
| **protocol permit** | Defines any specific protocol traffic as interesting for a particular dialer group |

**Table 15.5   ISDN interface configuration commands.**

| Command | Description |
|---|---|
| **interface bri** interface number | Chooses the router interface acting as a TE1 device |
| **encapsulation ppp** | Chooses PPP framing |
| **dialer-group** number | Assigns an interface to a specific dialer group |
| **dialer map protocol next hop** | Maps a layer 3 protocol to a next hop address with a specific name |
| **address name** hostname speed | Defines the connection speed |
| **number** dial-string | Defines the telephone number to dial |
| **dialer idle-timeout** number | Defines the number of seconds of idle time before the ISDN connection is terminated |

Table 15.5 shows the ISDN commands that must be configured on an interface.

Figure 15.3 presents a simple ISDN DDR configuration for router A and router B.

# Monitoring ISDN

The commands listed in this section enable you to monitor the activity and operation of ISDN and DDR configurations.

You can monitor ISDN and DDR configurations with the following commands:

➤ **show controller bri**

➤ **show interface bri**

➤ **show dialer**

Use the **show controller bri** command to display detailed information about the B and D channels. Listing 15.1 displays an example of the **show controller** command.

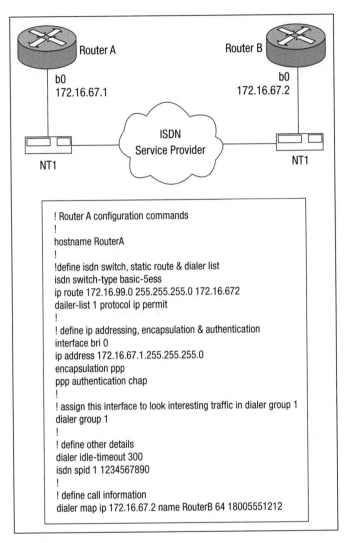

**Figure 15.3** DDR configuration example.

## Listing 15.1 The **show controller bri** command output.

```
RouterA# show controller bri 0
BRI unit 0
D Chan Info:
Layer 1 is ACTIVATED
idb 0x32089C, ds 0x3267D8, reset_mask 0x2
buffer size 1524
RX ring with 2 entries at 0x2101600 : Rxhead 0
```

```
00 pak=0x4122E8 ds=0x412444 status=D000 pak_size=0
01 pak=0x410C20 ds=0x410D7C status=F000 pak_size=0
TX ring with 1 entries at 0x2101640: tx_count = 0,
  tx_head = 0, tx_tail = 0
00 pak=0x000000 ds=0x000000 status=7C00 pak_size=0
0 missed datagrams, 0 overruns, 0 bad frame addresses
0 bad datagram encapsulations, 0 memory errors
0 transmitter underruns
B1 Chan Info:
Layer 1 is ACTIVATED
idb 0x3224E8, ds 0x3268C8, reset_mask 0x0
buffer size 1524
RX ring with 8 entries at 0x2101400 : Rxhead 0
00 pak=0x421FC0 ds=0x42211C status=D000 pak_size=0
01 pak=0x4085E8 ds=0x408744 status=D000 pak_size=0
02 pak=0x422EF0 ds=0x42304C status=D000 pak_size=0
03 pak=0x4148E0 ds=0x414A3C status=D000 pak_size=0
04 pak=0x424D50 ds=0x424EAC status=D000 pak_size=0
05 pak=0x423688 ds=0x4237E4 status=D000 pak_size=0
06 pak=0x41AB98 ds=0x41ACF4 status=D000 pak_size=0
07 pak=0x41A400 ds=0x41A55C status=F000 pak_size=0
TX ring with 4 entries at 0x2101440: tx_count = 0,
  tx_head = 0, tx_tail = 0
00 pak=0x000000 ds=0x000000 status=5C00 pak_size=0
01 pak=0x000000 ds=0x000000 status=5C00 pak_size=0
02 pak=0x000000 ds=0x000000 status=5C00 pak_size=0
03 pak=0x000000 ds=0x000000 status=7C00 pak_size=0
0 missed datagrams, 0 overruns, 0 bad frame addresses
0 bad datagram encapsulations, 0 memory errors
0 transmitter underruns
B2 Chan Info:
Layer 1 is ACTIVATED
idb 0x324520, ds 0x3269B8, reset_mask 0x2
buffer size 1524
RX ring with 8 entries at 0x2101500 : Rxhead 0
00 pak=0x40FCF0 ds=0x40FE4C status=D000 pak_size=0
01 pak=0x40E628 ds=0x40E784 status=D000 pak_size=0
02 pak=0x40F558 ds=0x40F6B4 status=D000 pak_size=0
03 pak=0x413218 ds=0x413374 status=D000 pak_size=0
04 pak=0x40EDC0 ds=0x40EF1C status=D000 pak_size=0
05 pak=0x4113B8 ds=0x411514 status=D000 pak_size=0
06 pak=0x416ED8 ds=0x417034 status=D000 pak_size=0
07 pak=0x416740 ds=0x41689C status=F000 pak_size=0
TX ring with 4 entries at 0x2101540: tx_count = 0,
  tx_head = 0, tx_tail = 0
```

```
00 pak=0x000000 ds=0x000000 status=5C00 pak_size=0
01 pak=0x000000 ds=0x000000 status=5C00 pak_size=0
02 pak=0x000000 ds=0x000000 status=5C00 pak_size=0
03 pak=0x000000 ds=0x000000 status=7C00 pak_size=0
0 missed datagrams, 0 overruns, 0 bad frame addresses
0 bad datagram encapsulations, 0 memory errors
0 transmitter underruns
```

*Note: Both B channels and the D channel are active.*

Use the **show interface bri** command to display BRI status, encapsulation, and counter information. Listing 15.2 displays an example of the **show interface** command.

### Listing 15.2   The **show interface bri** command output.

```
RouterA# show interface bri 0
BRI0 is up, line protocol is up (spoofing)
Hardware is BRI
Internet address is 172.16.67.1, subnet mask is 255.255.255.0
MTU 1500 bytes, BW 64 Kbit, DLY 20000 usec,
rely 255/255, load 1/255
Encapsulation PPP, loopback not set, keepalive set (10 sec)
Last input 0:00:07, output 0:00:00, output hang never
Output queue 0/40, 0 drops; input queue 0/75, 0 drops
Five minute input rate 0 bits/sec, 0 packets/sec
Five minute output rate 0 bits/sec, 0 packets/sec
16263 packets input, 1347238 bytes, 0 no buffer
Received 13983 broadcasts, 0 runts, 0 giants
2 input errors, 0 CRC, 0 frame, 0 overrun, 0 ignored, 2 abort
22146 packets output, 2383680 bytes, 0 underruns
0 output errors, 0 collisions, 2 interface resets, 0 restarts
1 carrier transitions
```

*Note: The encapsulation type is PPP, and two errors were received on the BRI.*

Use the **show dialer bri** command to display general diagnostic information for serial interfaces configured to support DDR. Listing 15.3 displays an example of the **show dialer** command.

### Listing 15.3   The **show dialer bri** command output.

```
RouterA# show dialer interface bri 0
BRI0 - dialer type = IN-BAND NO-PARITY
Idle timer (900 secs), Fast idle timer (20 secs)
Wait for carrier (30 secs), Re-enable (15 secs)
```

```
Time until disconnect 838 secs
Current call connected 0:02:16
Connected to 8986

Dial String Successes Failures  Last called  Last status
8986             0        0      never                     Default
8986             8        3      0:02:16      Success      Default
```

*Note:* *"IN-BAND" indicates that DDR is enabled and the router is currently connected. The Dial String table provides a history of logged calls.*

# Practice Questions

## Question 1

> If your router does not have a built-in BRI, which device will you need to connect to ISDN services? [Choose the two best answers]
>
> ❑ a. NT1
>
> ❑ b. TA
>
> ❑ c. TE1
>
> ❑ d. TE2

Answers a and b are correct. You need a TA to convert the serial signal from your router into a BRI signal and an NT1 to convert the BRI signal for use by the ISDN digital line. A TE1 is a device that *has* a built-in BRI and already transmits BRI signals, so answer c is incorrect. Answer d is incorrect because a device that does *not* have a built-in BRI is considered a TE2.

## Question 2

> How can you use ISDN? [Choose all that apply]
>
> ❑ a. To improve Internet response times
>
> ❑ b. To encapsulate other WAN services
>
> ❑ c. To add bandwidth for telecommuting
>
> ❑ d. To carry multiple network-layer protocols

Answers a, b, c, and d are all correct.

## Question 3

> What commands should you use to monitor ISDN or DDR activity? [Choose the three best answers]
>
> ❑ a. **show interfaces**
>
> ❑ b. **show controllers**
>
> ❑ c. **show dialer**
>
> ❑ d. **show bri**

Answers a, b, and c are correct. The **show interfaces** command displays status and statistics for each interface on the router, including BRI. The **show controllers** command displays detailed information about BRI channels. The **show dialer** command presents information about current dialer activity and simple call history. Answer d is incorrect because the **show bri** command is invalid.

# Question 4

According to ITU-T standards for ISDN protocols, which series of standards deals with switching and signaling?

○ a.  A-series

○ b.  E-series

○ c.  R-series

○ d.  Q-series

Answer d is correct. The Q-series standards address switching and signaling topics. Answers a and c are incorrect, because A-series and R-series do not exist for ISDN. Although E-series is a valid grouping of standards, it addresses telephone network and ISDN topics; therefore, answer b is incorrect.

# Question 5

What is the correct command to define all IPX traffic as "uninteresting" for dialer group 7?

○ a.  **dialer-group 7 no ipx**

○ b.  **dialer-group 7 no ipx all**

○ c.  **dialer-group 7 protocol no ipx**

○ d.  **dialer-group 7 protocol ipx deny**

Answer d is correct. The syntax for the **dialer-group** command requires a dialer-group, the keyword "protocol," the protocol you want to define (IP, IPX, AppleTalk, and so on), and the keyword "permit" or "deny" to indicate whether the protocol should be permitted or denied. Answers a, b, and c are incorrect because they each generate syntax error messages.

# Need to Know More?

 McNutt, Shawn, Mark Poplar, Jason Waters, and David Stabenaw: *CCNA Routing and Switching Exam Prep*. The Coriolis Group, Scottsdale, AZ, 2000. ISBN 1-57610-440-0. This book is a great complement to the CCNA Cram book. Chapter 13 covers ISDN.

 Downes, Kevin, Merilee Ford, H. Kim Lew, Steve Spanier, and Tim Stevenson. *Internetworking Technologies Handbook, 2nd Edition*. MacMillan Publishing Company, Indianapolis, IN, 1998. ISBN 1-57870-102-3. Chapters 12 and 13 present more information about PPP and ISDN.

 Reed, Kenneth. *Data Network Handbook*. Van Nostrand Reinhold Publishing, New York, NY, 1996. ISBN 0-442-02299-9. Chapter 11 provides more information about voice and data telecommunications.

 Syngress Media, with Richard D. Hornbaker, CCIE. *Cisco Certified Network Associate Study Guide*. Osborne/McGraw-Hill, Berkeley, CA, 1998. ISBN 0-07-882487-7. Chapter 10 addresses wide area networking.

 Using Cisco's documentation CD, you can immediately access Cisco's entire library of end-user documentation, selected product news, bug databases, and related information. The documentation CD-ROM is produced monthly.

 **www.cisco.com**, the official Cisco Web site, contains several Cisco white papers on topics such as PPP and ISDN configuration and troubleshooting.

 **www.cis.ohio-state.edu/hypertext/information/rfc.html**, the computer and information science Web site at Ohio State University, provides information about Internet Request for Comments (RFC) documents. You can review detailed information about the RFCs related to PPP and ISDN.

# Wide Area Networking: Frame Relay

**16**

## Terms you'll need to understand:

✓ Data terminal equipment (DTE)

✓ Data communication equipment (DCE)

✓ Frame Relay

✓ Frame check sequence (FCS)

✓ Discard eligibility bit

✓ Permanent virtual circuit (PVC)

✓ Data link connection identifier (DLCI)

✓ Local Management Interface (LMI)

✓ Nonbroadcast multiaccess (NBMA)

✓ Subinterface

## Techniques you'll need to master:

✓ Recognizing key Frame Relay terms and features

✓ Listing commands to configure Frame Relay LMIs, maps, and subinterfaces

✓ Listing commands to monitor Frame Relay activity in a router

This chapter continues the overview of wide area network (WAN) protocols and services. It discusses the use of Frame Relay networking and addresses Frame Relay configuration and monitoring commands.

# Frame Relay

Frame Relay is a high-speed, packet-switching WAN protocol. Packet-switching protocols enable devices to share the available network bandwidth. As its name implies, Frame Relay operates at layer 2 of the Open Systems Interconnect (OSI) model and runs on nearly any type of serial interface. Frame Relay encapsulates packets from the upper layers of the OSI model and switches them through the provider's network. Figure 16.1 provides a quick comparison of Frame Relay and the OSI model.

Frame Relay services have been streamlined to gain more throughput. Services such as flow control, robust congestion management, and error checking are left to upper layer protocols like Transmission Control Protocol (TCP); however, Frame Relay does include some error checking and congestion management.

Frame Relay uses cyclic redundancy checking (CRC) to perform error checking quickly. CRC produces a *frame check sequence* (*FCS*), which is appended to each frame that is transmitted. When a node receives the frame, it calculates a new FCS (based on the data portion of the frame) and compares it with the one contained in the frame. If the values are different, the frame is dropped.

Frame Relay manages congestion through the use of a *discard eligibility bit*. This bit is set to a value of 1 if the frame has lower importance than other frames; the DTE device is responsible for setting the bit and sets the bit to 1 for frames that have lower importance than other frames. Switches within the WAN provider's network may discard frames to manage congestion. However, the switches only discard frames with the discard eligibility bit set to 1; frames with bits set to 0 are still transmitted. This feature protects against critical data being dropped during periods of network congestion.

## Virtual Circuits

Communication in a Frame Relay network is connection-oriented, and a defined communication path must exist between each pair of DTE devices. Virtual circuits provide the bidirectional communication within Frame Relay networks. In essence, a virtual circuit is a logical connection established between two DTE devices. Many virtual circuits can be multiplexed into one physical circuit, and a single virtual circuit can cross multiple DCE devices within the Frame Relay network.

| OSI Reference Model | Frame Relay |
|---|---|
| Application | 0 |
| Presentation | 0 |
| Session | 0 |
| Transport | 0 |
| Network | 0 |
| Data Link | Frame Relay |
| Physical | Physical |

**Figure 16.1**    The OSI reference model and Frame Relay.

Virtual circuits can be grouped into two categories: *switched virtual circuits* (*SVCs*) and *permanent virtual circuits* (*PVCs*). SVCs are temporary connections and can be used when only sporadic data communication is necessary between DTE devices. SVCs require the connection to be set up and terminated for each session. Conversely, PVCs are permanent connections. They support frequent and consistent data communications across a Frame Relay network. When the PVC is established, DTE devices can begin transmitting data when they are ready. PVCs are used more widely in Frame Relay networks than SVCs.

# DLCI

A *DLCI* serves as the addressing scheme within a Frame Relay network. The service provider assigns a DLCI for each PVC, and the DLCI is locally significant within the network. In other words, the DLCI must be unique within the network like an Internet Protocol (IP) address. Two DTE devices that have a PVC established between them may or may not use the same DLCI value. Figure 16.2 illustrates how PVCs and DLCIs appear within a Frame Relay network. Table 16.1 clarifies how each router maps its ports to DLCI numbers.

There are two methods that can be used to map a DLCI to a network layer address (such as an IP address)—dynamically by inverse ARP or manually using the map command. Both methods are discussed in the Configuring Frame Relay section.

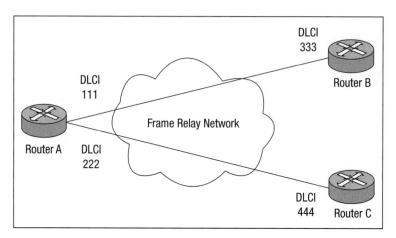

**Figure 16.2** PVCs with DLCIs.

| Table 16.1 DLCI mapping. | | |
|---|---|---|
| **From Router** | **To Router** | **Use DLCI** |
| A | B | 111 |
| A | C | 222 |
| B | A | 333 |
| C | A | 444 |

# LMI

*LMI* is a set of enhancements to the Frame Relay protocol specifications. Developed in 1990 by four companies (nicknamed the "Gang of Four"), LMI extensions offer several features for better management of complex Frame Relay networks. These extensions include global addressing, virtual circuit status messaging, and multicasting.

*Note: The "Gang of Four" includes Cisco Systems, StrataCom, Northern Telecom, and Digital Equipment Corporation.*

The LMI global addressing extension enables a DLCI to have global instead of local significance. With LMI, DLCI values are unique within a Frame Relay network, and standard address resolution protocols, such as Address Resolution Protocol (ARP) and reverse ARP (or inverse ARP), and discovery protocols can be used to identify nodes within the network. Virtual circuit status messaging improves the communication and synchronization between DTE and DCE devices. The status messages, which are similar to hello packets, report on the status of PVCs. LMI multicasting enables multicast groups to be assigned. Multicasting reduces overhead by allowing route updates and address resolution messages to be sent to specific groups of DTE devices.

Cisco supports the following Frame Relay LMI protocol variations:

➤ **ANSI**—American National Standards Institute

➤ **q933a**—International Telecommunication Union–Telecommunication standardization sector

➤ **cisco**—Gang of Four

# Configuring Frame Relay

Configuring a Cisco router to serve as a DTE device within a Frame Relay network involves configuring interfaces on the router. Table 16.2 lists the commands that you must execute to configure Frame Relay on an interface.

In configurations where inverse ARP is not used to dynamically discover network protocol addresses on the virtual circuit, the **frame-relay map** command must be used to map the layer 3 protocol address to the layer 2 DLCI.

Configure the **frame-relay map** command as follows:

```
Frame-relay map protocol protocol-address dlci [broadcast]
[cisco | ietf]
```

In this example, "protocol" is a supported protocol such as IP or Internet Packet Exchange (IPX). "protocol-address" is the destination protocol address. "dlci" is the DLCI number used to connect to the specified protocol address on the interface. "broadcast" (optional) forwards broadcasts to this address; although this is optional, it's usually a good idea to include it. "ietf" (optional) uses the Internet Engineering Task Force (IETF) form of Frame Relay encapsulation; use this parameter when the router or access server is connected to another vendor's equipment across a Frame Relay network. "cisco" (optional) is the Cisco encapsulation method.

## Nonbroadcast Multiaccess

Because Frame Relay connections are established by direct PVCs, Frame Relay cannot support broadcast transmissions. If broadcast services are required, a router

**Table 16.2   Frame Relay basic configuration.**

| Command | Description |
| --- | --- |
| encapsulation frame-relay [cisco I ietf] | Enables Frame Relay encapsulation; default setting is "cisco"; "ietf" (see RFC 1490) enables connections to non-Cisco equipment |
| frame-relay lmi-type [ansi I cisco I q933a] | Sets the LMI type; default setting is "cisco" |

must copy the broadcast, then transmit it on each of its PVCs. A term that describes this behavior is *nonbroadcast multiaccess* (*NBMA*). NBMA simply describes any multiaccess layer 2 protocol that does not provide a mechanism for broadcasting messages (such as route updates between routers). For broadcast messages to be communicated in an NBMA network, each router within the network serves as a peer and is part of the same subnet. In a Frame Relay network, broadcast messages must be duplicated and then sent out each PVC to each peer.

# Subinterfaces

A single, physical, serial interface can be configured with several virtual interfaces called *subinterfaces*. These subinterfaces can be configured on a serial line; different information is sent and received on each of its subinterfaces. Using subinterfaces, a single router can support PVCs to several other routers. Figure 16.3 depicts a simple Frame Relay network with subinterfaces.

Before configuring a subinterface for a Frame Relay network, the Frame Relay configuration on the physical interface must be complete. Execute the following command to create a subinterface and assign it a DLCI value:

```
Interface type .subinterface point-to-point
Frame-relay interface-dlci DLCI [broadcast]
```

In this command, "type" is the physical serial interface number, "subinterface" is the subinterface number, "dlci" is the DLCI number used to connect to the

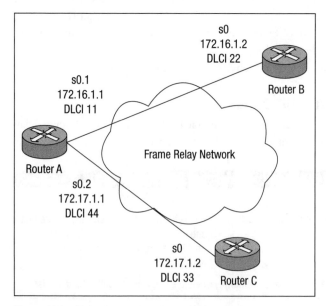

**Figure 16.3** Frame Relay network with subinterfaces.

specified protocol address on the interface, and "broadcast" (optional) forwards broadcasts to this address.

The proper syntax for creating and accessing a subinterface is the interface number followed by a period (.) followed by the subinterface number. For example, serial 0.11 indicates the subinterface 11 on serial interface 0.

A common practice in choosing subinterface numbers is to use the same number as the DLCI value.

# Monitoring Frame Relay

After the Frame Relay configuration is complete, you can use the **show interface** and **debug frame-relay** commands to monitor and troubleshoot the configuration. Listing 16.1 shows the output from the **show interface** command.

Listing 16.1   The **show interface** command output.

```
Router# show interface serial 0
  Serial0 is up, line protocol is up
  Hardware is MCI Serial
  Internet address is 172.59.1.1,
    subnet mask is 255.255.255.252
  MTU 1500 bytes, BW 1544 Kbit, DLY 20000 usec, rely 249/255,
    load 1/255
  Encapsulation FRAME-RELAY, loopback not set,
    keepalive set (10 sec)
  LMI enq sent   4, LMI stat recvd 0, LMI upd recvd 0,
    DTE LMI UP
  LMI enq recvd 268, LMI stat sent   264, LMI upd sent   0
  LMI DLCI 1023   LMI type is CISCO   frame relay DTE
  Last input 0:00:09, output 0:00:07, output hang never
  Last clearing of "show interface" counters 0:44:57
  Output queue 0/40, 0 drops; input queue 0/75, 0 drops
  Five minute input rate 0 bits/sec, 0 packets/sec
Five minute output rate 0 bits/sec, 0 packets/sec
    309 packets input, 6641 bytes, 0 no buffer
    Received 0 broadcasts, 0 runts, 0 giants
    0 input errors, 0 CRC, 0 frame, 0 overrun,
    0 ignored, 0 abort
```

```
0 input packets with dribble condition detected
268 packets output, 3836 bytes, 0 underruns
0 output errors, 0 collisions, 2 interface resets,
0 restarts
180 carrier transitions
```

*Note: The encapsulation type, DLCI, LMI type, and router status as DTE are displayed.*

Use the **show frame-relay pvc** command to display the status of the virtual circuit:

```
RouterA#show frame-relay pvc

PVC Statistics for interface Serial0 (Frame Relay DTE)

DLCI = 222, DLCI USAGE = LOCAL, PVC STATUS = ACTIVE, INTERFACE =
Serial0

   input pkts 50          output pkts 20          in bytes 11431
   out bytes 1474         dropped pkts 2          in FECN pkts 0
   in BECN pkts 0         out FECN pkts 0         out BECN pkts
0
   in DE pkts 0           out DE pkts 0
   pvc create time 04:14:12, last time pvc status changed 00:39:06
RouterA#
```

*Note: No packets have had their discard eligibility bits set.*

Use the **show frame-relay lmi** command to determine whether LMI is being transmitted successfully:

```
RouterA#show frame-relay lmi

LMI Statistics for interface Serial0 (Frame Relay DTE) LMI TYPE =
CISCO
   Invalid Unnumbered info 0        Invalid Prot Disc 0
   Invalid dummy Call Ref 0         Invalid Msg Type 0
   Invalid Status Message 0         Invalid Lock Shift 0
   Invalid Information ID 0          Invalid Report IE Len 0
   Invalid Report Request 0         Invalid Keep IE Len 0
   Num Status Enq. Sent 292         Num Status msgs Rcvd 292
   Num Update Status Rcvd 0         Num Status Timeouts 0
RouterA#
```

*Note: No LMI status messages have been lost.*

Use the **show frame-relay map** command to display mappings among protocol, protocol address, and DLCI:

```
RouterA#show frame-relay map
Serial0 (up): ip 172.59.1.1 dlci 222(0xDE,0x34E0), dynamic,
              broadcast, status defined, active
RouterA#
```

*Note: IP address 172.59.1.1 is mapped to DLCI 222, and the PVC is active.*

The **debug frame-relay** command enables you to monitor the Frame Relay activity closely. The **debug frame-relay lmi** command enables you to monitor LMI activity on a router closely. Listing 16.2 shows a sample output from the **debug frame-relay lmi** command.

**Listing 16.2    The debug frame-relay lmi command.**

```
RouterA#debug frame-relay lmi
Frame Relay LMI debugging is on

RouterA#
Serial0(out): StEnq, myseq 20, yourseen 67, DTE up
 datagramstart = 0x23A3820, datagramsize = 13

 FR encap = 0xFCF10309
00 75 01 01 01 03 02 14 43

Serial0(in): Status, myseq 20
RT IE 1, length 1, type 1
KA IE 3, length 2, yourseen 68, myseq 20
RouterA#
Serial0(out): StEnq, myseq 21, yourseen 68, DTE up
 datagramstart = 0x23A3820, datagramsize = 13
```

*Note: The sequence counters for the LMI transmission are being increased properly. Enabling a single debug command on a router does not use much of the router's system resources; however, enabling several debug commands may severely affect the router's ability to perform its functions. The* **no debug all** *command quickly disables all debug commands on a router.*

# Practice Questions

## Question 1

Which of the following commands will display Frame Relay information about serial interface 0?

- a. **sh frame-relay s0**
- b. **sh frame-relay interface s0**
- c. **sh interface s0**
- d. **sh ip interface brief**

Answer c is correct. The **sh interface s0** command displays the configuration and statistics for the serial 0 interface on the router. The **sh frame-relay s0** and **sh frame-relay interface s0** commands are invalid, so answers a and b are incorrect. The **sh ip interface brief** command displays IP addressing and status information for all interfaces, so answer d is incorrect.

## Question 2

Frame Relay operates at which layer of the OSI model?

- a. Transport
- b. Network
- c. Data link
- d. Physical

Answer c is correct. Frame Relay operates with the data link layer. Answers a and b are incorrect because Frame Relay does not include any specifications for layer 4 (transport) or layer 3 (network). Although Frame Relay can operate on several different physical media, it does not include specifications for layer 1 (physical); therefore, answer d is incorrect.

# Question 3

Which of the following devices can serve as a DTE device? [Choose the two best answers]

❑  a.  router

❑  b.  terminal

❑  c.  modem

❑  d.  CSU

Answers a and b are correct. Routers and terminals can be configured to act as DTE devices. Modems and CSUs cannot be configured as DTE devices, but they can be configured as DCE devices; therefore, answers c and d are incorrect.

# Question 4

Which of the following are common WAN services supported by Cisco? [Choose the best answers that apply]

❑  a.  ISDN

❑  b.  Frame Relay

❑  c.  PPP

❑  d.  BGP

❑  e.  HDLC

❑  f.  SDLC

Answers a, b, c, e, and f are correct. ISDN, Frame Relay, PPP, HDLC, and SDLC are all WAN services supported by Cisco equipment. Although BGP is supported by Cisco equipment, it is an exterior routing protocol, so answer d is incorrect.

## Question 5

Which of the following can be used to establish bidirectional communication between two DTE devices? [Choose the two best answers]

❑ a. CVC

❑ b. DVC

❑ c. PVC

❑ d. SVC

Answers c and d are correct. A permanent virtual circuit (PVC) remains established between two DTE devices, even when data is not being transmitted. A switched virtual circuit (SVC) is established only when two DTE devices need to transmit data; it is disconnected when the transmission is over. CVC and DVC are not related to virtual circuits between DTE devices, so answers a and b are incorrect.

## Question 6

Which of the following serves as the addressing scheme within a Frame Relay network?

○ a. DLCI

○ b. LMI

○ c. NBMA

○ d. SVC

Answer a is correct. A DLCI number serves as the addressing scheme and is assigned to each PVC. LMI provides several enhancements to Frame Relay specifications, so answer b is incorrect. Answer c is incorrect because NBMA describes how a router must send broadcasts within a Frame Relay network. An SVC is established to enable DTE to communicate; therefore, answer d is incorrect.

# Question 7

Cisco supports which of the following Frame Relay LMI protocol variations?
[Choose the three best answers]

❑ a.  IETF

❑ b.  ANSI

❑ c.  Q933A

❑ d.  Cisco

Answers b, c, and d are correct. Cisco supports LMI extensions from American National Standards Institute (ANSI), International Telecommunication Union–Telecommunication standardization sector (Q933A), and the Cisco's "Gang of Four." Answer a is incorrect because IETF is a type of frame encapsulation supported by Cisco that enables Cisco devices to communicate with non-Cisco devices across a Frame Relay network.

# Question 8

Frame Relay uses what mechanism to perform error checking?

○ a.  CRC

○ b.  LMI

○ c.  TA/NT1

○ d.  inverse ARP

Answer a is correct. Frame Relay uses CRC to derive the FCS, which is a calculated value based on the data portion of each frame. If a device calculates an FCS value that is different from the FCS value it receives, the frame is dropped. LMI is communicated between DTE and DCE devices and contains the status of the virtual circuit, so answer b is incorrect. Answer c is incorrect because a TA/NT1 is a DCE device and has nothing to do with error checking. Answer d is incorrect, because inverse ARP is the method by which DTE devices discover layer 3 protocol address information about each other.

## Question 9

DCE devices provide which of the following functions?

○ a.  Provide clock to the DTE

○ b.  Convert the data into a suitable format

○ c.  Switch the data across the provider's network

○ d.  All of the above

Answer d is correct. Answers a, b, and c are all functions of DCE devices.

## Question 10

Which of the following commands allow you to closely monitor Frame Relay activity? [Choose the two best answers]

❑ a.  **debug frame-relay lmi**

❑ b.  **debug frame-relay activity**

❑ c.  **debug frame-relay all**

❑ d.  **debug frame-relay verbose**

Answers a and d are correct. The **debug frame-relay lmi** command monitors link information between the DCE and DTE devices. The **debug frame-relay verbose** command displays detailed information. Answers b and c are incorrect because the commands are not valid.

# Need to Know More?

 McNutt, Shawn, Mark Poplar, Jason Waters, and David Stabenaw: *CCNA Routing and Switching Exam Prep*. The Coriolis Group, Scottsdale, AZ, 2000. ISBN 1-57610-440-0. This book is a great complement to the CCNA Cram book. Chapter 12 covers Frame Relay.

 Reed, Kenneth. *Data Network Handbook*. Van Nostrand Reinhold Publishing, New York, NY, 1996. ISBN 0-442-02299-9. Chapter 11 provides more information about voice and data telecommunications.

 Syngress Media, with Richard D. Hornbaker, CCIE. *Cisco Certified Network Associate Study Guide*. Osborne/McGraw Hill, Berkeley, CA, 1998. ISBN 0-07-882487-7. This book is a great study guide to reference when preparing for the CCNA exam.

 Using Cisco's documentation CD, you can immediately access Cisco's entire library of end-user documentation, selected product news, bug databases, and related information. The documentation CD-ROM is produced monthly.

 **www.cisco.com**, the official Cisco Web site, contains several Cisco white papers on topics such as Frame Relay configuration and troubleshooting.

 **www.cis.ohio-state.edu/hypertext/information/rfc.html**, the computer and information science Web site at Ohio State University, provides detailed specifications about Frame Relay (RFC 2427).

# Sample Test

This chapter provides pointers to help you to develop a successful test-taking strategy, including how to choose proper answers, how to decode ambiguity, how to work within the Cisco testing framework, how to decide what you need to memorize, and how to prepare for the test. In this chapter, 65 questions on subject matter pertinent to Cisco Exam 640-507, "CCNA Routing and Switching" are included. After this chapter, the test answer key is provided. Good luck!

# Questions, Questions, Questions

Have no doubt that you are facing a test full of specific and pointed questions. The version of the CCNA Routing and Switching exam that you are going to take is a fixed length. It includes 65 questions, and you are allotted 75 minutes to complete the exam. To pass, you are required to achieve a score of 822 or better on a scale of 300 to 1,000.

For this exam, questions belong to one of two basic types:

➤ Multiple-choice with a single answer

➤ Multiple-choice with multiple answers

Always take the time to read a question at least twice before selecting an answer. Not every question has only one answer; many questions require multiple answers. Therefore, it's important to read each question carefully, to determine how many answers are necessary or possible, and to look for additional hints or instructions when selecting answers. Such instructions often occur in brackets immediately following the question itself (as they do for all multiple-choice, multiple-answer questions). Some questions do not have any right answers, and you are forced to find the most correct choice.

# Picking Proper Answers

Obviously, the only way to pass any exam is to select enough of the right answers to obtain a passing score. Cisco's exams are not standardized like SATs and GREs; they are far more diabolical and convoluted. In some cases, questions are strangely worded, and deciphering them can be a real challenge. In those cases, you may need to rely on answer-elimination skills. You can almost always eliminate at least one answer out of the possible choices immediately because it matches one of these conditions:

➤ The answer does not apply to the situation.

➤ The answer describes a nonexistent issue, an invalid option, or an imaginary state.

➤ The answer may be eliminated because of the question itself.

After you eliminate all answers that are obviously wrong, you can apply your retained knowledge to eliminate other answers. Look for items that sound correct, but refer to actions, commands, or features that are not present or not available in the situation that the question describes.

If you're still faced with a blind guess among two or more potentially correct answers, reread the question. Try to picture how each of the remaining answers would alter the situation. Be especially sensitive to terminology; sometimes the choice of words ("remove" instead of "disable") can make the difference between a right answer and a wrong one.

If you've exhausted your ability to eliminate answers, but are still unclear about which of the remaining possibilities is correct, only then should you guess at an answer. An unanswered question offers you no points, but guessing gives you at least some chance of getting a question right; just don't be hasty when making a blind guess.

 Because you're taking a fixed-length test, you can wait until the last few minutes (just as you're about to run out of time or out of unanswered questions) before you start making guesses. Guessing should be your technique of last resort!

# Decoding Ambiguity

Cisco exams have a reputation for including questions that can be difficult to interpret, confusing, or ambiguous. In our experience with numerous exams, we consider this reputation to be completely justified. The Cisco exams are tough and deliberately made that way.

The only way to beat Cisco at its own game is to be prepared. You'll discover that many exam questions test your knowledge of things that are not directly related to the issue raised by a question. This means that the answers you must choose from, even incorrect ones, are just as much a part of the skill assessment as the question itself. If you don't have some knowledge of most aspects of CCNA Routing and Switching, you may not be able to eliminate obviously wrong answers, because these relate to a different area of CCNA Routing and Switching. In other words, the more you know about the question's topic, the easier it will be for you to tell right from wrong.

Questions often give away their answers, but you have to be Sherlock Holmes to see the clues. Subtle hints may appear in the question text in a way that seems almost irrelevant to the situation. You must realize that each question is a test unto itself and that you need to inspect and successfully navigate each question to pass the exam. Look for small clues, such as the mention of times, group permissions and names, and configuration settings. Little things like these can point at the right answer if they're properly understood; if missed, they can leave you facing a blind guess.

Another common difficulty with certification exams is vocabulary. Cisco has an uncanny knack for naming some utilities and features entirely obviously in some cases and completely inanely in other instances. Be sure to brush up on the key terms presented at the beginning of each chapter. You may also want to read through the Glossary at the end of this book the day before you take the test.

# Working within the Framework

The test questions appear in random order, and many elements or issues that receive mention in one question may crop up in other questions. It's not uncommon to find that an incorrect answer to one question is the correct answer to another question, or vice versa. Take the time to read every answer to each question, even if you recognize the correct answer to a question immediately. That extra reading may spark a memory or remind you about a Cisco router Internetwork Operating System (IOS) feature or function that helps you on another question elsewhere in the exam.

 For the newest generation of Cisco exams (including test 640-507 CCNA 2.0), you are no longer able to mark questions and review them later. Each question must be answered before you proceed onto the next, and you cannot refer back to questions that have already been answered.

# Deciding What to Memorize

The amount of memorization you must undertake for an exam depends on how well you remember what you've read and how well you know the material by heart. If you are a visual thinker and you can see the configuration commands in your head, you won't need to memorize as much as someone who's less visually oriented. The tests will stretch your recollection of router commands, protocols, and functions.

At a minimum, you'll want to memorize the following kinds of information:

➤ The basics of Internet Protocol (IP) addressing and subnetting

➤ The functions of each layer of the Open Systems Interconnect (OSI) model

➤ The pertinent commands for configuring Frame Relay

➤ The various **show** commands that will allow you to see the status of the subjects mentioned previously and throughout the book

If you work your way through this book while sitting at a Cisco router and try to manipulate this environment's features and functions as they're discussed throughout, you should have little or no difficulty mastering this material. Also, don't forget that the Cram Sheet at the front of the book is designed to capture the material that is most important to memorize; use this to guide your studies as well.

# Preparing for the Test

The best way to prepare for the test—after you've studied—is to take at least one practice exam; we've included one here in this chapter for that reason. The test questions are located in the pages that follow. Unlike the preceding chapters in this book, the answers don't follow the questions immediately; go to Chapter 18 to review the answers separately.

Give yourself 90 minutes to take the exam. Keep yourself on the honor system, and don't look at earlier text in the book or jump ahead to the answer key. When your time is up or you've finished the questions, check your work against Chapter 18. Pay special attention to the explanations for the incorrect answers; these can also help to reinforce your knowledge of the material. Knowing how to recognize correct answers is good, but understanding why incorrect answers are wrong can be equally valuable.

# Taking the Test

Relax. When you're sitting in front of the testing computer, there's nothing more you can do to increase your knowledge or preparation. Take a deep breath, stretch, and start reading that first question.

Don't rush; you have plenty of time to complete each question. You should have ample time to read each question twice and choose a well-formulated answer. Both easy and difficult questions are intermixed throughout the test in random order. Because you're taking a fixed-length test, don't cheat yourself by spending too much time on a hard question early on in the test, thereby depriving yourself of the time you need to answer the questions at the end of the test.

# Sample Test

## Question 1

What are the primary purposes of the OSI model network layer? [Choose the two best answers]

❑ a. Path determination

❑ b. Code formatting

❑ c. Flow control

❑ d. Packet switching

❑ e. Error notification

## Question 2

Which router commands, if executed from the global configuration prompt, will enable RIP routing for network 172.23.0.0?

○ a. **router rip 13** and **network 172.23.0.0**

○ b. **router rip all**

○ c. **router rip** and **network 172.23.0.0**

○ d. **network 172.23.0.0**

## Question 3

Which of the following are performed at the data link layer of the OSI model? [Choose the three best answers]

❑ a. Error notification

❑ b. Packet switching

❑ c. Physical addressing

❑ d. Establishing, maintaining, and terminating sessions

❑ e. Frame sequencing

## Question 4

Which of the following are examples of LAN protocols? [Choose the three best answers]

❑ a.  Frame Relay

❑ b.  token ring

❑ c.  Ethernet

❑ d.  FDDI

❑ e.  ISDN

## Question 5

Given the following physical address, what is the vendor code of this address?

BBD1.4822.53AA

○ a.  BBD148

○ b.  2253AA

○ c.  BBD1

○ d.  53AA

○ e.  4822

## Question 6

Which two answers are characteristics of connection-oriented communication? [Choose the two best answers]

❑ a.  Setup and maintenance procedures are performed to ensure delivery of messages.

❑ b.  A physical circuit exists between the two communicating devices.

❑ c.  It is a best-effort type of communication.

❑ d.  A virtual connection exists between the two devices.

## Question 7

Which of the following are examples of layer 3 addressing? [Choose the two best answers]

❑ a. 172.29.5.12

❑ b. CB255467.3000.B433.A232

❑ c. 0000.B333.A232

❑ d. A4XX

## Question 8

If you want to view the currently executing configuration file, which of the following commands should you use?

○ a. **show startup-config**

○ b. **show running-config**

○ c. **configure terminal**

○ d. **configure memory**

## Question 9

What command would be used to back up a running configuration file?

○ a. **router#copy tftp running-config**

○ b. **router>copy tftp running-config**

○ c. **router#copy running-config tftp**

○ d. **router>copy tftp running**

## Question 10

Which of the following commands would set an enable secret password on a Cisco router?

○ a. **router#enable secret** *password*

○ b. **router(config-line)#password phoenix**

○ c. **router(config)#enable secret** *password*

○ d. **router(config)#enable password**

# Question 11

Which of the following commands would create a text description on an interface of a router?

○ a.  **router#description** I am going to pass the CCNA exam

○ b.  **router(config)#description** I am going to pass the CCNA exam

○ c.  **router(config-line)description** I am going to pass the CCNA exam

○ d.  **router(config-if)#description** I am going to pass the CCNA exam

# Question 12

What are methods used to map a Frame Relay virtual circuit 's DLCI to a destination network layer address such as an IP address? [Choose the two best answers]

❑ a.  CIR

❑ b.  Inverse ARP

❑ c.  Manually

❑ d.  LMI

❑ e.  PVC

# Question 13

Which of the following are advantages of using ISDN BRI service? [Choose the three best answers]

❑ a.  Ability to simultaneously carry voice and data

❑ b.  Offers faster call setup as opposed to modem connections

❑ c.  Creates a permanent virtual circuit between two networks

❑ d.  Provides dedicated, full-time connection to the Internet

❑ e.  Provides end-to-end digital service

# Question 14

Which of the following services is used to copy files between Cisco routers?

- ○ a. SMTP
- ○ b. SNMP
- ○ c. TFTP
- ○ d. RARP
- ○ e. HTTP

# Question 15

Which of the following are characteristics of TCP? [Choose the three best answers]

- ❑ a. Performs error and duplication checking
- ❑ b. Performs acknowledgment windowing to increase efficiency of bandwidth use
- ❑ c. Initiates a three-way handshake
- ❑ d. Provides logical addressing

# Question 16

What is the function performed by Address Resolution Protocol?

- ○ a. Maps a known physical address to a logical address
- ○ b. Maps a known logical address to a physical address
- ○ c. Communicates error messages and control messages between devices
- ○ d. Obtains physical and logical addresses from a TFTP server

# Question 17

Which best describes the process of connection-oriented services?

- ○ a. Repackaging data for transmission on a different physical network
- ○ b. Flow control/sequencing/data transfer
- ○ c. A data link is permanently established
- ○ d. Connection establishment/data transfer/connection termination

# Question 18

Which of the following functions do both UDP and TCP perform? [Choose the two best answers]

- ❏ a.  Provides destination and source port numbers
- ❏ b.  Initiates a three-way handshake
- ❏ c.  Allocates dynamic datagram size
- ❏ d.  Performs checksum
- ❏ e.  Acknowledges datagram receipt

# Question 19

An IP address is listed below in decimal format. Please indicate the corresponding binary value of this IP address:

172.16.8.8

- ○ a.  10101100.00010000.00001000.00001000
- ○ b.  10101100.00100000.11100000.00000100
- ○ c.  10101100.00010000.00000010.00000111
- ○ d.  11001100.00001111.00011001.00001000

# Question 20

Given the Ethernet specification 100BaseFL, what do each of the following parts mean: 100, Base, and FL?

- ○ a.  LAN speed / signaling method / media type
- ○ b.  LAN speed / media type / signaling method
- ○ c.  LAN speed / topology / media type
- ○ d.  LAN speed / signaling method / topology

## Question 21

Which of the following addresses are class C addresses? [Choose the two best answers]

❑ a. 221.15.130.254

❑ b. 10100000.11000000.11111111.11110000

❑ c. 11010001.11001100.10101010.00001111

❑ d. 127.0.0.0

## Question 22

Encapsulation, or tunneling, can be described as which of the following?

○ a. Taking frames from one network system and placing them inside frames from another network system

○ b. Stripping data off of a packet as it moves up the protocol stack

○ c. Creating a stream of ones and zeros for transmission across a physical wire

○ d. The exchange of route summary messages between routers

## Question 23

With an IP address and subnet mask of 172.10.10.4 255.255.255.128, what is the full range of IP addresses in this subnet?

○ a. 172.10.10.1 through 172.10.10.254

○ b. 172.10.10.129 through 172.10.10.254

○ c. 172.10.10.0 through 172.10.10.127

○ d. 172.10.10.1 through 172.10.10.12

# Question 24

With an IP address and subnet mask of 172.10.10.4 255.255.255.128, what is the number of possible subnets?

○ a.  510

○ b.  254

○ c.  1,024

○ d.  14

○ e.  4,094

# Question 25

Which of the following commands identifies an IP standard access list?

○ a.  **ip access-group 400 out**

○ b.  **ip access-group 11 out**

○ c.  **ip access-group 145 out**

○ d.  **ip access-group 105 out**

○ e.  **ipx access-group 805 in**

# Question 26

If you are extremely security conscious, which PPP authentication protocol should you implement?

○ a.  CHAP

○ b.  DDR

○ c.  PAP

## Question 27

Which of the following cannot be used to permit or deny traffic with IP extended access lists?

○ a. TCP port number

○ b. Destination IP address

○ c. IP sequence number

○ d. Source IP address

## Question 28

What is the valid range for an IPX extended access list?

○ a. 0 through 99

○ b. 100 through 199

○ c. 800 through 899

○ d. 900 through 999

## Question 29

Which of the following commands can be used to show access lists? [Choose the three best answers]

❑ a. **show ip interfaces**

❑ b. **show ipx interfaces**

❑ c. **show access-lists**

❑ d. **show access lists**

# Question 30

Which of the following are disadvantages of using a bridge to segment a LAN? [Choose the two best answers]

❏ a. Increases the latency period to forward frames by 20 percent

❏ b. A bridge logically segments a LAN and, therefore, isolates non-local devices from local traffic

❏ c. A bridge can extend the physical distance of a LAN by amplifying the electrical signal of the physical media

❏ d. Introduces the possibility of bridging loops

# Question 31

What is maintained in a bridge's forwarding table?

○ a. A device's IP address and the IP network on which the device resides

○ b. A device's MAC address and the physical segment on which the device resides

○ c. A device's MAC address and the next physical segment to forward a frame to while in route to the physical segment on which the device resides

○ d. The IP network and the MAC address of devices

# Question 32

What is the name of the protocol used to pass VLAN information between switches?

○ a. Switching

○ b. ISL

○ c. Frame tagging

○ d. Spanning tree

## Question 33

How many of the following are disadvantages of routing in comparison with bridging and switching? [Choose the two best answers]

- ❏ a. Routing provides the functionality to allow complex networks with dissimilar technologies to be connected
- ❏ b. Increased latency
- ❏ c. Reduced security
- ❏ d. Increased complexity

## Question 34

Frame tagging is used to tag a frame with a unique VLAN ID between switches.

- ○ a. True
- ○ b. False

## Question 35

Which of the following switching methods provides error-checking capabilities?

- ○ a. Store-and-forward switching
- ○ b. Frame-tag switching
- ○ c. Cut-through switching
- ○ d. ISL switching

## Question 36

You have connected six PCs to a Fast Ethernet switch. Each PC is plugged into a single switch port. All PCs are equipped with 10/100 NICs. How much bandwidth is available to each PC?

- ○ a. 16.6Mbps
- ○ b. 0.6Mbps
- ○ c. 100Mbps
- ○ d. 10Mbps

## Question 37

Which of the following are not services provided by the transport layer?
[Choose the three best answers]

- ❑ a. Establishing a session
- ❑ b. Ensuring that the segment sent is error-free
- ❑ c. Ending a session
- ❑ d. Keeping the sending and receiving station from sending segments at the same time

## Question 38

Which of the following addresses represents a class D IP address that is used for multicast applications?

- ○ a. 255.255.0.0
- ○ b. 10.1.1.0
- ○ c. 224.0.1.1
- ○ d. 192.0.0.255

## Question 39

Which PPP authentication protocol uses a two-way handshake?

- ○ a. PAP
- ○ b. CHAP
- ○ c. LCP
- ○ d. NCP

## Question 40

How do devices on different VLANs communicate?

- ○ a. Through a layer 2 switch
- ○ b. Through a bridge
- ○ c. Through a router
- ○ d. Through a layer 2 switch with properly configured access lists
- ○ e. Through a switch that supports ISL

# Question 41

Which of the following commands will display Frame Relay information about serial interface 1?

○ a.  **sh frame-relay s1**

○ b.  **sh frame-relay interface s1**

○ c.  **sh interface s1**

○ d.  **sh ip interface brief**

# Question 42

Given the following output from the **show interface** command,

```
Ethernet0 is administratively down, line protocol
     is down
```

what can you assume about this interface?

○ a.  Ethernet0 is operational.

○ b.  Ethernet0 is not plugged into the network.

○ c.  There is a hardware problem with the Ethernet0 interface.

○ d.  Ethernet0 has been disabled or shut down.

# Question 43

Frame Relay operates primarily at which layers of the OSI model?

○ a.  Transport and network

○ b.  Network and data link

○ c.  Data link and physical

## Question 44

What key or keys would you press to complete a partially entered command?

- ○ a. Ctrl+E
- ○ b. Tab
- ○ c. Shift+Right Arrow
- ○ d. Ctrl+A
- ○ e. Up Arrow

## Question 45

Which of the following is an interior routing protocol? [Choose the three best answers]

- ❑ a. RIP
- ❑ b. IGRP
- ❑ c. OSPF
- ❑ d. BGP

## Question 46

Which of the following is a valid IPX address for network 4d?

- ○ a. 4d80.c747.b122
- ○ b. 4d.0080.c747.b122
- ○ c. 4d.172.16.101.123
- ○ d. 4d

## Question 47

Which command, when executed successfully, verifies that two routers are routing packets between them successfully? [Choose the three best answers]

- ❑ a. **ping**
- ❑ b. **show interface**
- ❑ c. **trace**
- ❑ d. **telnet**

## Question 48

To enable IPX, what is the first IPX configuration command that must be executed on a router?

○ a. **ipx routing**

○ b. **ipx protocol**

○ c. **ipx interface**

○ d. **ipx network**

## Question 49

What was the primary purpose for the creation of the OSI model?

○ a. So that mainframe networks could interoperate with newer client/server networks

○ b. To help computer vendors create interoperable network equipment

○ c. As a learning tool for people who were new to network engineering

○ d. To reduce the burden on software programmers

## Question 50

How are collisions handled by Fast Ethernet when running in full duplex mode?

○ a. When a collision is detected, data is retransmitted after a random waiting period.

○ b. The NIC checks to make sure that the line is free before transmitting, so no collisions are created.

○ c. There are no collisions.

○ d. When a collision is detected, data is retransmitted at predetermined intervals.

## Question 51

Which router commands, if executed from the global configuration prompt, will enable IGRP routing for autonomous system 77 and network 172.25.0.0?

○ a. **router igrp 77** then **network 172.25.0.0**

○ b. **router igrp 172.25.0.0**

○ c. **router igrp** then **network 172.25.0.0**

○ d. **network 172.25.0.0**

## Question 52

Which of the following is not a solution to problems experienced by dis-tance vector routing protocols?

○ a.  Split horizon

○ b.  Route poisoning

○ c.  Counting to infinity (loops)

○ d.  Maximum hop count

○ e.  Hold-down timers

## Question 53

The presentation layer provides which of the following services? [Choose the three best answers]

❑ a.  Data representation

❑ b.  Data compression

❑ c.  Dialog management

❑ d.  Data transmission

❑ e.  Data encryption

# Question 54

Which of the following prompts indicates that the router is in user mode?

○ a.  Router>

○ b.  Router#

○ c.  Router(config)#

○ d.  Router:

# Question 55

What is the purpose of ICMP?

○ a.  To report errors and provide other information relevant to IP packet processing

○ b.  To map a known IP address to a physical address

○ c.  To pass mail messages between devices

○ d.  To obtain data on remote devices

# Question 56

Which of the following router commands displays a list of keywords needed for the **show** command?

○ a.  **sh?**

○ b.  **sh ?**

○ c.  **show?**

# Question 57

When you first log in to a Cisco router under normal circumstances, what router mode are you in?

○ a.  RXBOOT

○ b.  Privileged

○ c.  Global configuration

○ d.  User

# Question 58

---

Examine the following output from the initial configuration dialog on a Cisco 2500 router:

```
Configuring interface Serial 0:
Is this interface in use? [yes] <Return>
Configure IP on this interface? [yes] <Return>
Configure IP unnumbered on this interface? [no] :
    <Return>
IP Address for this interface: 172.29.3.4
Number of bits in subnet field [8]: <Return>
Class B network is 172.29.0.0, 8 subnet bits; mask
    is
    255.255.255.0
```

What does the information contained in brackets represent?

○ a.  Allowable answers

○ b.  An answer that was previously entered

○ c.  The default answer

○ d.  The answer that was entered manually by the person configuring this router

# Question 59

---

To display a brief description of the help system in privileged mode, which of the following keys or commands must be typed at the prompt?

○ a.  Help

○ b.  F1

○ c.  Ctrl+H

○ d.  ?

## Question 60

Which of the following layers is most concerned with the representation of data?

○ a. Application

○ b. Presentation

○ c. Session

○ d. Transport

## Question 61

Which of the following devices will segment a LAN into separate collision domains? [Choose the three best answers]

❑ a. Hub

❑ b. Bridge

❑ c. Switch

❑ d. Router

❑ e. Repeater

## Question 62

With what is the application layer primarily concerned?

○ a. Providing services for user applications

○ b. Data representation

○ c. Dialog management

○ d. Data transport

# Question 63

A packet, frame, and bits conversion process includes which layers (in order)?

○ a.  Session, transport, network

○ b.  Network, data link, physical

○ c.  Presentation, session, transport

○ d.  Network, transport, data link

# Question 64

Which of the following represent the reason the industry uses a layered model? [Choose the best answers that apply]

❏ a.  Network operations and troubleshooting can be simplified.

❏ b.  Standard interfaces can be defined for vendor compatibility.

❏ c.  Enhancements for one layer can be isolated from the other layers.

❏ d.  Designs and development efforts can be made in a modular fashion.

❏ e.  Complex internetworking components can be divided into discrete subsets.

# Question 65

Which of the following layers is most concerned with end-to-end communication?

○ a.  Application

○ b.  Presentation

○ c.  Session

○ d.  Transport

# Answer Key

| | | | |
|---|---|---|---|
| 1. a, d | 18. a, d | 35. a | 52. c |
| 2. c | 19. a | 36. c | 53. a, b, e |
| 3. a, c, e | 20. a | 37. a, c, d | 54. a |
| 4. b, c, d | 21. a, c | 38. c | 55. a |
| 5. a | 22. a | 39. a | 56. b |
| 6. a, d | 23. c | 40. c | 57. d |
| 7. a, b | 24. a | 41. c | 58. c |
| 8. b | 25. b | 42. d | 59. a |
| 9. c | 26. a | 43. c | 60. b |
| 10. c | 27. c | 44. b | 61. b, c, d |
| 11. d | 28. d | 45. a, b, c | 62. a |
| 12. b, c | 29. a, b, c | 46. b | 63. b |
| 13. a, b, e | 30. a, d | 47. a, c, d | 64. a, b, c, d, e |
| 14. c | 31. c | 48. a | 65. d |
| 15. a, b, c | 32. b | 49. b | |
| 16. b | 33. b, d | 50. c | |
| 17. d | 34. a | 51. a | |

## Question 1

Answers a and d are correct. The network layer of the OSI model performs both path determination and packet switching. Path determination is the process of identifying the best path to a destination across an internetwork. Packet switching is the process of moving a packet from one network interface to another. Answer b is incorrect because code formatting occurs at the presentation layer of the OSI model, not the network layer. Answer c is incorrect because flow control occurs at the data link or transport layer. Answer e is incorrect because the network layer does not perform any error notification.

## Question 2

Answer c is correct. The **router rip** command enables RIP routing and the **network 172.23.0.0** command enables the router to advertise that network to other routers. Answers a and b are incorrect because the **router rip** command does not require an autonomous system or additional parameters. Answer d is incorrect because you must first enter routing protocol configuration mode before configuring a network to be advertised.

## Question 3

Answers a, c, and e are correct. The data link layer performs error notification, physical addressing, and frame sequencing, among other things. Answer b is incorrect because packet switching is performed at the network layer. Answer d is incorrect because establishing, maintaining, and terminating sessions occurs at the session layer.

## Question 4

Answers b, c, and d are correct. Token ring, Ethernet, and FDDI are all layer 2 LAN protocols. Answers a and e are incorrect because Frame Relay and ISDN are WAN protocols; however, they both do function at layer 2 of the OSI model.

## Question 5

Answer a is correct. The first six digits of the physical address represent the vendor code. Answer b is incorrect because the last six numbers of the physical address represent the serial number, not the vendor code. Answers c, d, and e have no meaning on their own and are, therefore, incorrect.

# Question 6

Answers a and d are correct. Both a virtual connection and setup and maintenance functions are performed during connection-oriented communication. Answer b is incorrect because a physical circuit is not necessary for connection-oriented communication. Answer c is a characteristic of connectionless communication, not of connection-oriented communication, and is, therefore, incorrect.

# Question 7

Answers a and b are correct. Answer a is an example of an IP logical address or a network layer address. Answer b is an example of an IPX logical address or a network layer address. Answer c is incorrect because it is an example of a physical or layer 2 address, not a network or layer 3 address. Answer d has no meaning and is, therefore, incorrect.

# Question 8

Answer b is correct. The command to display the executing configuration/running configuration file to a console terminal is **show running-config**. Answer a is incorrect because this command displays the backup configuration/startup configuration file. Answers c and d are incorrect because these are used to modify configuration files, not to show configuration files.

# Question 9

Answer c is correct. When backing up a running configuration file, the file needs to be copied from the router to a TFTP server. Answer a is incorrect because it would copy a file from a TFTP server to the router, when the goal is the opposite. Answer b is incorrect because the command is being executed from user EXEC mode. Answer d is incorrect because the command is executed from user EXEC mode, and it is in the wrong format.

# Question 10

Answer c is correct. The **enable secret** command is the correct command. Answer b is incorrect because the word "password" is not used for setting an enable secret password. Answer a is incorrect because the enable secret password is set while in configuration mode, not privileged EXEC mode. Answer d is incorrect because this command is used to set the enable password, not the enable secret password.

## Question 11

Answer d is correct. The command description is executed from the interface configuration mode and is the correct command to create a text description on an interface of a router. Answer a is incorrect because the command is executed from privileged EXEC mode. Answer b is incorrect because the command is executed from global configuration mode. Answer c is incorrect because the syntax of "router(config-line)" is incorrect.

## Question 12

Answers b and c are correct. A local DLCI is mapped to a network layer address dynamically using inverse ARP or manually by configuring a static map in the map table. Answer a is incorrect because CIR is the rate at which Frame Relay transfers data. Answer d is incorrect because LMI is a signaling standard. Answer e is incorrect because a PVC is a permanently established virtual circuit.

## Question 13

Answers a, b, and e are correct. ISDN BRI service includes the ability to carry voice and data simultaneously, offers faster call setup than modem connections, and provides end-to-end digital service. Answer c is incorrect because PVCs are used by Frame Relay. Answer d is incorrect because an ISDN BRI connection is not a dedicated, full-time connection.

## Question 14

Answer c is correct. TFTP is a scaled down version of FTP used to copy files between Cisco routers or to TFTP servers. Answer a is incorrect because SMTP is a mail protocol, not a file transfer protocol. SNMP is network management protocol, not a file transfer protocol; therefore, b is incorrect. RARP is a protocol used to map an unknown logical address to a known physical address; therefore, d is incorrect. HTTP is used for Web browsing; therefore, e is incorrect.

## Question 15

Answers a, b, and c are correct. Error and duplication checking, acknowledgment windowing, and the three-way handshake are some of the characteristics of TCP. IP performs logical addressing in the TCP/IP suite; therefore, answer d is incorrect.

# Question 16

Answer b is correct. ARP maps a known logical address to an unknown physical address. Answer a is incorrect because it describes RARP, not ARP. Answer c is incorrect because it has nothing to do with ARP. Answer d is incorrect because ARP does not retrieve logical addresses, nor does a TFTP server have to be in the picture.

# Question 17

Answer d is correct. Connection-oriented services have no permanently established connection; therefore, for two devices to communicate via a connection-oriented network environment, they must establish a connection, transfer data, then terminate the connection. Answer b is incorrect because it describes specific methods used by some protocols to ensure reliable data transport. Answer c is incorrect because this describes connectionless communication. Answer a is incorrect because this is not a function of connection-oriented services. Answer a describes the process of encapsulation.

# Question 18

Answers a and d are correct. Destination and source port numbers are provided in both the UDP and TCP headers, and both TCP and UDP provide for a checksum in the header to verify accurate delivery. Answer b is incorrect because only TCP performs the three-way handshake. Answer c is incorrect because UDP does not set datagram sizes dynamically, but assigns each datagram the same size. Only TCP provides reliability in its data transport; therefore, answer e is incorrect because UDP does not generate acknowledgments for the receipt of datagrams.

# Question 19

Answer a is correct, because the dotted decimal value 172.16.8.8 is equivalent to the binary value 10101100.00010000.00001000.00001000. Answers b, c, and d are incorrect because these binary values are not equivalent to 172.16.8.8.

# Question 20

Answer a is correct. The Ethernet naming convention breaks down into three components that summarize its characteristics: LAN speed, signaling method, and media type. 100BaseFL means 100Mbps LAN speed, baseband signaling, and fiber optic media.

## Question 21

Answers a and c are correct. Answer a can be identified as correct because it has a decimal value between 192 and 223. Answer c can be identified as correct because the first three binary digits are 110. Answer b can be eliminated because the first three binary digits are 101, not 110. Answer d can be eliminated because the dotted decimal value is not between 192 and 223.

## Question 22

Answer a is correct. Tunneling refers to the process of taking frames from one network system and placing them inside frames from another network system. Answer b is incorrect because stripping data from a packet is a function of de-encapsulation. Answer c is incorrect because this is a function of the data link layer of the OSI model. Answer d is incorrect because it does not accurately describe the process of encapsulation or tunneling.

## Question 23

Answer c is correct. An IP address of 172.10.10.4 255.255.255.128 indicates a class B address with a nine-bit subnet mask. The valid range in dotted decimal notation for this IP address is 172.10.10.0 through 172.10.10.127. Answers a, b, and e can be eliminated because they do not fall within this range of IP addresses.

## Question 24

Answer a is correct. The number of subnets can be derived by using the formula 2n-2. A class B address of 172.10.10.4 with a nine-bit subnet mask indicates that nine bits are used for identifying networks. Therefore, take 2 to the power of 9 and subtract 2 to yield the number of networks. Answers b, c, d, and e are not the correct result of the formula and can, therefore, be eliminated.

## Question 25

Answer b is correct. The command in answer b identifies an IP standard access list by the access list number 11, which is the proper numeric range for identifying an IP standard access list. Answer a is incorrect because it uses the access list number 400. The access list number 400 is not reserved for IP standard access lists. Answer c is incorrect because the access list number 145 is reserved for IP extended access lists, not IP standard access lists. Answer d is incorrect because the number 105 is reserved for IP extended access lists, not IP standard access lists. Answer e is incorrect because it is an IPX access list, not an IP access list.

## Question 26

Answer a is correct. CHAP uses a three-way handshake and transmits encrypted data between remote and local hosts. Answer b is incorrect because DDR is not a PPP authentication protocol. Answer c is incorrect because PAP transmits authentication data in clear text from the remote host to the local host.

## Question 27

Answer c is correct. The IP sequence number cannot be used to permit or deny traffic with IP extended access lists. IP extended access lists can permit or deny traffic using TCP port number, destination IP address, and source IP address; therefore, answers a, b, and d are incorrect.

## Question 28

Answer d is correct. IPX extended access lists are identified by a numeric range between 900 and 999. Answers a, b, and c are incorrect because they do not fall within the correct numeric range for IPX extended access lists.

## Question 29

Answers a, b, and c are correct. The **show ip interfaces, show ipx interfaces,** and **show access-lists** commands can all be used to show access lists. Answer d is incorrect because the **show access lists** command is not in the correct format.

## Question 30

Answers a and d are correct. Bridges increase frame-forwarding rates at approximately 20 percent in comparison with repeaters or physical media. In addition, implementing bridges to segment a layer 2 network introduces the possibility of bridging loops in a network. Answers b and c are incorrect because these are actually advantages of bridges.

# Question 31

Answer c is correct. A bridge only maintains a device's physical MAC address and the next physical segment to forward a frame to while in route to the destination device. Answer a is incorrect because bridges do not maintain IP addresses. Answer b is incorrect because bridges don't maintain the physical segment on which a device resides, but only maintain the next physical segment to forward a frame to while in route to the destination device. Answer d is incorrect because bridges do not maintain IP networks.

# Question 32

Answer b is correct. ISL is a communication protocol used between switches to communicate common VLANs between devices. Answer a is incorrect because a switch is a physical device, not a protocol. Answer c is incorrect because frame tagging is a process employed by switches, not a protocol. Answer d is incorrect because the spanning tree protocol is used to eliminate loops in bridged networks.

# Question 33

Answers b and d are correct. Routers increase the latency of forwarding packets/frames between networks. In addition, the increased functionality provided by routers often increases the complexity of networks. Answers a and c are incorrect because these are actually advantages of routing in comparison with bridging and switching.

# Question 34

Answer a is correct. Frame tagging is used to tag a frame with a unique VLAN ID between switches.

# Question 35

Answer a is correct. Store-and-forward switching is a method of forwarding frames by copying the entire frame into the buffer of the switch and making a forwarding decision. Answer a is correct because store-and-forward switching provides error checking that is not provided by cut-through switching. Answers b and d are not switching methods and are, therefore, incorrect. Answer c is incorrect because cut-through switching does not provide error-checking capabilities.

## Question 36

Answer c is correct. A Fast Ethernet switch provides dedicated bandwidth to each port. This is unlike hubs, which share bandwidth among all ports. By definition, Fast Ethernet runs at 100Mbps. Note that if these PCs were connected through a single switch port, they would share the 100Mbps available to that port; however, the question states that each PC is given its own switch port.

## Question 37

Answers a, c, and d are correct. The session layer provides services to establish sessions, end sessions, and manage the dialogue between the sending and receiving stations. Ensuring that the segment sent is error free *is* handled within the transport layer; therefore, answer b is incorrect.

## Question 38

Answer c is correct. The Internet Assigned Numbers Authority (IANA) has assigned various class D addresses as well known addresses for use by multicast applications. 224.0.1.1 is one such address, and it should be recognizable from the other choices as the only IP address that is a class D. Answer a is incorrect because this is a subnet mask, not an IP address. Answer b is incorrect because this is a class A IP address. Answer d is incorrect because this is a class C IP address.

## Question 39

Answer a is correct. PAP only uses a two-way handshake to allow the remote host to identify itself to the local host. Answer b is incorrect because CHAP uses a three-way handshake in its procedure. LCP and NCP are not authentication protocols; therefore, answers c and d are incorrect.

## Question 40

Answer c is correct. Devices on separate VLANs require a router to communicate, just as devices on separate LANs would. Answers a and b are incorrect because neither a layer 2 switch nor bridge provides inter-VLAN communication. Answer d is incorrect because access lists will not allow inter-VLAN communication. Answer e is incorrect because ISL is required for truck connections, not inter-VLAN communication.

## Question 41

Answer c is correct. The **sh interface s1** command displays the configuration and statistics for serial interface 1 on the router. Answers a and b are incorrect because the **sh frame-relay s1** and **sh frame-relay interface s1** commands are invalid. Answer d is also incorrect because the **sh ip interface brief** command displays IP addressing and status information for all interfaces, not Frame Relay information.

## Question 42

Answer d is correct. The most common reason to see this message is because the interface was manually shut down through an IOS command. Answer a is incorrect because an operational interface would not give this message. Answer b is incorrect because the network connection may or may not be present given the output from the **show interface** command. Answer c is incorrect because this message does not mean there is a hardware problem.

## Question 43

Answer c is correct. Frame Relay operates within the data link layer and over the physical layer. Answers a and b are incorrect because Frame Relay does not contain any layer 3 (network) or layer 4 (transport) information.

## Question 44

Answer b is correct. Pressing Tab will complete a partially entered command. Answer a is incorrect because it will place the cursor at the end of a line. Answer c is incorrect because it is not an IOS command. Answer d is incorrect because it will place the cursor at the beginning of a line. Answer e is incorrect because it will recall the most recent command from the command history buffer.

## Question 45

Answers a, b, and c are correct. RIP, IGRP, and OSPF are interior routing protocols used to communicate route information within an autonomous system. Answer d is incorrect because BGP is designed to communicate route information between autonomous systems; therefore, it is an exterior routing protocol.

# Question 46

Answer b is correct. It is a complete IPX logical address for network 4d and node 0080.c747.b122. Answer a is incorrect because it is a node address and does not contain network information. Answer c is incorrect because it contains an IPX network number (4d), but also includes an IP address. Answer d is incorrect because it is only the IPX network number and is not a valid IPX logical address.

# Question 47

Answers a, c, and d are correct. The **ping** and **trace** commands verify routing by sending and receiving packets across the network. For the **telnet** command to be successful, packets must be sent and received properly, so it also verifies that packets are being routed. Although the **show interface** command displays the status of the interfaces on a router, it does not indicate whether packets are reaching their destination; therefore, answer b is incorrect.

# Question 48

Answer a is correct. The **ipx routing** command enables IPX routing within the router; the other commands can be executed after IPX has been enabled. Answer d is incorrect because the **ipx network** command assigns a network number to a router interface. Answers b and c are also incorrect because the **ipx protocol** and **ipx interface** commands are not valid commands.

# Question 49

Answer b is correct. Although many additional benefits have been realized by the networking industry, including the use of the OSI model as an educational tool, the International Organization for Standardization (ISO) released the OSI reference model with the primary purpose of helping computer vendors create interoperable network equipment.

# Question 50

Answer c is correct. When in full-duplex mode, there are dedicated wires used for sending and receiving; therefore, collisions are not possible. Answer a is incorrect because this is the behavior of standard or half-duplex Ethernet operation. Answers b and d are incorrect because neither is valid in any instance of Ethernet.

## Question 51

Answer a is correct. The **router igrp 77** command enables IGRP routing for autonomous system 1, and the **network 172.25.0.0** command enables the router to advertise that network to other routers. Answers b and c are incorrect because the **router igrp** command requires an autonomous system to be specified. Answer d is incorrect because you must first specify a routing protocol and then enter routing protocol configuration mode before configuring a network to be advertised.

## Question 52

Answer c is correct. Counting to infinity can result from the slow convergence inherent with distance vector protocols. Answers a, b, d, and e are incorrect. Split horizon, route poisoning, maximum hop count, and hold-down timers are techniques used to reduce the occurrence and impact of the counting-to-infinity situation.

## Question 53

Answers a, b, and e are correct. The presentation layer concerns itself with data representation, data compression, and data encryption. Because the session layer handles dialogue management, answer c is incorrect. The transport layer handles data transmission, so answer d is incorrect.

## Question 54

Answer a is correct. A greater than sign (>) after the hostname (in this case, Router) indicates that the router is in user mode. Answer b is incorrect because a pound sign (#) immediately following the hostname indicates that the router is in privileged mode. The text "(config)#" after the hostname indicates that the router is in global configuration mode; therefore, answer c is incorrect. A colon (:) after the hostname is not a valid router mode indicator, so answer d is incorrect.

## Question 55

Answer a is correct. ICMP reports errors and provides other information relevant to IP packet processing. Answer b is incorrect because this is the function of ARP. Answer c is incorrect because this is the function of SMTP. Answer d is incorrect because this is the function of SNMP.

# Question 56

Answer b is correct. The **sh ?** command displays the keyword needed to complete the **show** command. The **sh?** and **show?** commands display the commands beginning with the text "sh" and "show," respectively; therefore, answers a and c are incorrect.

# Question 57

Answer d is correct. Upon login, the router is placed in user mode. Answer a is incorrect because RXBOOT mode is for router recovery. Answer b is incorrect because you must first enter user mode before entering privileged mode. Answer c is incorrect because global configuration mode is enabled after you have entered privileged mode.

# Question 58

The correct answer is c. Bracketed items represent the default answer in dialog sessions within the Cisco IOS. You can press Enter to accept the default answer, or something else to change it. Answer b is incorrect because even though this might be the case in some scenarios, answer c is better. Answer a is incorrect because the information in brackets is certainly allowable, but listing allowable answers is not why the information is there. Answer d is incorrect because this will never be the case in a configuration dialog.

# Question 59

Answer a is correct. The **help** command displays a brief description of the help system for any command mode. Answer b is incorrect because pressing F1 will not provide help on a Cisco router. Answer d is incorrect because the question mark (?) displays the list of possible commands when it is typed at the prompt, regardless of the router's current mode. The Ctrl+H keystrokes display nothing; therefore, answer c is incorrect.

# Question 60

Answer b is correct. The presentation layer's chief concern is data representation. The application layer provides services for user applications, so answer a is incorrect. The session layer mainly performs session management; therefore, answer c is incorrect. Answer d is incorrect because the transport layer handles different aspects of data transport that include end-to-end communication, sending segments from one host to another, and reliable transport.

## Question 61

Answers b, c, and d are correct. Bridges, switches, and routers all segment a LAN into separate collision domains. Only routers, however, segment broadcast domains. Answer a is incorrect because all devices on a hub are in the same collision domain. Answer e is incorrect because a repeater provides no network segmentation.

## Question 62

Answer a is correct. The application layer provides services for user applications. Answer b is incorrect because the presentation layer's chief concern is data representation. The session layer mainly performs session management, so answer c is incorrect. The transport layer focuses primarily on aspects of data transport; therefore, answer d is incorrect.

## Question 63

Answer b is correct. The network layer converts segments into packets. The data link layer converts packets into frames. The physical layer converts frames into bits. Answer a is incorrect because the session layer sends *data* to the transport layer. Answer c is incorrect because the transport layer converts data into segments. Answer d is incorrect because the layers are out of order; the transport layer communicates with the network layer, and the network layer communicates with the data link layer.

## Question 64

Answers a, b, c, d, and e are correct.

## Question 65

Answer d is correct. The transport layer handles different aspects of data transport, including end-to-end communication, sending segments from one host to another, and reliable transport. Answer a is incorrect because the application layer provides services for user applications. Because the presentation layer's chief concern is data representation, answer b is incorrect. The session layer mainly performs session management; therefore, answer c is incorrect.

# Glossary

**advanced distance vector protocol**

A routing protocol that combines the strengths of distance vector and link state routing protocols. Cisco's EIGRP is considered an advanced distance vector protocol.

**application layer**

The highest layer of the OSI model (layer 7). It is closest to the end user and selects appropriate network services to support end-user applications such as email or FTP.

**area**

See *autonomous system*.

**ARP (Address Resolution Protocol)**

Used to map a known logical address to an unknown physical address. A device performs an ARP broadcast to identify the physical address of a destination device. This physical address is then stored in cache memory for later transmissions.

**autonomous system**

A group of networks under common administration and sharing a routing strategy. Sometimes referred to as a *domain* or *area*.

**bandwidth**

The available capacity of a network link over a physical medium.

**BGP (Border Gateway Protocol)**

An exterior routing protocol that exchanges route information between autonomous systems.

**boot field**

The lowest four binary digits of a configuration register. The value of the boot field determines the order in which a router searches for Cisco IOS software.

**BRI (basic rate interface)**

An ISDN interface that contains two B channels and one D channel for circuit-switched communication for data, voice, and video.

**bridge**

A device used to segment a LAN into multiple physical segments. A bridge uses a forwarding table to determine which frames need to be forwarded to specific segments. Bridges isolate local traffic to the originating physical segment, but forward all nonlocal and broadcast traffic.

### buffering
A method of flow control used by the transport layer that involves the memory buffers on the receiving hosts. The transport layer of the receiving system ensures that sufficient buffers are available and that data is not transmitted at a rate that exceeds the rate at which the receiving system can process it.

### carrier detect signal
A signal received on a router interface that indicates whether the physical layer connectivity is operating properly.

### CDP (Cisco Discovery Protocol)
A Cisco proprietary protocol that operates at the data link layer. CDP enables network administrators to view a summary protocol and address information about other directly connected Cisco routers (and some Cisco switches).

### channel
A single communication path on a system. In some situations, channels can be multiplexed over a single connection.

### CHAP (Challenge Handshake Authentication Protocol)
An authentication protocol for PPP that uses a three-way, encrypted handshake to force a remote host to identify itself to a local host.

### CIDR (Classless Interdomain Routing)
Implemented to resolve the rapid depletion of IP address space on the Internet and to minimize the number of routes on the Internet. CIDR provides a more efficient method of allocating IP address space by removing the concept of classes in IP addressing. CIDR enables routes to be summarized on powers-of-two boundaries, thus reducing multiple routes into a single prefix.

### CIR (Committed Information Rate)
The rate at which a Frame Relay link transmits data, averaged over time. It is measured in bits per second.

### classful addressing
Categorizes IP addresses into ranges that are used to create a hierarchy in the IP addressing scheme. The most common classes are A, B, and C, which can be identified by looking at the first three binary digits of an IP address.

### CO (central office)
The local telephone company office where all local loops in an area connect.

### configuration register
A numeric value (typically displayed as hexadecimal) used to specify certain actions on a router.

### congestion
A situation that can occur during data transfer if one or more computers generate network traffic faster than it can be transmitted through the network.

### connectionless network services

Involves using a permanently established link. Path selection and bandwidth allocation are done dynamically.

### connection-oriented network services

Involves using a non-permanent path for data transfer. In order for two systems to communicate, they must establish a path that will be used for the duration of their connection.

### console

A terminal attached directly to the router for configuring and monitoring the router.

### convergence

The process where all routers within an internetwork exchange route information and eventually agree on optimal routes through the internetwork.

### counting to infinity

A routing problem where the distance metric for a destination network is continually increased because the internetwork has not fully converged.

### CPE (customer premise equipment)

Terminating equipment such as telephones or modems supplied by the service provider, installed at the customer site, and connected to the network.

### CRC (cyclic redundancy check)

An error-checking mechanism where the receiving node calculates a value based on the data it receives and compares it with the value stored within the frame from the sending node.

### CSMA/CD (carrier sense multiple access/collision detection)

A physical specification used by the Ethernet to provide contention-based frame transmission. CSMA/CD specifies that a sending device shares a physical transmission media and must listen to determine if a collision occurs after transmitting.

### cut-through switching

A method of forwarding frames based on the first six bytes contained in the frame. It provides higher throughput than store-and-forward switching because it requires only six bytes of data to make the forwarding decision. Cut-through switching does not provide error checking like its counterpart store-and-forward switching.

### DARPA (Defense Advanced Research Projects Agency)

A government agency designed to develop advanced defense capabilities. It is now known as ARPA.

### DCE (data communication equipment)

The device at the network end of a user-to-network connection that provides a physical connection to the network, forwards traffic, and provides a clocking signal used to synchronize data transmission between the DCE and DTE devices.

### DDR (dial-on-demand routing)

A technique where a router can initiate and terminate a circuit-switched connection over ISDN or telephone lines to meet network traffic demands.

## de-encapsulation

The process by which a destination peer layer removes and reads the control information sent by the source peer layer in another network host.

## default mask

A binary or decimal representation of the number of bits used to identify an IP network. The class of the IP address defines the default mask. A default mask is represented by four octets of binary digits. The mask can also be presented in dotted decimal notation.

## default route

A network route established (that usually points to another router) to receive and attempt to process all packets for which no route appears in the route table.

## delay

The amount of time necessary to move a packet through the internetwork from source to destination.

## demarc

A point of demarcation between the carrier's equipment and the CPE.

## discard eligibility bit

A bit that can be set to indicate that a frame may be dropped if congestion occurs within the Frame Relay network.

## distance vector protocol

An interior routing protocol that relies on distance and vector or direction to choose optimal paths. A distance vector protocol requires each router to send all or a large part of its route table to its neighboring routers periodically.

## DLCI (data link connection identifier)

A value that specifies a PVC or SVC in a Frame Relay network.

## DNS (Domain Name System)

A system used to translate fully qualified hostnames or computer names into IP addresses, and vice versa.

## domain

See *autonomous system*.

## dotted decimal notation

A method of representing binary IP addresses in a decimal format. Dotted decimal notation represents the four octets of an IP address in four decimal values separated by decimal points.

## DTE (data terminal equipment)

The device at the user end of the user-to-network connection that connects to a data network through a DCE device.

## dynamic route

A network route that adjusts automatically to changes within the internetwork.

## EGP (Exterior Gateway Protocol)

An exterior routing protocol that exchanges route information between autonomous systems. EGP has become obsolete and is being replaced by BGP.

## EIGRP (enhanced interior gateway routing protocol)

A Cisco-proprietary routing protocol that includes features of both distance vector and link state routing protocols. It is considered to be an advanced distance vector protocol.

### encapsulation

Generally speaking, the process of wrapping data in a particular protocol header. In the context of the OSI model, the process by which a source peer layer includes header and/or trailer control information with a PDU destined for its peer layer in another network host. The information encapsulated instructs the destination peer layer how to process the information.

### EXEC

The user interface for executing Cisco router commands.

### exterior routing protocol

A routing protocol that conveys information between autonomous systems; it is widely used within the Internet. BGP is an example of an exterior routing protocol.

### Flash

Router memory that stores the Cisco IOS image and associated microcode. Flash is erasable, reprogrammable ROM that retains its content when the router is powered down or restarted.

### flat routing protocol

A routing environment where all routers are considered peers and can communicate with any other router in the network as directly as possible. A flat routing protocol functions well in simple and predictable network environments.

### flow control

A mechanism that throttles back data transmission to ensure that a sending system does not overwhelm the receiving system with data.

### FCS (frame check sequence)

Extra characters added to a frame for error control purposes. It is the result of a CRC.

### Frame Relay

A switched, data link layer protocol that supports multiple virtual circuits using HDLC encapsulation between connected devices.

### frame tagging

A method of tagging a frame with a unique user-defined VLAN. The process of tagging a frame allows VLANs to span multiple switches.

### FTP (File Transfer Protocol)

A protocol used to copy a file from one host to another host, regardless of the physical hardware or operating system of each device. FTP identifies a client and server during the file transfer process. In addition, it provides a guaranteed transfer by using the services of TCP.

### full-duplex

A physical transmission process on a network device where one pair of wires transmits data, while another pair of wires receives data. Full-duplex transmission is achieved by eliminating the possibility of collisions on an Ethernet segment, thereby eliminating the need for a device to sense collisions.

### function

A term that refers to the different devices and hardware tasks they perform within ISDN.

## global configuration mode

A router mode that enables simple router configuration commands to be executed such as router names, banners, and passwords. Global configuration commands affect the whole router, rather than a single interface or component.

## GNS (Get Nearest Server)

A request sent by an IPX client to locate the closest active server of a particular service. Depending on where the service can be located, either a server or a router can respond to the request.

## half-duplex

A physical transmission process whereby one pair of wires is used to transmit information and the other pair of wires is used to receive information or to sense collisions on a physical media. Half-duplex transmission is required on Ethernet segments with multiple devices.

## handshake

The process of one system making a request to another system prior to a connection being established. Handshakes occur during the establishment of a connection between two systems and address matters such as synchronization and connection parameters.

## HDLC (High-level Data Link Control)

A bit-oriented, synchronous data link layer protocol that specifies data encapsulation methods on serial links.

## header

Control information placed before the data during the encapsulation process.

## hierarchical routing protocol

A routing environment that relies on several routers to compose a backbone. Most traffic from nonbackbone routers traverses the backbone routers (or at least travels to the backbone) to reach another nonbackbone router. This is accomplished by breaking a network into a hierarchy of networks where each level is responsible for its own routing.

## hold-down

The state into which a route is placed so that routers will not advertise or accept updates for that route until a timer expires.

## hop count

The number of routers a packet passes through on its way to the destination network.

## hostname

A logical name given to a router.

## HSSI (high-speed serial interface)

A physical standard designed for serial connections that require high data transmission rates. The HSSI standard allows for high-speed communication that runs at speeds up to 52Mbps.

## ICMP (Internet Control Message Protocol)

A protocol that communicates error messages and controls messages between devices. Thirteen different types of ICMP messages are defined. ICMP allows devices to check the status of other devices, to query the current time, and to perform other functions such as ping and traceroute.

### IGRP (Interior Gateway Routing Protocol)

A Cisco-proprietary distance vector routing protocol that uses hop count as its metric.

### initial configuration dialog

The dialog used to configure a router the first time it is booted or when no configuration file exists. The initial configuration dialog is an optional process used to simplify the configuration process.

### integrated routing

A technique where a router routing multiple routed protocols shares resources. Rather than using several routing protocols to support multiple routed protocols, a network administrator can use a single routing protocol to support multiple routed protocols. EIGRP is an example of a routing protocol that supports integrated routing.

### interdomain router

A router using an exterior routing protocol such as BGP to exchange route information between autonomous systems.

### interfaces

Router components that provide the network connections where data packets move in and out of the router. Depending on the model of router, interfaces exist either on the motherboard or on separate, modular interface cards.

### interior routing protocol

A routing protocol that exchanges information within an autonomous system. RIP, IGRP, and OSPF are examples of interior routing protocols.

### intradomain router

A router using an interior routing protocol such as IGRP to convey route information with an autonomous system.

### IP (Internet Protocol)

One of the many protocols maintained in the TCP/IP suite of protocols. IP is the transport mechanism for TCP, UDP, and ICMP data. It also provides the logical addressing necessary for complex routing activity.

### IP extended access list

A way of filtering IP traffic on a router interface based on the source and destination IP address or port, IP precedence field, TOS field, ICMP-type, ICMP-code, ICMP-message, IGMP-type, and TCP established connections.

### IP standard access list

A way of filtering IP traffic on a router interface based on the source IP address or address range.

### IPX (Internet Packet Exchange)

The layer 3 protocol used within NetWare to transmit data between servers and workstations.

### IPX extended access list

A way of filtering IPX traffic on a router interface based on the source and destination IPX address or address range, IPX protocol, and source and destination sockets.

## IPX SAP filter

A way of filtering SAP traffic on a router interface. SAP filters are used to filter SAP traffic origination or traffic destined for specific IPX addresses or address ranges.

## IPX standard access list

A way of filtering IPX traffic on a router interface based on the source IPX address or address range.

## ISDN (Integrated Services Digital Network)

A communication protocol offered by telephone companies that permits telephone networks to carry data, voice, and other traffic.

## ISL (inter-switch link)

A protocol used to allow VLANs to span multiple switches. It is used between switches to communicate common VLANs between devices.

## keepalive frames

PDUs transmitted at the data link layer and that indicate whether the proper frame type is configured.

## LAN protocols

Protocols that identify layer 2 protocols used for the transmission of data within a LAN. The three most popular LAN protocols used today are Ethernet, token ring, and FDDI.

## LCP (Link Control Protocol)

A protocol that configures, tests, maintains, and terminates PPP connections.

## link state packet

A broadcast packet that contains the status of a router's links or network interfaces.

## link state protocol

An interior routing protocol where each router sends only the state of its own network links across the network, but sends this information to every router within its autonomous system or area. This process enables routers to learn and maintain full knowledge of the network's exact topology and how it is interconnected. Link state protocols use a shortest path first algorithm.

## LLC (logical link control sublayer)

A sublayer of the data link layer. The LLC sublayer provides the software functions of the data link layer.

## LMI (Local Management Interface)

A set of enhancements to the Frame Relay protocol specifications.

## load

An indication of how busy a network resource is. CPU utilization and packets processed per second are two indicators of load.

## local loop

The line from the customer's premises to the telephone company's CO.

## logical addressing

Network layer addressing is most commonly referred to as logical addressing versus the physical addressing of the data link layer. A logical address consists of two parts: the network part and the node part. Routers use the network part of the logical address to determine the best path to the network of a remote device. The node part of the logical address is used to identify the specific node to forward the packet on the destination network.

## logical AND

A process of comparing two sets of binary numbers to result in one value representing an IP address network. The logical AND is used to compare an IP address against its subnet mask to yield the IP subnet on which the IP address resides.

## MAC address

A physical address used to define a device uniquely.

## MAC (media access control) layer

A sublayer of the data link layer that provides the hardware functions of the data link layer.

## metric

The relative cost of sending packets to a destination network over a specific network route. Examples of metrics include bandwidth, delay, and reliability.

## MIB (management information database)

A database that maintains statistics on certain data items. The protocol SNMP uses MIBs to query information about devices.

## multicasting

A process of using one IP address to represent a group of IP addresses. Multicasting is used to send messages to a subset of IP addresses in a network or networks.

## multipath routing protocol

A routing protocol that loads balances over multiple optimal paths to a destination network when the costs of the paths are equal.

## multiplexing

A method of flow control used by the transport layer in which application conversations are combined over a single channel by interleaving packets from different segments and transmitted.

## NBMA (nonbroadcast multiaccess)

A multiaccess network that either does not support broadcasts or for which sending broadcasts is not feasible.

## NCP (NetWare Core Protocol)

A collection of upper-layer server routines that satisfy requests from other applications.

## NCP (Network Control Program)

A collection of protocols that establish and configure different network layer protocols for use over a PPP connection.

## NetBIOS (Network Basic Input/Output System)

A common session-layer interface specification from IBM and Microsoft that enables applications to request lower-level network services.

## NetWare

A popular LAN operating system developed by Novell Corporation that runs on a variety of different types of LANs.

## NetWare shell

An upper-layer NetWare service that determines whether application calls require additional network services.

## network discovery

When a router starts up, this is the process by which it learns of its internetwork environment and begins to communicate with other routers.

### NIC (network interface card)
A board that provides network communication capabilities to and from a network host.

### NLSP (NetWare Link State Protocol)
A link state routing protocol used for routing IPX.

### NOS (Network Operating System)
A term used to describe distributed file systems that support file sharing, printing, database access, and other similar applications.

### NVRAM (non-volatile random access memory)
A memory area of the router that stores permanent information, such as the router's backup configuration file. The contents of NVRAM are retained when the router is powered down or restarted.

### OSI (Open Systems Interconnect) model
A layered networking framework developed by the International Organization for Standardization. The OSI model describes seven layers that correspond to specific networking functions.

### OSPF (open shortest path first)
A hierarchical link state routing protocol that was developed as a successor to RIP.

### packet switching
A process by which a router moves a packet from one interface to another.

### PAP (Password Authentication Protocol)
An authentication protocol for PPP that uses a two-way, unencrypted handshake to enable a remote host to identify itself to a local host.

### parallelization
A method of flow control used by the transport layer in which multiple channels are combined to increase the effective bandwidth for the upper layers.

### path length
The sum of the costs of each link traversed up to the destination network. Some routing protocols refer to path length as *hop count*.

### PDU (protocol data unit)
A unit of measure that refers to data that is transmitted between two peer layers within different network devices. Segments, packets, and frames are examples of PDUs.

### peer-to-peer communication
A form of communication that occurs between the same layers of two different network hosts.

### physical connection
A direct physical connection between two devices.

### ping
A tool for testing IP connectivity between two devices. A ping sends multiple IP packets between a sending and a receiving device. The destination device responds with an ICMP packet to notify the source device of its existence.

## POP (point of presence)

A physical location where a carrier has installed equipment to interconnect with a local exchange carrier.

## PPP (Point-to-Point Protocol)

A standard protocol the enables router-to-router and host-to-network connectivity over synchronous and asynchronous circuits such as telephone lines.

## presentation layer

Layer 6 of the OSI model. The presentation layer is concerned with how data is represented to the application layer.

## PRI (primary rate interface)

An ISDN interface that contains 23 B channels and one D channel for circuit-switched communication for data, voice, and video. In North America and Japan, a PRI contains 23 B and 1 D channel. In Europe, it contains 30 B channels and 1 D channel.

## privileged mode

An extensive administrative and management mode on a Cisco router. This router mode permits testing, debugging, and commands to modify the router's configuration.

## protocol

A formal description of a set of rules and conventions that defines how devices on a network must exchange information.

## PSTN (public switched telephone network)

A term used to identify the circuit-switching facilities maintained for voice analog communication.

## PVC (permanent virtual circuit)

A virtual circuit that is permanently established and ready for use.

## RAM (random access memory)

A memory area of a router that serves as a working storage area. RAM contains data such as route tables, various types of cache and buffers, as well as input and output queues and the router's active configuration file. The contents of RAM are lost when the router is powered down or restarted.

## RARP (Reverse Address Resolution Protocol)

Provides mapping that is exactly opposite to ARP. RARP maps a known physical address to a logical address. Diskless machines that do not have a configured IP address when started typically use RARP. RARP requires the existence of a server that maintains physical to logical address mapping.

## reference point

An identifier of the logical interfaces between functions within ISDN.

## reliability

A metric that allows the network administrator to assign arbitrarily a numeric value to indicate a reliability factor for the link. The reliability metric is a method used to capture an administrator's experience with a given network link.

## RIP (Routing Information Protocol)

A widely used distance vector routing protocol that uses hop count as its metric.

### ROM (read only memory)

An area of router memory that contains a version of the Cisco IOS image, usually an older version with minimal functionality. ROM also stores the bootstrap program and power-on diagnostic programs.

### ROM monitor

A mode on a Cisco router where the executing software is maintained in ROM.

### ROM monitor mode (RXBOOT)

A router maintenance mode that enables router recovery functions when the IOS file in Flash has been erased or is corrupt.

### route aggregation

A process of combining multiple IP address networks into one superset of IP address networks. Route aggregation is implemented to reduce the number of route table entries required to forward IP packets accurately in an internetwork.

### route poisoning

A routing technique where a router immediately marks a network as unreachable as soon as it detects that the network is down. The router broadcasts the update throughout the network and maintains this poisoned route in its route table for a specified period of time.

### route table

An area of a router's memory that stores the network topology information used to determine optimal routes. Route tables contain information such as destination network, next hop, and associated metrics.

### routed protocol

Provides the information required for the routing protocol to determine the topology of the internetwork and the best path to a destination. The routed protocol provides this information in the form of a logical address and other fields within a packet. The information contained in the packet allows the router to direct user traffic. The most common routed protocols include IP and IPX.

### router modes

Modes that enable the execution of specific router commands and functions. User, privileged, and setup are examples of router modes that allow you to perform certain tasks.

### routing algorithm

Well-defined rules that aid routers in the collection of route information and the determination of the optimal path.

### routing loop

An event where two or more routers have not yet converged and are propagating their inaccurate route tables. In addition, they are probably still switching packets based on their inaccurate route tables.

### routing protocols

Routing protocols use algorithms to generate a list of paths to a particular destination and the cost associated with each path. Routers use routing protocols to communicate among each other the best route to use to reach a particular destination.

## RS-232

A physical standard used to identify cabling types for serial data transmission for speeds of 19.2Kbps or less. RS-232 connects two devices communicating over a serial link with either a 25-pin (DB-25) or 9-pin (DB-9) serial interface. RS-232 is now known as EIA/TIA-232.

## running configuration file

The executing configuration file on a router.

## SAP (Service Advertisement Protocol)

An IPX protocol that serves as a means to inform network clients of available network resources and services.

## SDLC (synchronous data link control)

Primarily used for terminal-to-mainframe communication. SDLC requires that one device is labeled as the primary station and all other devices are labeled as secondary stations. Communication can only occur between the primary station and the secondary station.

## session

A dialogue between presentation layers on two or more different systems.

## session layer

Layer 5 of the OSI model. It is concerned with establishing, managing, and terminating sessions between applications on different network devices.

## setup mode

The router mode triggered on startup if no configuration file resides in NVRAM.

## shortest path first

See *link state protocol*.

## single-path routing protocol

A routing protocol that uses only one optimal path to a destination.

## sliding windows

A method by which TCP dynamically sets the window size during a connection, allowing either device involved in the communication to slow down the sending data rate based on the other device's capacity.

## SMTP (Simple Mail Transfer Protocol)

Used to pass mail messages between devices. It uses TCP connections to pass the email between hosts.

## socket

The combination of the sending and destination TCP port numbers and the sending and destination IP addresses defines a socket. Therefore, a socket can be used to define any UDP or TCP connection uniquely.

## spanning tree protocol

Used to eliminate all circular routes in a bridged or switched environment while maintaining redundancy. Circular routes are not desirable in layer 2 networks because of the forwarding mechanism employed at this layer.

## split horizon

A routing mechanism that prevents a router from sending information that it received about a network back to its neighbor that originally sent the information. This mechanism is very useful in preventing routing loops.

## SPX (Sequence Packet Exchange)

The layer 4 protocol used within NetWare to ensure reliable, connection-oriented services.

## startup configuration file

The backup configuration file on a router.

## static route

A network route that is manually entered into the route table. Static routes function well in very simple and predictable network environments.

## store-and-forward switching

A method of forwarding frames by copying the entire frame into the buffer of the switch and making a forwarding decision. Store-and-forward switching does not achieve the same throughput as its counterpart, cut-through switching, because it copies the entire frame into the buffer instead of copying only the first six bytes. Store-and-forward switching, however, provides error checking that is not provided by cut-through switching.

## subinterface

One of possibly many virtual interfaces on a single physical interface.

## subnetting

A process of splitting a classful range of IP addresses into multiple IP networks to allow more flexibility in IP addressing schemes. Subnetting overcame the limitation of address classes and allowed network administrators the flexibility to assign multiple networks with one class of IP addresses.

## switch

Provides increased port density and forwarding capabilities compared with bridges. The increased port densities of switches allow LANs to be microsegmented, thereby increasing the amount of bandwidth delivered to each device.

## TCP (Transmission Control Protocol)

One of the many protocols maintained in the TCP/IP suite of protocols. TCP provides a connection-oriented and reliable service to the applications that use its services.

## TCP three-way handshake

A process by which TCP connections send acknowledgments between each other when setting up a TCP connection.

## TCP windowing

A method of increasing or reducing the number of acknowledgments required between data transmissions. This allows devices to throttle the rate at which data is transmitted.

## Telnet

A standard protocol that provides a virtual terminal. Telnet enables a network administrator to connect to a router remotely.

## TFTP (Trivial File Transfer Protocol)

A protocol used to copy files from one device to another. TFTP is a stripped-down version of FTP.

## tick

A measure of network delay time, about $1/18^{th}$ of a second. In RIP version 2, ticks serve as the primary value used to determine the best path.

### traceroute

An IP service that allows a user to utilize the services of UDP and ICMP to identify the number of hops between sending and receiving devices and the paths taken from the sending to the receiving device. Traceroute also provides the IP address and DNS name of each hop. Typically, traceroute is used to troubleshoot IP connectivity between two devices.

### trailer

Control information placed after the data during the encapsulation process.

### transport layer

Layer 4 of the OSI model is positioned between the upper and lower layers of the model. It is concerned with segmenting upper layer applications, establishing end-to-end connectivity through the network, sending segments from one host to another, and ensuring the reliable transport of data.

### trunk

A switch port that connects to another switch to allow VLANs to span multiple switches.

### tunnel

Takes packets or frames from one protocol and places them inside frames from another network system. See *encapsulation*.

### UDP (User Datagram Protocol)

One of the many protocols maintained in the TCP/IP suite of protocols. UDP is a layer 4, best-effort, delivery protocol and, there-fore, maintains connectionless network services.

### user mode

A display-only mode on a Cisco router. Only limited information about the router can be viewed within this router mode; no configuration changes are permitted.

### V.35

V.35 is a physical standard used to identify cabling types for serial data transmission for speeds up to 4Mbps. The V.35 standard was created by the International Telecommunication Union-Telecommunication (ITU-T) standardization sector.

### virtual connection

A logical connection between two devices created through the use of acknowledgments.

### VLAN (virtual local area network)

A method of assigning devices to specific LANs based on the port to which they attach on a switch, not on physical location. VLANs extend the flexibility of LANs by allowing devices to be assigned to specific LANs on a port-by-port basis versus a device basis.

### VLSM (Variable Length Subnet Masking)

Provides more flexibility in assigning IP address space. (A common problem with routing protocols was the necessity of all devices in a given routing protocol domain to use the same subnet mask.) Routing protocols that support VLSM allow administrators to assign IP networks with different subnet masks. This increased flexibility saves IP address space because administrators can assign IP networks based on the number of hosts on each network.

## WAN protocols
Identify layer 2 protocols used for the transmission of data within a WAN.

## well-known ports
A set of ports between 1 and 1,023 that are reserved for specific TCP/IP protocols and services.

# Index

# Better, Faster, Louder!

## *Get certified on the go with EXAM CRAM™ AUDIO TAPES*

**A+ Exam Cram Audio Review**
ISBN: 1-57610-541-5
$39.99 U.S. • $59.99 Canada
Four hours of audio instruction
Cassettes • Available Now

**Network+ Exam Cram Audio Review**
ISBN: 1-57610-534-2
$39.99 U.S. • $59.99 Canada
Four hours of audio instruction
Cassettes • Available Now

**MCSE Core Four Exam Cram Audio Review**
ISBN: 1-57610-631-4
$39.99 U.S. • $59.99 Canada
Four hours of audio instruction
Cassettes • Available Now

## AUDIO TAPES

Hear what you've been missing with Exam Cram Audio Review tapes. Each set contains four cassettes jam-packed with the certification information you must have to pass your exams. Exam Cram Audio Review tapes can be used on their own or as a complement to our Exam Cram Study Guides, Flash Cards, and Practice Tests.

## FLASH CARDS

Exam Cram Flash Cards are the pocket-sized study tool that provide key questions on one side of each card and in-depth answers on the other. Each card features a cross-reference to the appropriate chapter in the corresponding Exam Cram Study Guide or other valuable resource. Each pack includes 100 cards 100% focused on exam material, along with a CD-ROM featuring electronic versions of the flash cards and a complete practice exam.

## PRACTICE TESTS

Each book contains several practice exams with electronic versions on the accompanying CD-ROM. Each practice question is followed by the corresponding answer (*why the right answers are right and the wrong answers are wrong*). References to the Exam Cram Study Guide and chapter or other valuable resource in which the topic is discussed in depth are included. The CD-ROM presents exams in an interactive format, enabling you to practice in an environment similar to that of the actual exam.

**The <u>Smartest</u> Way to Get Certified
Just Got Smarter™**

# The Coriolis Exam Cram Personal Trainer
## An exciting new category in certification training products

The Exam Cram Personal trainer is the first certification-specific testing product that completely links learning with testing to:

• **Increase your comprehension**

• **Decrease the time it takes you to learn**

No system blends learning content with test questions as effectively as the Exam Cram Personal Trainer.

Only the Exam Cram Personal Trainer offers this much power at this price.

Its unique Personalized Test Engine provides a real-time test environment and an authentic representation of what you will encounter during your actual certification exams.

### Much More Than Just Another CBT!

Most current CBT learning systems offer simple review questions at the end of a chapter with an overall test at the end of the course, with no links back to the lessons. But Exam Cram Personal Trainer takes learning to a higher level.

### Its four main components are:

• The complete text of an Exam Cram study guide in an HTML format,

• A Personalized Practice Test Engine with multiple test methods

| | |
|---|---|
| **Adaptive:** | 25-35 questions |
| **Fixed-length:** | Four unique exams on critical areas |
| **Random:** | Each randomly generated test is unique |
| **Test All:** | Drawn from the complete database of questions |
| **Topic:** | Organized by Exam Cram chapters |
| **Review:** | Questions with answers are presented |

**Scenario-based questions:** Just like the real thing

• A database of nearly 300 questions linked directly to an Exam Cram chapter

• Over two hours of Exam Cram Audio Review

### Plus, additional features include:

• **Hint:** Not sure of your answer? Click Hint and the software goes to the text that covers that topic.

• **Lesson:** Still not enough detail? Click Lesson and the software goes to the beginning of the chapter.

• **Update feature:** Need even more questions? Click Update to download more questions from the Coriolis Web site.

• **Notes:** Create your own memory joggers.

• **Graphic analysis:** How did you do? View your score, the required score to pass, and other information.

• **Personalized Cram Sheet:** Print unique study information just for you.

---

**MCSE Networking Essentials Exam Cram Personal Trainer**
ISBN:1-57610-644-6

**MCSE NT Server 4 Exam Cram Personal Trainer**
ISBN: 1-57610-645-4

**MCSE NT Server 4 in the Enterprise Exam Cram Personal Trainer**
ISBN: 1-57610-646-2

**MCSE NT Workstation 4 Exam Cram Personal Trainer**
ISBN:1-57610-647-0

**A+ Exam Cram Personal Trainer**
ISBN: 1-57610-658-6

$69.99 U.S. • $104.99 Canada

Available: March 2000

**CORIOLIS**™
*Certification Insider Press*

**The <u>Smartest</u> Way to Get Certified**
**Just Got Smarter**™